Quilting

For Fun & Profit™

Sylvia Ann Landman

PRIMA HOME

An Imprint of Prima Publishing

Library of Congress Cataloging-in-Publication Data

Landman, Sylvia.
    Quilting for fun & profit / Sylvia Landman.
        p.   cm.
    Includes index.
    ISBN 0-7615-2037-6
    1. Needlework industry and trade. 2. Handicraft industries. 3. Home-based businesses. 4. Quilting—Economic aspects.
    I. Title. II. Title: Quilting for fun and profit.
    HD9936.5 AZL363 1999
    746.46'.068—dc21   99-39223
                                                                              CIP

99 00 01 02 ii 10 9 8 7 6 5 4 3 2 1

How to Order

Single copies may be ordered from Prima Publishing,
P.O. Box 1260BK, Rocklin, CA 95677; telephone (916) 632-4400.
Quantity discounts are also available. On your letterhead, include
information concerning the intended use of the books and
the number of books you wish to purchase.

Visit us online at www.primalifestyles.com

Contents

The FOR FUN & PROFIT™ Series

Introduction

UNLIKE OTHERS WHO MAY HAVE gained an appreciation for quilting from their mother or grandmother, my quilting passion came to me uninvited and unexpectedly in my late thirties with a phone call from a total stranger one Sunday afternoon.

My caller identified herself as an entrepreneur who wanted to establish the largest, most comprehensive needlework and quilt show in Northern California, even though she herself knew nothing about these crafts. Someone had referred me to her as the "Needlework Lady" of Marin County, California, where I live, and she said she wanted to hire me as a consultant to deal with the details of the unfamiliar needlework she sought to promote.

At that time, I was well-established as a knitting, crocheting, sewing, and embroidery teacher. I was writing columns on these topics and felt that no new craft could possibly capture my attention as much as those to which I was already devoted. But things began to change the day I was asked to serve not only as a consultant for the needlework and quilt show, but as judge as well.

"I design and judge needlework," I said, "but I do not quilt." Not to worry, I was told, as two quilt judges had been hired. Needlework and quilting enthusiasts began to arrive at our large Civic Center Auditorium a few days before the show, treasures in hand, eager to exhibit and vie for cash prizes. Quilts arrived, most of them folded with their wrong sides out. Nothing impressive here, I thought. Two days later, I went to the auditorium to begin judging the needlework entries and saw the quilts that had been hung, judged, and displayed the day before. My life changed forever.

Row upon row of quilts of all types and colors hung majestically from invisible nylon cords attached to the ceiling. The stimulation of it all overwhelmed me! After completing my judging, I drove the few miles home only to return with my jogging shoes on. I spent the remainder of the day walking through each row, marveling at the wonder of all those talented artisans' imaginations. As they say, I was hooked.

The next day, I returned to see the quilt show after it opened to the public, checkbook in hand. I went home with enough quilting books to fill three shopping bags. I could not wait to learn more about this idea of cutting up fabric and sewing it back together again into a work of art. I recall staying up until the wee hours of the morning reading my new books and learning about quilt history.

I continue to read and learn today, even as I write my own books and columns about quilting. Recently I attended my second full week of quilting inspiration and study at an Empty Spools Seminar in Asilomar, California (see next chapter). Where else would one go taking an ironing board, iron, sewing machine and laundry baskets full of fabrics to sew and quilt a mere twelve hours per day? Marvelous quilting artists from all over the world came to share their secrets with all of us. This, of course, has led me to another passion I said I would never attempt: dyeing and marbling fabric. But that's another book, isn't it?

A Language All Their Own

Through the years, quilters have developed a language all their own to explain their fascination with making, buying, using, and collecting quilts; wearing quilted clothing; and attending quilt shows so far from home that tour busses have a new profit sideline carrying quilters from one show to another. Certain words and phrases that mean one thing to the average person have an entirely different meaning to a quilter.

Take "addiction," for example. To a quilter, this word means a compulsive, psychological need for increasing amounts of fabric, thread, and completed quilts. Large collections known as "stashes" may become habit forming, but ownership of same provides both comfort and pleasure. Many sweatshirts embellished with lettering shout to the world, "She who dies with the most fabric, wins!"

Articles and books on how to manage a fabric stash abound. Prewash or store immediately after purchase? Store by color or fabric content? Store on shelves or in plastic bags? My particular favorite: After you have filled up the space under beds with boxes of fabric, consider filling up your car trunk and telling everyone you lost the key (until you need a particular color, that is).

"Stash" does not limit itself to fabric, of course. Quilters have thread stashes, too. At one quilting seminar I attended, a thread addict wore a different sweatshirt each day, designed with spools of thread of varying colors and types positioned as carefully as flowers in an arrangement. Its wearer, Patsy Shields, works for Sulky, Inc., a thread manufacturer. When I asked her why she enjoyed working for the company, she replied enthusiastically, "I just love thread! Fabric comes alive when embellished with decorative threads."

Patsy stores her thread in two large clear plastic boxes the size of suitcases. They have little compartments just the right size to hold a spool of thread. Designed to hold collections of little toy cars, they are available in toy shops. "These are perfect for my thread collection. I never know which color or weight I may need at a given moment, so I carry them all with me wherever I go."

"Theme" is another word that has special meaning to quilters, who not only make quilts in their favorite colors, patterns, and sizes, but with a special theme as well. On the Internet, where thousands of quilters network today, people often exchange fabrics to maintain a theme. "I will trade one-half yard of cat fabric for zebra fabric," one may write, while another says, "I need fabric with airplanes for my son, in exchange for a yard of red roses on black." Fabric exchanges like this go on internationally as well as in the United States. How about fabric from a quilter in Zimbabwe in exchange for those multi-colored frog designs so popular here?

That quilting is fun, and often addictive, cannot be denied. The serious question is this: What if you want to keep quilting after you have layered every bed with five quilts, given some to all your friends and relatives until they feel saturated, donated one to a church raffle, and even covered your walls with them?

I'm reminded of a male student I had in one of my college small business classes. In the back of the room, I had a few copies of both *Crafting for Dollars* and *Make Your Quilting Pay for Itself*. He wanted a copy of the latter, which prompted me to ask if he was a quilter himself. "No," he replied. "But my wife loves quilting and can't stop. I want to buy this book so she will get the idea of letting her obsession pay for itself. I sure can't afford it any more, and I do not see her quilting slowing down."

Brief History of Quilting

Quilting is one of the most pure American art forms. To America's early pioneers, quilts were an absolute necessity and a valuable part of a woman's dowry. (In those days, men actually looked for potential wives based on the size of their dowries. The more quilts, the better.) Quilts provided warmth to the early settlers who lived in drafty cabins on the prairie and to families huddled in covered wagons traveling to California. Babies, as well as the newly deceased, were commonly wrapped in quilts.

Creating warmth was the primary intent, yet quilting became one of the earliest recycle processes before the term came to signify ecological concerns late in the twentieth century. Thrifty housewives saved old clothing and cut less-worn portions into small pieces. Joining these artistically resulted in a larger quilt top, also called patchwork. Old blankets often became "fillers," and an old sheet became the bottom layer. Often, several of these quilts would be stacked on a bed to keep sleepers warm during freezing weather. (Today's quilters layer quilts for an entirely different reason: because they have a quilt on every bed and wall and don't know where else to put them.)

Very old quilts in museums around the country reveal a few interesting secrets. Yes, quilts consist of three layers: the fancy and beautiful top layer; the middle layer made of cotton, wool, or old blankets for warmth; and the "backing" relegated to leftover fabrics in the old days. But antique quilts often had a fourth layer added right over the backing when it became worn and thin. In fact, at a gathering for quilt historians I attended, an old quilt rested on a clean sheet, upside down, exposing its crumbling fourth layer. Its threadbare condition enabled us to see a wonderful example of repressed Victorian passion. Rather than a wool or cotton batting, the middle layer was made of paper. Not just any paper, but a collection of love letters cut into diamond shapes and then inserted between fabric layers. I could only stand so much after reading little snippets saying, "Darling, I cannot go further without . . ." and, "Charity doesn't know yet, but I will tell her all about it when. . . ."

Today, people quilt more as an art form and a hobby than to satisfy a sense of thrift. Scrap bags filled with pieces of old clothing, patiently waiting until a new quilt was needed, have left us. Today's quilters astound their non-quilting friends by purchasing new fabric, only to cut it up and re-sew the resulting pieces into decorative, elaborate designs. They sew and quilt with an amazing variety of threads, ribbons, and braids in hundreds of different colors. And this is part of what makes quilting today so much fun.

How to Use This Book

This book's goal is twofold: (1) to help you get started in a craft that has given millions of people enormous pleasure over the years, and (2) to show you how to profit from your quilting if this is your desire. In the first section of this book, you will have fun as you learn quilting basics, step by step. Later, if you decide to start selling the things you're making, the second section of the book gives you everything you need to know to set up a small quilting business in your home.

Yes, you can keep your day job and still enjoy both quilting and the profit it may bring. This book includes some copyright-free patterns to help you learn from scratch or polish old skills. Try making a few of these for sale at your next church bazaar.

Once you get going in quilting, I predict you'll be hungry for more information, so to satisfy that desire, the last chapter of this book lists magazines, organizations, books, and Internet sites that will boggle your mind. Is there really all that much to say about quilts? Yes . . . and I have 239 quilt books in my personal library to prove it!

Basic Tools for Quilting

1 Quilting needles
2 Straight pins
3 Saftey pins
4 Scissors
5 Tape measure
6 Thread
7 Variety of rulers
8 Marking tools
9 Batting
10 Template material
11 Thread snips
12 Thimble
13 Rotary cutter
14 Self-healing cutting mat

Part One

For Fun

The Joy of Quilting

▼▼

DID YOU HAVE COLORING books as a child? I did, and I loved them so much it really annoyed me when Mom asked me to put my colors away and come to dinner. I liked having the freedom to make flowers any color I chose from my crayon box. I colored giraffes blue and gave people green hair, and was teased for coloring outside the lines.

I didn't know it then, but that was the start of a lifelong fascination with colors that would eventually lead me into stitchery and the wonderful world of quilting. Now that I'm a "big girl," quilting has replaced my colors and coloring books, and I predict that, like me, you'll soon be having as much fun playing with fabrics and colors as I do.

We have lots of company, too. As you will soon learn, quilting today is an international obsession for fabric lovers around the world. And, thanks to the Internet and e-mail communication, quilters everywhere can exchange information and ideas every day if they wish. (More about this topic later!)

Quilting for Pleasure

Whether you are already familiar with quilting or are a complete beginner, this book is all you need to get going in a hobby that is likely to give you thousands of hours of enjoyment in years to come. Quilting offers the same pleasure to everyone who enjoys unbridled creativity with fabric and thread. Men who quilt become no less obsessed than women. Even children enjoy quiltmaking. Today, quilters young and old alike "color" both inside and outside the lines, and so can you.

Traditional quiltmakers still make blue and white quilts using patterns handed down from generation to generation, and you may enjoy doing this as well. Or perhaps you favor "art quilts" and "wearable art," which allow you to express anything you can imagine. Fairies and mermaids, biblical themes, flowers, maps, and lacy hankies all become fair game to the uninhibited quilter. Baltimore Album quilts, those wonderful, dimensional baskets overflowing with

BOMs and Mystery Quilts

Serious quilters may belong to several BOMs, an interesting concept for quilters that began in 1993 and has now swept across the United States. It's similar to the Book-of-the-Month Club, except that quilt enthusiasts sign up and pay in advance to receive a pattern each month to make a quilt "block of the month," sight unseen.

Speaking of unseen, have you ever heard of a "Mystery Quilt"? Quilters sign up to make a mystery quilt, unseen by anyone other than the designer. Clubs, shops, and magazines feature these suspenseful designs where one receives instructions to cut and sew a few sections at a time, with no idea of the ultimate design. At the end, like Agatha Christie's books, all becomes clear, and finishing instructions bring it all together. You'd better like it because you've just finished it!

fantasy-like flowers, satisfy the soul of the romanticist who wants to reproduce Victorian designs. There's something for everyone.

What about you? What style, color, or design will best express your sense of beauty and visual joy? What sort of quilt will give you that smug sense of accomplishment when asked, "Did you make that yourself?" What would you enjoy playing with most? Stars? Colors? Animals? Laces? Why not capture what you love most in a quilt? Perhaps you'd like to transfer the faces of loved ones to a quilt that will be passed down in your family for generations to come. A friend of mine is working on such an heirloom for her parents' fiftieth anniversary. The quilt features a family tree in cloth. Who could receive anything more precious than this?

Playing with Color

One of the great joys of quilting lies in the use of colors. Making a quilt will give you an opportunity to indulge in your favorite colors and prints with no justification required. No, your quilt need not match the walls, drapes, or carpeting. I have seen magnificent pieces swirling with rainbows and those limited to only shades of blue. Bold, primary colors threaten some quilters while others delight in making only white-on-white quilts. Personally, I love stained glass so much that I have more or less majored in designing stained-glass quilts. Tiffany lamps have always inspired me, as have art books of real stained glass. I paint and dye fabric to achieve the effects I want and glaze each little piece with special paint that makes it glisten just as glass does. At times, I cannot stop stitching the "leading" between colorfully streaked fabric patches.

Yes, "leading." Just as stained glass artisans separate sections of stained-glass windows with strips of lead (called *leading*), quilters use strips of black or charcoal bias tape to surround individual sections of a colorful quilt. (As a child, I always outlined all the pictures in my coloring books because I felt it added something to each design. I still feel that way.)

For the ultimate color project, you might want to consider making a "watercolor quilt." These quilts have become very popular and now appear everywhere. More than a dozen books have been published on this topic within the last few years, and there are several Web sites dedicated to watercolor quilts only (see Resources). These quilts use thousands of two-inch fabric squares in colors ranging from lights, mediums, medium darks, and plain darks to neutrals, florals, leaves, water, and so on. Using a "design wall" (see next chapter), a quilter places individual fabric squares within each marked square on the design wall in the manner of a jigsaw puzzle, creating a sort of "Monet-esque" impressionist design. My first watercolor quilt took four months of moving squares from here to there, painting some and dyeing others until I felt happy with the result. I thought I worked slowly, but exemplary designers say such quilts often take a year or more to complete.

Many quilters make watercolor quilts from their favorite fabric scraps. Although this kind of quilt project isn't featured in this book, you might want to keep it in mind for the future as you begin to collect fabric scraps.

The Benefits of Quilting

What keeps people quilting in addition to the fun and pleasure of it all? Many factors contribute to the quilting frenzy all over the world. First, the deeply embedded sense of thrift in all of us loves to say, "I made this quilt from fabric scraps!" Today, we even have a special term for this: a Scrap quilt! Quilters in grandmother's day could only dream of what we call "scraps" today, but quilters still love to make quilts from remnants left from other quilts.

In her book *Scrap Quilts,* quilting professional Judy Martin offers techniques and patterns old and new for making quilts from "collected" fabrics. Most quilters find that collecting a fabric stash is not only fun, but thrifty. However, we talk ourselves into thinking that if we buy three or four yards of a fabric we love, dozens of times per year, that finally using a few of them becomes "thrifty." Nothing much is said about the hundreds of yards we keep on hand for future thrift.

In addition to tying us to the past when we reproduce grandmother's patterns, quilting satisfies our need for play by letting us work with beautiful fabrics and threads. Watching dramatic patterns evolve from merely cutting and rejoining little triangles and squares can be fascinating. Quilting offers few limitations, and you are always the artist in total control. A non-fattening hobby, quilting also permits you to indulge yourself endlessly! You can make a blue giraffe or a fairy with green hair but, today, we call these modernistic or impressionist fiber-art quilt forms. Sounds impressive, don't you think?

You may or may not consider yourself a creative person, but I guarantee that quilting will release and excite your natural creativity. After visiting a quilt show, I am always impressed to observe how far others can stretch their imaginations. I have enjoyed children's quilting, with their unbridled freedom of expression. I have seen memorial quilts where photos of long-dead family members are transferred to fabric, then surrounded with ribbons, beads, and neat lines of stitching. Some seem more like an oil painting, so realistically do they portray landscapes, animals, and human faces.

An added bonus of quilting is that it allows you to suit your mood at any given moment. I love the flexibility quilting gives me! I can become studious and make a quilt as a teaching aid for my workshops, or switch to work on a whimsical small quilt for a new baby in the family. I have made romantic quilts and geometric quilts, and one to memorialize a dear friend. Christmas brings on new designs and provides just the excuse I need to buy more fabric and start a new project. Wait until you have quilted for a while, and you'll know exactly what I mean.

Lest you get too excited thinking about future projects, remember that quilting is also relaxing. Watching your favorite colors glide beneath your fingers will satisfy your need for tactile beauty. Stitching steadily and rhythmically by hand or machine will also soothe your mind and soul after a hard day's work.

Did you know???

There are 14 million quilters in the United States. Of these, 650,000 describe themselves as "dedicated quilters," spending $1,400 or more on quilt-related books and products.

Quilting on Vacation

Many quilters are so devoted to their quilting that they indulge themselves while on vacation. Every quilting magazine describes cruises, schools, seminars, exhibitions, vacations, clubs, and organizations to help feed a quilter's passion, and you'll find a list of such publications in Resources. If you really want to delve into quilting, here are just a few things you might do on a "quilter's vacation":

- Travel to Alaska, the Caribbean, Europe, or Mexico aboard a cruise ship, taking classes from quilting professionals (I've taught this way and have fond memories of threading needles for 30 passengers swaying back and forth).

- Attend "Quilt Camp in the Pines," located on the campus of Northern Arizona University in Flagstaff, and choose classes from more than a dozen quilting superstars.

- Enjoy a week of quilting events at an Empty Spools Seminar, one of the most popular seminars for quilters, held annually for several weeks in the Asilomar, California, conference center. Here you can listen to the ocean while you're both sewing and sleeping there. Let me tell you what I did for six glorious days at the last Empty Spools Seminar I attended:

Day 1: We learned to paint our own fabric to make a quilted wall-hanging or art-to-wear garment by dyeing silk, muslin, and yes, even cheesecloth, into lovely, landscape backgrounds awaiting our special touches.

Day 2: We made our own subtly shaded applique fabric with a magical texture created by painting wet fabric laid on plastic bags. I never recognized the creative wrinkles in plastic bags before, but I'm looking at them in a new way now. We began cutting interesting shapes from our "original fabric" creations. I opted to cut butterflies flitting everywhere on my garment-to-be.

Day 3: We learned to make dimensional flowers with petals. Imagine a gorgeous iris with one or two petals standing away from its center, outlined in gold braid. Wow!

Day 4: We learned to cut away portions of our work and replace the openings with machine-made lace webs of gold and silver threads shaped on covered wire. Accordion-pleated hand-painted silk proved not as difficult as I expected. The instructor showed us her techniques in about ten minutes. Wretched excess, but simply beautiful!

Day 5: We studied our compositions and added special touches, such as swirling tendrils, "mounds" of sand, and photo-transfers of real leaves. (A few enterprising students brought their lettuce leaves from lunch to class, saving them the trouble of hunting for tree leaves outside. These, too, made their way onto our works-in-progress.)

Day 6: We learned to add bobbin stump work and bobbin curls with heavy gold and silver threads to create three-dimensional design elements on quilts and wearable art.

Each evening after dinner, we gathered in a large hall to see slides of quilts made by the teacher/designers, hear quilt jokes, buy fabric and books, and participate in quilting contests. If each day didn't totally exhaust you, you could march back to your classroom and sew and quilt some more until past midnight then start over again the next day. To me, every day of this seminar offered a new textile dessert, each better than the last!

Quilt Shows and Festivals

There are many exciting quilt shows and festivals that greatly increase the fun and pleasure of quilting as a hobby or business. *Quilter's Newsletter,* the most popular consumer magazine for quilt enthusiasts, lists upcoming quilt shows to be held in every state in every issue. You will always find one near you. In addition, quilting guilds meet across the country to offer classes, techniques, help, and encouragement. Associations such as the American Quilting Society and the National Quilting Association publish magazines and quilt books, sponsor nationwide seminars, and keep every quilter hobbyist or professional well-informed and stimulated. They sponsor contests of all types to make quilters continue to stretch their skills.

Today, we see new associations cropping up in Japan, Australia, and Britain, plus a host of other countries. Quilters in these

A Serious Pincushion!

One of the most enjoyable parts of attending a quilting seminar is meeting other fabric and fiber addicts like yourself and seeing their work. At one seminar, I spotted an ornate, exotic something-or-other from across the classroom. I simply had to approach its owner to ask about this object. "Well," said Peggy Diamanti, "This is my serious pincushion!"

Peggy explained why her quilting pincushion was so outrageously exotic. "I really need to keep my sewing supplies very tidy in drawers and closets. Everything else in my house accumulates and overflows everywhere, but I don't mind this so long as my precious sewing supplies remain in order at all times."

The pincushion itself was barely visible, buried beneath the weight of Peggy's pin collection. Like an exotic porcupine, it was studded with fancy sewing pins with different colored heads. Clustered together, pins of one color formed soft petal shapes. Red petals gave way to pearl-tops, followed by blue and silver pins swirling around one another. Beautiful, pastel-colored flower pins inserted so close together looked like sea shells. Clearly, this was more than a sewing notion—it was an *objet d'art*. Now, I ask you, where else can you find such delight and fun in even the most humble quilting tool? Even the supplies are fun. Ask Peggy. She'll tell you!

countries can't wait to express their own identities via American-style quilting. (When you see glorious quilts from other countries, know that they are copying us, not the other way around.) These associations also have national seminars and guilds and frequently invite American quilting stars to come visit them and teach. Their need is insatiable! Quilting is not just for Americans anymore.

The International Quilt Market

To understand just how big the quilting industry is, travel to Houston in the fall and attend the annual International Quilt Market, the largest trade show in the world for the quilting industry.

Shop owners, teachers, writers, designers, and manufacturers come from all over the world and completely overwhelm attendees who love quilting and sewing. American and international retailers occupy nearly 600 booths in the 250,000-square-foot exhibit hall at the George R. Brown Convention Center, and quilters can choose from as many as 300 classes.

The International Quilt Festival

Although the Quilt Market is a trade show for professionals, all sewers, dollmakers, and quiltmakers are invited to attend the Quilt Festival, a consumer show held in conjunction with the Market a day or two later in the same location. This show is open to hobbyists and admirers and anyone who cares to come. The first time I attended the International Quilt Festival, I felt totally bewildered just looking down the countless rows of booths containing the latest tools, fabrics, notions, patterns, and books. Attending classes taught by the stars of the quilting world intimidated me, but I went anyway. To my surprise, I learned new techniques I thought I had known before. What a neophyte! One can always learn more and that's the most valuable bit of knowledge this event taught me.

Today, I still feel humbled when I attend this and other major quilt events. I always wear my sturdy running shoes and bring a rolling cart to prepare seriously for the quilting version of "The Greatest Show on Earth" in Houston.

Of course, Houston is no longer the only home of the International Quilt Market and Festival. Springtime brings us not only one but two more big quilting shows. You can attend an event on either of the U.S. coasts in Portland, Oregon, or Providence, Rhode Island. *The Insider,* published by Quilts, Inc. (the parent company of the International Quilt Market), noted in one issue that "The first and foremost reason to come to Quilt Market is to see what products are hot in the industry, things you simply cannot see or buy anywhere else and to see them first."

The Fairfield Fashion Show

Fairfield Processing Corp. began its business decades ago, producing that middle layer between a quilt's top and bottom—what we call batting. Their fashion show is held in conjunction with the Houston quilt shows. No, you will not see ordinary clothes there; handmade maybe, but not ordinary. I call them "fantasy clothes."

Quilters and seamstresses who come to the attention of Fairfield Processing Corp. receive an invitation to design something spectacular for the next year's show. The problem is, everything in the show is already spectacular so each year designers continue to try to out-do themselves. Following the initial presentation at the Houston show each year, the garments travel for display at other major quilting events throughout the country.

Manufacturers of beads, silk thread, laces, and exotic fabrics offer a selected Fairfield designer any product they request, which, in turn, appears on the fantasy garments in the show itself. What an effective marketing idea! Fashions with names such as "Volga Melody," "Fiesta Sunrise," and "My Secret Garden" float down the runways.

Wearable art seen at a Fairfield show features luxurious fibers such as chiffon, crushed velvet, raw silk noil, ultra-suede, and Middle Eastern batiks. Embellishments include sequins, pearls, gold and silver thread, silk braid, jeweled buttons, silk linings, lace, and more, much more. Attending a Fairfield fashion show is more than fun it's a fantastic experience reminiscent of clothing depicted in the beautifully illustrated *Grimm's Fairy Tales*.

Quilting Is Big Business!

In 1994, Quilter's Newsletter and the International Quilt Market and Festival in Houston, Texas, commissioned the first exclusive survey of the U.S. quilting market. Released in 1996 as *The First National Survey of Quilting in America,* it revealed that 14.7 percent (14,091,000) of American homes house a quilter.

According to this survey, quilters were expected to spend $476 million on tools and supplies plus a staggering $353 million on fabric during the following year. A newer survey is under way, but, nonetheless, statistics like these erase the notion that quilting is a frivolous hobby.

Your Quilting Options

As you will soon learn, you are not limited to making quilts only. Once you've learned the basic techniques of quilting—and this is easy to do—you will be able to turn quilt squares into a variety of items, from garments and bags to wall hangings, pillows, and other decorative accessories and gifts. In chapter 5, you will find several copyright-free quilt block patterns and projects you can make for both fun and profit.

Increasingly, dedicated quilters are discovering the additional pleasure of earning money from something they love so much. Maybe selling one of your original designs to a quilting magazine will thrill you for a lifetime. Perhaps you would feel satisfied to just sell a few baby quilts, pot holders, and pillows at your annual Christmas boutique.

If so, in chapter 6 you will find information to help you decide just how serious you want to become about quilting as a hobby or a way to earn extra money. If you dream of becoming a quilting professional like Judy Martin, Jinny Beyers, Virginia Avery, or Judy Simmons, remember they were once beginners, too. You also have the opportunity to join others whose work resides in the Quilters Hall of Fame.

As you will learn in the second half of this book, there are many exciting "quilting roads" you might explore if profit is your goal. Only you can set limits on how far you want to go.

Whether you quilt only for fun, or for both fun and profit, one thing is certain: In quilting, you will never run out of new ideas and patterns to try, new techniques to experiment with, new tools and supplies to play with, new books to read, or new friends to meet. And that's what makes quilting such an adventurous and satisfying craft!

Getting Started

▼▼▼

WHETHER YOU PLAN TO QUILT only for fun, or for both fun and profit, you need certain basic supplies, and the longer you quilt, the more supplies you are likely to need or want. This chapter describes the basic tools, equipment, and supplies commonly used by quilters. Initially, you can do without some of the things on my list, but if you're serious about quilting, you won't want to be without them for long.

Sewing Machine

Unless you plan to quilt and sew entirely by hand, you will need a sewing machine. Purists say that Grandmother did not cheapen her quilting by using a machine because she took pride in her handiwork. But think what she would have said if she could have seen today's computerized machines! They come loaded with more sewing and stitching information than I have gathered in my head

Summary List of Essential Quilting Tools and Supplies

- Sewing machine

- Working and cutting surfaces

- Ironing supplies

- Scissors and other cutting equipment (different sizes/types for different jobs)

- Sewing notions (needles, thimbles, regular and silk pins, basting, sewing, and quilting thread)

- Measuring tools (rulers, yardsticks, quilting guides, and measuring tapes)

- Marking tools (pens, chalk, and pencils in several colors)

- Template materials (commercial or hand made)

- Stencils (commercial or hand made)

- Drafting materials (paper, compasses, protractors, French curves, and graph and freezer paper which are optional for beginners)

- Design wall

- Batting

- Fabric

after more than 30 years of professional sewing and quilting experience. Would she have said no to one of them? I doubt it. Grandmothers did not have the choices we have today, though they would have surely used all the help they could find.

A computerized sewing machine is not mandatory, of course. As a matter of fact, until recently, I used only a Singer made and purchased in 1957. (These machines were made to last!) I still use it, although it only sews back and forth and zigzag. Eventually, however, I began to long for a smart machine with a built-in computer, screen, and stitching memory. If you long for a super-duper model as I did, buying one from your first earnings can be a realistic goal, but let me warn you: If you have not used a computerized machine before, your confidence may be in for a shock when you try one for the first time.

No one knew less than I did about my second sewing machine when I first bought it. I found that jokes about new buyers who cannot turn the machine on are quite true. Even lowering the needle challenged me. I had to join an online machine quilting group to learn how to thread my automatic-threader feature! Old or new, if your machine knows more than you do, learn all about it, and keep your machines in good condition by having a professional technician service them regularly.

Working and Cutting Surfaces

You will need a large work surface for cutting fabric and laying out projects. Desks, tables, and cutting boards are nice, but many of us still use the floor. It's always around. (See next chapter for tips on how to set up an efficient work space.)

Ironing Supplies

Reliable irons, ironing boards, and other pressing equipment are critical in making any kind of quilted project. If you do not have an ironing board, here's how to make a "quilter's ironing box." Find a sturdy, corrugated, cardboard box at least 13 inches wide. Cut a section from one side and trim to exactly 12 1/2 inches square. (You'll learn why this is important when you begin making blocks in chapter 5.) Now cut heavy flannel or an old towel at least two inches bigger than the cardboard and cover the padded layer with a square of favorite fabric from your stash. (No, it's not wasteful—you will be looking at it lovingly quite frequently.) Pull both layers taut over the edges of the cardboard and secure with strapping tape. Voila! You have created a mini-ironing board that can sit beside you as you press those little pieces of fabric.

Scissors, Shears, and Other Cutting Equipment

Scissors and shears in several sizes are a must. Those used for quilting deserve special care and should be reserved for cutting fabric only. All my scissors and shears are absolutely off limits to anyone else in the house. No longer should you let your teens cut just anything with your fabric shears. Hide them if you must.

Keep a separate pair of scissors handy for cutting paper and patterns. Cutting paper with fabric shears will dull the blades, so why not use an old, dull pair to start with? You also need little, sharp scissors for use in clipping threads at your machine and when you hand stitch.

Optional: Grandmother never had a rotary cutter, but no serious quilter would be without this equipment today. Rotary cutters cut through fabric like rolling cutters cut through pizza. But you must always rotary cut on a special, self-healing mat unless you plan to cut your breadboard in half. (Rotary blades used to cut fabric on wood will last only about 10 minutes before they go dull.) It's a good idea to always keep spare blades on hand. Better yet, keep a rotary blade sharpener with your sewing notions like I do.

Sewing Notions

You will need ordinary sewing notions, some of which you may already have, and sewing needles, machine needles (if you have a sewing machine), thimbles, regular and silk pins, and lots of basting, sewing, and quilting thread. Gone are the days when you could buy cotton thread only in black, white, and a few colors. Today's quilters have an incredible variety of threads from which to choose, with choices that boggle the mind: silk, rayon, metallic threads, braids, ribbon, variegated colors, and even more exotic threads such as invisible, iridescent, and pearlized nylon thread.

If someday you decide you'd like to earn extra money by doing machine quilting for other quilters, don't overlook the wonderful book, *Machine Quilting with Decorative Threads,* by Marine Noble and Elizabeth Handpicks. The authors analyze, review, and test literally every thread on the market, explaining how to distinguish the good threads from the mediocre.

Optional: As your thread collection grows, you will need something to store it in. Remember the quilter I mentioned in the introduction who carries special, plastic mini-suitcases to cart her thread collection around? You can start with cartons, pizza boxes, small fishing tackle boxes, or wall racks, if you prefer.

Measuring Tools

Wait until you see what quilting companies have designed for quilters to use when they take measurements! Rulers come in triangular, square, and even hexagon shapes and often feature both metric and English markings. Some appear with boldly colored marks that are easy to see. Some even have slits that you can run a pencil between to mark a straight line. You will be astounded when you see how many types and sizes of measuring tools you can find in today's shops. See chapter 4 for more details.

Handy Hint

If you have been sewing for a while, you may still have some thread on old wooden spools. Before using this thread, test it by snapping it between your hands. If it breaks too readily or comes apart, save it for basting only. In buying new thread, be careful about buying generic threads in chain stores that sell at four or five for a dollar. Most are inferior, uneven in color, break easily, and fuzz and pill like old Orlon sweaters. Unless such a sale features well-known brands advertised in quilting and sewing magazines, take care. Professional quilters who tote those big thread boxes around do not fill them with low-quality thread.

Quilting requires meticulous measuring, and by meticulous, I mean absolutely exact. Check your rulers, yardsticks, quilting guides, and measuring tapes to make sure each tool measures accurately. For example, I have a 12-inch ruler that actually measures 12 1/2 inches when compared to other measuring sticks.

Marking Tools

Grandmother could use only an ordinary pencil to mark her quilt squares, but you have many more options available. Buy marking pens, chalk, and pencils in several colors for making marks that you know you can remove on fabric. No one wants their marking lines to outlast their quilts, so study each type of tool with care.

You may use pencils made specifically for marking quilts, the marks of which can be brushed off as you stitch. Consider also the excellent soapstone and chalk sticks available today. Of all these implements, however, invisible pens are my top choice. No, the pens are not invisible, but the ink is, eventually. Residents of humid areas can buy blue felt quilting pens. Their marked lines remain in place until you pat them down with a very wet sponge or spray them with water from a pump bottle.

Purple felt pens fare better in dry climates. Because the marks disappear in a few hours, you'd better stitch quickly. When you use these pens in humid areas (I've done this during the rainy season), the lines disappear in just minutes because of the moisture in the air.

By all means, test the tool you choose for marking on a scrap of the same fabric you will use in the quilt. Does it come off when you spray it or put it through the washer? When you use a special quilter's eraser? If so, use it. If not, save it for paper only. Tragic stories of permanent markings that stubbornly refuse to leave the quilt are a frequent topic of discussion on quilting chat groups on the Internet. Unless you want to end up in tears after you've completed your quilt, test first!

Note: Details about marking methods and how to use marking tools, plus my unofficial survey of pens and markers, will be found in chapter 4.

Template Materials (Commercial or Handmade)

When placed on your fabric, templates help you cut the shape you need. You trace around them with a marker to ensure that all your fabric pieces (in the quilting world, we call them patches) measure exactly the size you intend.

You can go from one extreme to another here. Templates galore are listed in chapter 4. Fabric and quilt shops sell white, clear, or colored plastic sheets intended for cutting templates. You can even buy template plastic marked with grid lines to help you cut evenly and square.

Commercial templates are an optional purchase. Grandmother did not have this luxury item. If she had a handy husband a century ago, he would have cut her templates from tin or copper sheets. Some of these are still around, admired but not used. If on her own, Grandmother would have used whatever was at hand, such as cardboard, postcards, manila envelopes, paper, and, later, empty plastic milk or bleach bottles. You can use these, too.

Did you know???

Most quilters, men and women alike, wear a thimble when quilting even though they may not for other types of sewing. The continual pushing of the needles through several layers can make your finger quite sore. Almost all wear a thimble on their middle finger, sometimes on both hands at once.

Stencils
(Commercial or Handmade)

Stencils or stencil-making materials (plastic or cardboard plus a craft knife) are musts. They enable quilters to quilt the blank spaces between and around design elements on their quilts, by hand or machine. Stencils offer many design ideas, from traditional feather and leaf sprays to modern heart, rainbow, floral, and flowing ribbon shapes. Enjoy buying and using these but note that you may also mark plain grid lines on the straight or diagonal for all-over quilting lines. You will find more information about stencils and making your own in chapter 4.

Drafting Materials
(Optional for Beginners)

Quilters who design their own quilts keep drafting equipment, paper, compasses, protractors, French curves, and graph and freezer paper on hand. As you probably know, compasses and protractors ensure square corners, perfect circles, and precise triangles. French curves, little wavy plastic tools, ensure smooth, perfect arcs and will improve your flower stems and flowing lines.

Butcher or freezer paper, which is slightly sticky on one side, is wonderful stuff that is unsurpassed for appliquéing many quilting shapes. You simply iron the shiny side of the paper onto your fabric and it behaves like sticky notes do, remaining in place while you trace, cut, and press. Peel it off when you are done and use it somewhere else. Now quilting companies produce the wonderful stuff and call it *quilters freezer paper.*

Color Wheels

A color wheel gives you combinations of colors that will work with any primary color you've chosen. Several brands of cardboard wheels are available. An inner dial on the color wheel enables you to "dial up" a primary color and see which colors blend or contrast with that color. You can also lay a piece of yarn or fabric on the wheel and identify from one to four coordinated colors that will compliment it.

Design Walls

Now that quilting has reached art-form status, fabric artists should buy or make a design wall near their sewing space. Quilting superstars have them built into studio walls permanently. Imagine a white wall where you can place and adhere countless little fabric squares for a watercolor quilt. Because it takes months to move these around until a grand design emerges, you need to keep them in place to study them while your dazzling creation is under way.

Imagine a vertical tray attached to your wall where you can stick pieces of commercial picture puzzles while you work on them. Even as a part-time quilter, you may never again settle for moving little irregular pieces of painted cardboard around when you can play with favorite fabrics instead! That's what a design wall can do for you.

Optional: As mentioned in chapter 1, you can also buy a commercial design wall, which is simply a large piece of self-adhering felt marked with grid lines two inches apart.

Handy Hint

If you do not have a spare wall in your house, here's how to make an inexpensive portable design wall. Buy a four-foot-square piece of fiberboard from a lumberyard. Cover it with self-adhering quilt batting and store it beneath a bed or behind a door when not in use. Prop it on a chair or against other furniture when it is needed. Having no more walls to spare, (wall quilts cover all of mine), this is precisely how I use my home-made design wall.

Batting

"Batting" is the middle layer between a quilt top and its bottom, and it's available wherever fabric is sold. Start collecting batting in several varieties of thickness and fiber contents for different quilt projects. You may want fat batts for puffy comforters, or flat pure wool or cotton batting for traditional quilts or clothing. Today, you can even buy self-adhering batting that eliminates basting the layers together. The batting simply sticks on the underside of your quilt top. Some quilters complain that hand or machine needles drag through the layers as they become coated with the sticky stuff, but you can test for yourself and decide. If you plan to make quilted pillows, stuffed toys, or dolls, you will also need polyester fiber-fill for stuffing.

A large collection of batting will take up a lot of space unless it's properly stored, but you'll find tips on how to do this in the next chapter.

Fabric

Now, I don't have to tell you to start collecting fabric, do I? Many people who love fabrics become quilters just to justify buying all that material. In the beginning, you are likely to buy fabric when you find needed materials on sale at a shop or chain store nearby. Although buying this way will save a few dollars, you may have to settle for limited merchandise as well.

In her book *From Fiber to Fabric,* Harriet Hargrave tells you all you could possibly want to know about how to choose fabric and batting and how to determine quality. Hargrave explains clearly why very low-priced, flat-fold fabric sold in chain stores is not always a bargain. Arguments continue between newer quilters who want to buy fabric at $2 per yard and quilting and sewing shops that sell the same fabric for $8 or $9 per yard. Believe me, differences become apparent when you check the thread-count and see how evenly design patterns are registered onto the fabric. Many are too limp to retain their shape when cutting, marking, and stitching. Cheapest is not always best. Here are a few things to consider when choosing the fabric for a quilt project:

- Decide whether the finished item needs to be washed periodically, or if it will be dry cleaned. Select fabric accordingly.

- For items that need to be washed, choose 100% cotton (most favored by quilters). It's easy to work with, washes well, and holds its shape. (Note that cotton fabrics come in varying thicknesses and densities.)

- Cotton/polyester blends can be used, but they aren't as dense or firm as 100 percent cotton, and they can be more difficult to work with due to their somewhat slippery nature. These fabrics are also more difficult to stitch/quilt through.

- If the finished item won't be washed, you can use any fabric you like, so long as it can be successfully pieced or quilted. Silk, satin, and metallic fabrics can add dazzling touches to quilts, garments, and accessory items that will only be dry-cleaned.

Quilt books and magazines offer a wealth of information on the various types and kinds of fabrics you can use. Many stores now specialize in fabric especially for quilters and can offer purchasing guidance. To start a "fabric stash," you should purchase at least one-quarter yard of basic colors and three to four yards of fabrics you love. Most quilters still pre-wash, iron, then store their fabric, but a growing number prefer to not wash it at all, allowing it to retain the manufacturer's sizing. You should not store fabric in plastic bags as it invites mildew. Boxes and shelves are a better choice. (See next chapter for some specific fabric-storing tips.)

Until you can qualify to buy fabric at wholesale prices (see sidebar), you can save money by ordering from sewing discount supply catalogs, such as Clotilde, which offers quilting and sewing items at 20 percent less than retail.

How to Buy Fabric at Wholesale

Once you begin to sell your work as a quilting professional, you can save money on fabric by buying it wholesale. To do this, you need to obtain a seller's permit (see discussion under sales tax in chapter 11). Let me explain how the wholesale purchasing process works so you'll understand how to proceed if you later decide to start a small quilting business.

Having a seller's permit does not mean that all wholesalers (also called distributors) will sell to you. Some will refuse your order because it is too small. One solution to this problem is to subscribe to *Craft Supply Magazine*, a trade journal focused on home-based crafters. Subscriptions are available to all qualified buyers actively engaged, even part-time, in professional crafting. Their annual directory issue declares hundreds of sources of wholesale craft supplies. This market has grown so much that various craft shows around the country are now aimed at very small (one person) craft business owners, and most vendors at these shows will sell their products one or two at a time.

Additional wholesalers will be found in the annual directories published by Craftrends and Craft & Needlework Age (see Resources for more information.) You won't find these magazines in shops and bookstores because they are not consumer publications. They are trade journals published solely for craft business owners and available by subscription only.

In addition to using your seller's permit for purchasing wholesale items used to make products for sale, you can use it to gain admission to wholesale trade shows. Shows like these are the most important gathering places for wholesalers to display and demonstrate their merchandise to you, the potential retailer. If you listen, you will find that they will provide you with a rich education on their products, competitors' products, and the craft quilting market in general. Consumers may not buy at wholesale trade shows, but your seller's permit will identify you as a serious businessperson interested in buying supplies to make your products.

See chapter 7 for tips on how to successfully deal with wholesalers.

Setting Up Your Personal Workspace

▼▼▼

A QUILTING STUDIO? I DON'T have space for a quilting studio," you say. But you do! A "studio" is nothing more than a creative environment where you can design and work at your craft. Referring to whatever space you use for your quilting as a "studio" may be the first step in giving it the respect it deserves.

This chapter explains how to transform an area of your home into a comfortable, organized work space that is all your own, whether it's a whole room or just a small corner. You'll learn how to maximize your efficiency by designing your quilting space, not merely assigning it "leftover" space.

Although any available space can be transformed by a little creative design, converting a spare bedroom is the ideal solution. It's already heated, cooled, and ventilated like the rest of your home. Bathrooms and closet storage cry out to hold your supplies. The bedroom our last child vacated when leaving home today houses my working studio. Our former double garage is now a spacious home office. If you don't have this kind of space to work with, there are still many things you can do to create a comfortable and efficient working area.

Fabric Cutting Surfaces

As the place where you lay out and cut fabrics, your work surface comes first. How about an older dining or kitchen table if space allows? If possible, center it in the room, permitting you to walk, reach, and work from all four sides.

If your space is too small to leave a work table set up permanently, investigate today's collapsible, heavy cardboard cutting tables that enable you to cut, draft, and lay out large projects. When not in use, these temporary work surfaces fold for hiding under beds or behind doors. Consider camping tables with folding legs, too. Set them up when you need them; take them down when you are finished.

Your Sewing/Working Area

Most quilters want more space around their sewing machine than is typically offered by standard table models. To increase space, consider modifying an old-fashioned, heavy office desk. Cover the top surface with floor tiles, cementing them down or using the kind that have peel-off adhesive backings. Spruce up your desk by adding colorful tole or sponge-painted designs.

You might also wish to consider one of the modern tilt tables to angle your machine toward you. This will eliminate the need for you to hunch over the machine. A friend saved the $60 price of the special tilt table by resting the back of her sewing machine on two ordinary doorstops (wedges covered with rubber that prevent doors from closing shut). Now, why didn't I think of that before spending $60?

My economy move was to remodel an old army desk, cut an opening into the front, and drop the machine's base into the opening. This provided me with a large, flat surface to feed quilts and garments through the arm of my sewing machine. Unexpectedly, I discovered an extra bonus. The shallow middle drawer meant for pencils and small office items was exactly the right depth to store spools of thread.

I found the large double drawer on one side (originally meant for hanging files) perfect for filing sewing patterns. We paid $5 for the desk and $8 for floor tiles, then spent a day sanding and painting. Voila! I now have a custom work space that permits easy sewing on art-to-wear garments and even the largest quilts.

Two sliding boards or leaves beside the center drawer have become my friends. Secretaries used them to hold typewriters, but I pull mine out to create an L-shaped space around the machine to hold a quilt, as I bind it, for example. The added work surface supports the full weight of the quilt, preventing it from dragging as it glides through the presser foot of my machine.

Using Corners

Appropriate corners of rooms if you do not have an entire room for your sewing and quilting. Stack racks or shelves from floor to ceiling. Open bins nesting into one another are particularly practical, as their contents remain on view while all but the top bin are protected from dust by the bin above. This is a great way to store yarns, fabric, dolls, quilt batting, and more.

Watch for storage buys when small shops close their doors or remodel. Look for notices advertising fixtures for sale. Adjustable shelving and bins used to display goods in shops also work well in home studios, and many are designed and shaped specifically for corner placement.

Think about plant stands, too. Many corner styles offer half-circle shelves arranged in tiers from floor to

Handy Hint

To get the most use out of a desk drawer, don't just toss notions into them. Instead, buy plastic organizers meant for silverware storage in the kitchen. Choose styles with rectangular segments not spoon-shaped slots. These organizers also hold large spools of thread on their side or small spools standing up. Fill the spaces with marking tools, rulers, seam rippers, scissors, and rotary cutters. Craft and quilting stores also sell storage containers in many styles, sizes, and colors, featuring removable trays and small compartments. Keeping everything in order means you will not lose valuable quilting time looking for your tools.

ceiling. Or check out open-board shelving, which rests on wall-supported brackets. They cost little yet remain adjustable and moveable. Place them anywhere you find spare wall space. When planning for storage or display, make every inch count!

Your Closet: The Perfect Storage Space

For a quilter, nothing beats a closet with shelves from floor to ceiling. If you have closet space in a converted bedroom, consider it a treasure. Remove the door to create a walk-in storage closet. Sturdy shelves should already be in place overhead, but consider adding one or more shelves above the existing shelf to expand storage to the ceiling of the closet. Try to vary the space between shelves to allow narrow spaces for flat items such as your stencil collection, and larger spaces for pillow forms, bulky items, and batting.

Do you remember that I promised to tell you where you could store batting? Well, this is the place. Batting is expandable stuff that seems to have a life of its own, so I've found the best place for it is on the uppermost shelf against the ceiling. I keep mine rolled tightly, held in place with several rubber bands. This permits me to see the weight and fiber of the batting, but eliminates the springiness of unrolled batting that lets it spread everywhere. I am height-impaired (a short person) and, as such, I have a reaching tool in my studio that will grasp anything from a paper clip on the floor to a roll of batting close to the ceiling. Buy these in shops that sell supplies for arthritic folks or in catalogs specializing in convenient gadgets for "mature" persons (like me).

Building shelves inside the closet works well, but instead I bought old bookcases and fit them into the closet. My shelves are not beautiful, just unfinished fiberboard, but who can tell? Now that the shelves are overflowing with neat piles of my fabric stash, I can no longer see what the shelves look like. I guarantee that by the time you fill the shelves, yours will not be visible either.

Clear, plastic, sweater boxes stack easily on shelves, permitting viewing and easy retrieval of contents. These boxes in my studio closet act like drawers, enabling me to pull out exactly the one I want while eliminating the need to remove and look into each box. This is where I store my fabric scraps, sorted by color for easy reference.

One plastic "drawer" contains only white and off-white remnants, neatly pressed. The next holds pastels. Next, more plastic boxes of small, medium, and large prints. The lower boxes contain solid and darker fabrics. I can see the contents at all times, yet the drawers keep the fabrics organized and clean.

Sweater boxes also hold ribbons, reels of lace, and other trims. Flat-folded yardage sits on narrow shelves spaced a foot apart. Before storing, I wash and press each length, labeling each piece with fabric content. By storing flat folds this way, you can avoid landslides when the length you want is on the bottom of a tall stack.

Other Storage and Space-Saving Ideas

Handy Hint

Although the contents may not be visible, traditional dressers offer storage as their prime function. My old dresser holds stencils in one drawer, threads and yarn in the next two, and template materials and measuring tools in the last. To give your studio a unified, decorated look, consider painting or decorating all pieces of old furniture with a common theme.

Many years ago, I purchased from a hardware store a 12-inch-wide desktop cabinet that was designed to hold screws and nails in tiny, nesting drawers. If buying new boxes for your notions is beyond your budget just now, maybe you can convert one from your garage or household workspace that is now filled with nails and small tools. Bear in mind that clear plastic drawers allow you to see the contents without a search and that divided boxes work well for storing buttons, bobbins, cotton floss, and other small notions.

If you don't have space for boxes and cabinets, consider using the walls around your sewing machine. You can find hanging racks to hold notions, and can use pegboard and hooks from which to hang scissors, shears, and even small plastic bags filled with notions, ribbons, laces, and other tools.

To further preserve space, think about track lights or lamps clamped to the sides of bookshelves rather than wasting floor space

Idea Notebooks

Binders. Frankly, I cannot live without them. Dozens of binders hold my magazine collections as well as my design ideas. I have entire bookcases filled with bulging binders.

What's in them? First, I fill each binder with top-loading plastic pages. I can slip everything from a scrap of paper to a magazine into them, keeping everything in its proper place. I label all my binders so I know exactly what they contain. Here's what presently resides in my three quilting-idea binders (I have others for garment-making, knitting, crochet, doll-making, and so on.):

- Greeting cards with pleasing designs

- Wallpaper samples

- Postcards

- Gift wrap

- Stationery. (Don't be surprised that, as you take your quilting more seriously, friends and relatives will seek stationery with quilting designs just for you. Save them!)

- Samples of sewing or embroidery stitches worked on small fabric squares

using table-base styles. Footrests beneath your work table can double as containers. I have several cardboard boxes meant to store file folders, and, believe me, each one is full of fabric and yarn, not folders!

Filing Systems

As a quilter, you will probably collect magazines, books, and patterns that you will use in a variety of ways. To find what you're looking for at any given time, you must set up an efficient system for

- Photographs of beautiful things such as flowers, sea and landscapes, fish, and so on.

- Tear-sheets from quilting magazines showing quilts that caught my eye

- Tear-sheets from home furnishing, department store, and bed-linen catalogs. (Yes, even if the quilts you find within are machine-made or mass produced, it's the idea that counts. What style, design, and color of quilts did they find popular enough to reproduce?)

- Ads from news magazines giving me color ideas. (I once designed a quilt based on an ad for a folding pocket knife. No, the quilt does not depict a knife, but I did try to capture the clever use of black and charcoal shades against a cranberry and ruby-red background. I also use automobile ads as design sources because they use color so well.)

- Photos of stained-glass windows. (Remember my special interest in stained-glass quilts? One of my quilts featured on the cover of a quilt magazine came directly from a tracing I made of the real stained-glass window in my office.)

- Snippets of fabrics, ribbons, and lace that I may combine in a quilt or garment in the future. (One of my largest quilts began this way. I gathered swatches of velvet fabric, old, lace doilies, and interesting beads. Collected over a 15-year period, these items eventually became my "Victorian Crazy Quilt," published in *Lady's Circle Patchwork Quilts* in 1996 (no longer in publication).

filing and retrieving information. Following are some special tips on how to do this.

Publications

Second to hoarding fabric, most quilters save magazines. But how do you find the one you read three months ago that contains the information you need now? Saving publications in a random pile is inefficient, and searching through all of them for specific research material or a pattern can be frustrating. You need to find a way to simplify this job.

As you read a magazine, note on the cover what you found of value within its pages. (Steel-tipped pens will write on the heavy, coated paper stock used for magazine covers.) Below you will find a few "shorthand codes" to help you create a retrieval system. On the cover of the next magazine you read, write codes similar to those below:

Write	Example
Copy p. 21	about setting borders
Write p. 34	to request information about product
Do p. 42	call the 800 number and order this book.
Save p. 61	refer to this ad for color idea
Study p. 75	good article about storing fabric paint
Tear p. 103	add to idea binder

This system tells you immediately why you saved a publication. Now you can stop wasting time thumbing through countless issues looking for an idea you remember but cannot locate. I toss magazine issues without notations on the covers. This means I found nothing in them worth saving after the initial reading. The only exception to this rule occurs when I want to collect all the issues of a particular publication.

Slip cases sold by magazine publishers to hold a year's subscription can be both expensive and bulky. Consider instead plastic magazine holders. What humble gems! These three-hole punched plastic strips come in sets of 12 and sell for less than $4. Place them in a binder labeled with the magazine's name. Open each magazine to its centerfold. Slip each magazine, annotated as described previously, through the plastic slit. That's all there is to it. No need to punch holes in the magazine. You can remove it when you need to, replace it easily, and store your collection neatly and permanently.

Perhaps you want only a single page from a magazine. If so, place the page immediately into your idea binder discussed previously. Do not allow small bits of paper to collect. Assign them a place from the beginning.

What if you want to catalog specific information but prefer not to tear up a valuable publication? Photocopy what you need and store it in the appropriate binder or file. But remember you may only make photocopies for your own personal use. (See chapter 11 for information about the copyright law and the legal rights of publishers.)

Books

I find I must own my reference library, so all my information is available to me anytime, night or day. Frequently, you will find me roaming through my studio in the wee hours of the morning because I want to read or reference a specific book. Such a collection is only as good as how quickly you can find what you need.

The first step to getting your books organized is to make a list of all titles by topic (preferably on your computer). I keep separate lists for books on quilting, knitting, crochet, and color. Each time I buy a new book, I add it to one of my lists, and I carry them with me to seminars and workshops and when I visit bookstores. They tell me what already exists in my collection so I can avoid duplicate purchases.

On bookshelves, organize your books by topic rather than simply stacking them randomly. Group the books together on the shelf as they appear on your list. Make a list of titles you still want to buy. Carry it with you, always ready to expand your library in a planned way, not on impulse.

Patterns

Storing patterns presents a different challenge. Sewing patterns, like road maps, can try the patience of a saint to refold and replace in their original envelopes. Make patterns uniform and easy to store by first removing them from their envelopes. Tape or paste the cover of the pattern envelope on the outside of a manila folder once you have opened it. Refold and press the pattern sections to fit inside the folder and label it.

Purchase inexpensive cardboard file boxes that accommodate manila folders perfectly. (Remember, if you have no room to store the box, you can use it as a footrest beneath your desk, worktable, or computer station.)

Last, the ultimate secret of organization: Always return each item you use from your studio to its proper place so you can find it next time. An organized studio invites you to do your best work. For more ideas on creating the perfect sewing/quilting area, consider the book *Sewing Room Design,* listed in Resources.

Office Furnishings

If you decide to start a quilting business, you will definitely need a little office space somewhere in your home. No matter how small you plan to keep your business, you will eventually have paperwork to do. You must write checks, make calls, and answer correspondence. Initially, you can do what many former hobbyists turning professional do: keep everything in a box and periodically spread it out on your dining table. As your business grows, however, you may need a permanent space from which to actually run your quilting business, beginning with a comfortable office desk and chair.

Selecting a Desk

This should be a top priority. You can spend a fortune on a new, modern desk from an office furniture company, or you can save money by customizing an older desk. If possible, select one with drawers on each side of the center knee well. If you are buying a new desk, try sitting at it before you buy it and make sure the space between the columns of drawers accommodates your knees and legs comfortably.

A common mistake people make when choosing a desk is selecting one with an inadequate working surface. Consider all the items you will need. Will you be using a computer or a typewriter? What about a phone? These items consume a lot of desk space, and you must be careful to also allow enough open space on which to work.

One of my first remodeling mistakes was to select a desk with a surface that was too shallow. I found myself fumbling around trying to turn pages of books I had balanced on my lap because there was no room to lay them on the desk. There was no place to make handwritten notes or to shuffle papers. I had to place books I needed to use on a chair and even the floor.

Here is a simple, inexpensive solution if you already have a desk you find too small: Purchase a sheet of plywood or fiberboard; cut it wider and deeper than the surface of the desk; cover it with inexpensive, adhesive shelf paper or wallpaper, or paint it; place it on top of the existing desk; and, voila, you have expanded your desk's work area.

LINDA'S STORY

Linda Schmidt, a quilt and garment designer, began her home-based quilting and textile business in 1993. Linda says she lives her life the same way she makes quilts: a little of this, a little of that. She plays the flute, guitar, and piano, hikes, reads, makes wearable art, quilts, cooks, cleans, holds an outside job, goes to her children's games, and "simply does what all mothers do," according to Linda.

People seeing Linda's quilts for the first time often believe they are seeing an oil painting on fabric. Depicting animals and landscapes in a realistic, meticulously shaded, and precise way has become Linda's trademark.

Recently, I attended a large quilt show. While passing several of Linda's quilts on display, I heard over and over again, "Oh, there's Linda's work. I can spot it a mile away." I agree that her quilts are like no others. She does not use traditional methods, nor does she make traditional quilts. Linda does not begin by joining small squares and triangles together;

Reserve the desktop for active work. Do not allow stacks of paper and correspondence to collect there. Organize the drawers for office essentials such as stationery, forms, stamps, pens, pencils, and so on. Consider plastic utensil trays for your desk drawers to eliminate continually searching for items you cannot find. Stackable trays on a corner of your desk will make it easy to separate correspondence, bills, announcements, invoices, and other important business papers.

instead, she makes what I call "fabric portraits."

I asked Linda to advise readers of this book just starting or renewing their quilt interests. Her response: "Learn, work, do it, and finish it! Make quilts for your church and local shows. Make the effort to display your work in other shows after a while. Make baby gifts and wearable art, make dolls and crazy quilts, take classes and teach others, spread the word and cover your little piece of the world with color, grace, and beauty. You never know when a quilt you make will touch someone, bring someone hope, or say something to them that no one else has ever said before."

Copiers and computer printers need not take up valuable prime space on your desk, but can be positioned farther away on a separate table. That way, you have a chance to stand up and stretch your back when you use them.

If you keep your phone within reach of your filing cabinet, you need only swivel in your chair to search for information from file drawers when needed. This way, you will never need to put callers on hold.

Selecting a Chair

Though many famous businesspeople began on a card table and folding chair, you will not find these comfortable for long. Humans did not always spend most of their lives in a sitting position.

Take a book with you when you shop for a chair. That's right, try a chair on for size before you buy it, just as you did your desk. Select a chair because it fits your body, not because it fits your budget. Sit and read for at least 15 minutes when testing a chair, and evaluate its features carefully, for you will spend many hours sitting in it.

Note the depth of the seat pan. People with long legs require a deeper seat than those with short legs. A seat pan that is too long will impede circulation behind your knees.

Last, look for a chair with a back rest that rocks back and forth, enabling you to lean forward, and that will permit you to raise and lower the back as well. Keep in mind that chairs with a five-wheel base will provide a good deal of stability when you swivel around.

As a full-time writer and quilter, I count on my carefully chosen furniture and equipment to keep me working comfortably. Not all was new when I found it, however; secondhand stores filled my needs, and if you, too, find yourself with a limited budget, you can do the same as you grow into your new quilting activities.

Did you know???

There really is a building for outstanding quilters called *The Quilter's Hall of Fame*. Like its sports and music counterparts, this organization honors those that excel in the field it celebrates. Located in the Marie Webster House in Marion, Indiana, The Quilter's Hall of Fame houses the very best quilts from top designers throughout the country.

Quilting How-To's

▼▼▼

WHEN I TEACH A BEGINNERS' quilting class, my students are surprised to learn that all they need to bring to the first class is a notebook and pen. No quilting yet. I use the entire first three-hour lesson just to prepare them for the second class, which begins with the first steps in making a quilt. In this chapter and the next, you will learn about my favorite quilting method, known as "quilt-as-you-go" (QAYG), and how to:

- Select fabrics and colors
- Select the right marking and measuring tools
- Transfer quilting designs to fabric
- Accurately cut fabric shapes
- Baste and quilt

The QAYG Quilting Method

Among all the pleasures associated with this beautiful craft, quilters agree that making quilts does not provide instant gratification. It takes time and is definitely not a "quick and easy" craft. Understand that those glorious blue-ribbon winners you see at quilt shows may have taken months or a year to complete. This, in itself, contributes to the endearing quality of quilts. People marvel when they see what talented artisans can do with fabric, thread, and time. To love quilts is also to acknowledge the devotion quiltmakers put into their art.

If you are a new quilter, each block may take you a day or two to cut out and piece together. Like coloring in books when you were small, you may find yourself playing with your favorite fabric colors while time slips away. You may choose to combine your blocks into a four-, six-, or nine-block quilt or make individual projects of each block, as shown in the next chapter. When every block in a single quilt is a different design and/or color, the finished product is called a *sampler quilt*.

Sampler quilts, similar to my four-block quilt shown in the next chapter (see the color insert for reference), are delightful projects for beginners and experienced quilters alike. Because each block is different from the next, think of a sampler quilt as something of a buffet. You can experiment with several blocks within one project and determine what you enjoy most and wish to repeat in the future. Possibly, you will make a particular block and decide that it will become your "one and only."

If you are not ready to make a sampler quilt, you may prefer to finish each block individually and make them up as pillows, table mats, or small wall hangings. You will find specific directions for all of these in chapter 5.

Whether you decide to make individual projects or a sampler quilt with your blocks, you will learn to quilt in a wonderfully convenient way without a frame. To make your quilting experience truly portable, we will use the QAYG method, also called *lap quilting*.

QAYG quilts have a good record. Because this type of quilt is portable, quilters complete them more quickly than they do quilts worked on frames. You can take them with you while you wait for appointments or when you travel in airplanes or cars. Take them on vacation or merely move them from the living room to bed. Quilt wherever and whenever you please! Using small bits of time means more quilting gets done.

This is important for those who cannot devote full time to their quilting hobby, as well as those who have physical problems of any kind. QAYG quilting is perfect for me because I have arthritic problems. Painful joints do not do well when I'm sitting for long periods

Old vs. New Quilting Methods

In earlier days, busy women quilted differently. Large groups of quilters came together to quilt many of the beauties seen in museums today. Stretching the quilt "sandwich" (top, batting, and backing) onto large frames required many pairs of hands. Larger rooms held large frames in corners. Old photographs show innovative women attaching their frames to large chains in the ceilings. When not in use, frames were whisked up and out of the way.

Today, quilting is more often a solitary activity. Apartment and condominium dwelling makes quilting on big frames challenging; even if you own a house, living with a large frame for months at a time can be a major annoyance. QAYG quilts have ended all that, allowing a quilter to sit in her favorite easy chair and make even a king-sized quilt with individual blocks in a small basket nearby.

QAYG quilts have yet another advantage in that they hold your interest longer as you work. Traditional quilters begin a quilt by cutting out all the fabric pieces. Next, they press them all. After that, they mark each one and, at last the fun part, they join the small fabric patches together. In this quilting method, each step feels endless before the next begins. One must complete the entire quilt top before the most favored part, the hand or machine quilting, begins.

QAYG quilters can work to suit their mood. For example, working on three blocks at once suits me very well. I may cut pieces for one block one day, while a second block requiring hand piecing waits nearby. I may choose to hand quilt a third block the same day. Varying activities this way holds your interest longer and keeps you quilting for greater periods of time.

in one position over a frame. But with QAYG quilts, I can enjoy quilting in my reclining chair, and even in bed.

Selecting Fabrics and Colors

Selecting fabrics and colors for a new quilt can be a great pleasure. Start thinking about your fabric color scheme now. Successful quilting projects take time to plan. Following are some ideas to get you started.

Fabric Choices

Polyester and cotton/polyester fabric blends, while ideal for making garments, can seriously hinder the quiltmaking process. As a beginner, I did not believe that 100% cotton would make my quilting easier, even though it is advised by experts. Thus, my first quilt had 50-50 blends and a few patches of 100% polyester. Each stitch was a struggle, with the fabric fibers resisting each one. Now, like other experienced quilters, I've learned my lesson and use only 100% cotton fabrics.

Believe me, my fingers knew the difference! Easier stitching and more even hand quilting results with 100% cotton fabrics. Polyester fabrics, with their crease resistance, do just what they are supposed to do: resist your creasing them. It is impossible to press seam allowances flat. Try them if you must, but remember, I have warned you.

Avoid sheer, plaid, stretchy, double knit, napped, satin, and silk fabrics. Wait until you have a special need for these harder-to-manage materials.

Color Choices

Choose colors carefully to ensure they will work together. It's helpful to use a color wheel, as mentioned in chapter 2. Color schemes that feature red, yellow, and blue (the primary colors) always provide a clean, bright look. Green, a secondary color made from mixing yellow and blue together, still adds the restful feeling blue usually invokes, even in its green and blue-green variations. You may use all solid fabrics, or all prints, or come up with your own combination.

Also consider a monochromatic color scheme. This means choosing only one color in several values. Choose perhaps two dark blues, one solid and one print. Try adding a medium blue and a pale blue. Quilts made of many values of blue create a peaceful feeling. Rustic browns bring nature indoors. Pinks will produce a feminine atmosphere. Got the picture?

Warm and cool contrasts can be very effective, too. Choose two colors from the warm half of the color wheel (red, orange, and yellow) and two from the cool half (green, blue, and purple). For example, you might combine a deep blue and blue-green with orange and red-orange.

Excitement is created by the use of complementary colors. Find a color you like on the color wheel. That color's complement lies directly opposite it and, together, they create contrast and movement.

How to Make a Color Reference Folder

Here's a little project that will help you shop for the fabrics you need. If you are planning your quilt around an existing "stash" of fabrics, make a color reference folder that includes snips of all the colors you are considering. Arrange solid colors by lights, mediums, and darks and prints by small, medium, and large sizes. When the blend provides a satisfying feeling, tape them in place.

If you have no fabrics on hand, make a color folder of sample papers. Tear areas from magazines that illustrate colors that please you and paste them inside a manila folder, collage style, adding and subtracting as needed until the combination pleases you. With this tool in hand, you will have a clearer idea of colors you like and the effect you want to achieve.

If the result feels too strong for you, you can soften it with the color's near complements, also called its split-complements. Because violet's direct complement is yellow, its split complements, the two colors beside the complement, are yellow-green and yellow-orange. Sound strange? Take a look at pansies, violets, and the majestic iris; they illustrate nature's way of using complementary colors and split complements.

Now that you are ready to choose colors in a knowledgeable way, you won't feel overwhelmed by choices on your first trip to the fabric store. (See also sidebar, "How to Make a Color Reference Folder.")

Calculating Yardage Requirements

All blocks for your sampler quilt will measure 12 inches square. You will also add 2-inch lattice strips, called "sashing strips," to bring the size of each block to a 16-inch square. For reference, table 1 will give you approximate yardage requirements for the QAYG method, using blocks to make small items, such as wall hangings, up to larger items, such as bed-sized quilts.

Yardage Requirements

Quilt Top	# of Blocks	Backing Yardage
Wall Hanging (4 blocks)	2 across, 2 down–2 yards	1 yard
Crib (9 blocks)	3 across, 3 down–4 yards	3 yards
Twin (12 blocks)	3 across, 4 down–7 yards	5 yards
Double (16 blocks)	4 across, 4 down–9 yards	7 yards
Queen (20 blocks)	4 across, 5 down–11 yards	9 yards
King (24 blocks)	4 across, 6 down–13 yards	11 yards
California King (30 blocks)	5 across, 6 down–16 yards	13 yards
California King (Alternate) (35 blocks)	5 across, 7 down–19 yards	15 yards

Table 1. Yardage Requirements

Finished quilt sizes may be altered further by:

- Adjusting the finished width of the lattice strips
- Adding or reducing the width of borders
- Adding multiple borders

No hard and fast rule can predict exactly how much fabric your quilt will consume. Many variables come into play, such as marking and cutting methods and how one cuts large prints for small patches. Do not forget to allow an extra bit of fabric in the event you make an error or two.

Note: If you decide to make a bed quilt, measure your bed and the width, length, and thickness of the mattress to determine finished sizes. Do not forget the amount of overhang you want at the head, foot, and sides. You could make the quilt large enough to reach the floor or only cover the mattress sides. The latter requires a dust ruffle between the mattress and box spring to cover it and the bed frame.

A Helpful Yardage Formula

Balancing the colors, values, and prints of your final quilt is both a challenge and a delight. If you feel unsure of how much to buy of what, consider the following "formula":

Calculate the total number of yards you need. Let's say that you would like to make a crib blanket that would use 4 yards for the quilt top, as an example. Shop first for the main color (MC), which will unify the variety of blocks in your quilt. Will it be a dark, light, or medium color value? Does it tie in with the fabrics you already have? Having chosen your MC, you can buy fat quarters of other fabrics to balance the remainder of your quilt. Plan to use one-half of your total yardage for the MC. All lattice strips and the border around the outer blocks would be made of the MC. To further unify your quilt, plan to use your MC in at least one-third of the blocks. Even a tiny triangle or square of MC appearing frequently in the quilt will tie this important color and fabric to the lattice strips.

Divide the remaining fabrics (2 yards, in our example) into further groupings. Consider the remaining fabric with these elements in mind:

- Vary the print sizes. Use tiny calicos, medium-sized prints, and one or two larger, splashy prints. You might also consider space-dyed or marbled fabric for added interest.

- Vary the color values. Three or five is an easy number with which to work. Dark values contain the darkest colors closest to black, such as navy, maroon, deep violet, dark brown, and bottle green. Light values are those closest to white, such as pastel groups, cream, ecru, and small prints on pale backgrounds. Medium values fall in between.

Choose your backing fabric last (3 yards in our example). It should be a color and/or print that appears somewhere on the quilt surface or at least relates to it. Usually, the color of the quilting thread matches the backing fabric.

Preparing Fabric for Cutting

Before fabric can be marked for cutting, it must be properly prepared. To do this:

1. Gather all your fabrics and look them over in varied lighting situations.
2. Remove any that you find are not blending with the others.
3. Prewash all fabrics, including the main color and backing fabric, in hot water to remove sizing and fabric finishes.

4. Discard any fabric that gives even a hint of not being colorfast.

5. Iron all fabrics.

Now you're ready to cut strips, piece blocks, make a "sandwich," and get ready to mark your quilt lines! For more discussion on piecing, see chapter 5.

Selecting the Right Quilt Markers

You will recall my earlier discussion about the vast array of tools, pencils, and pens to mark those all-important lines on your completed quilt top. Our grandmothers had limited choices, but you have many—so many, in fact, that you may feel overwhelmed when trying to select the right one. In trying to make the right choice, you need to take the following into consideration:

Handy Hint

When you press seams, always try to alternate the directions of the seam allowances. When you join rows, all seam allowances from one row will fall in opposite directions from the next, avoiding having to sew through eight layers of fabric at once.

- You want to mark a line that is easy to follow as you stitch.
- You want to have a fine line to delineate flowing feathers and intersecting lines. (You don't want broad lines because they will make you unsure of exactly where to stitch.)
- You want the lines to remain visible until you complete the quilting process.
- You want assurance that chemicals and dyes used in manufacturing marking products will not harm fabric fibers and threads.
- You want the lines to disappear completely from the finished product when the quilting process is completed.

Wow! What a tall order! The following information, which includes a special study I did, will help you decide which marking tool you'd like to use.

A Study of Marking Pens

While writing this book, I conducted a special test of all the marking tools available from Dritz Quiltery, a manufacturer that offers the greatest number of choices. I traced through one complete stencil motif with each tool, observing both ease of use and clarity of line. I chose one of the most difficult marking problems: marking curved lines on solid, black broadcloth.

First, I tried Quilter's Mark-B-Gone Pens. These felt-tipped pens come in pink, blue, and white. Pink lines were too hard to see on black, blue were impossible. (However, these colors work well on light-colored fabrics, both prints and solids.) The white Mark-B-Gone made a clear line that was easy to see, but I would not choose it to mark an entire quilt. The tip is too broad, making quilting lines wider than I like. Also, the pen leaves a crumbly residue here and there. Because these specks would not be covered with stitches, you must take care to shake them off rather than press them in with the stencil.

Next, I tried Quilter's White Water-Soluble Marking Pencil for the second motif, with better results. The line was finer, neater, and easy to see, but still a little broader than I prefer. The pencil behaved well, and the line disappeared when rubbed lightly with a clean, damp sponge after quilting.

The Quilter's Yellow Marking Pencil made a strong, non-smearing, sharp, yellow line. However, it does not make its exit as easily as the pencil mentioned above. The package instruction suggests you press only as hard as you need to see the line. Perhaps a washing or two will take away all traces.

When I used the Quilter's Silver Marking Pencil, I knew immediately it would be my favorite. Because I prefer to make QAYG quilts and often mark the quilt after the batting and backing has been added, I need a marker that works equally well on both firm and soft surfaces. The fine point of this marker produces a thin, delicate line without much pressure. Thus, marking on a batted surface is easy. The fine point also fits easily into the stencil grooves. A damp sponge erases it with no trace, and because the silver color is less glaring than white, it is nearly invisible even if you do not remove it at all.

To complete my study of marking pencils, I also tried water-soluble pens, or disappearing ink pens. These have been around a while and come in purple and blue inks that are easy to see. If you apply less pressure, the felt-tip pens produce a finer line than if you push hard. Newer water-soluble pens come with a regular point as well as one marked "fine line point."

Controversy has arisen over disappearing ink pens and the blue, water-soluble felt pens made by some companies. Some quilters warn that although the lines disappear with a light water sponging, they may return, uninvited, years in the future. Concern about the chemical they leave in the fiber keeps some quilters from using them. I, however, have used them with great success. My oldest quilt, marked in 1980, still shows no telltale signs of blue ink reappearing. The quilt resides on a bed that is in constant use. Nearly 20 years later, I confess I have decided not to worry about it any longer.

EZ International makes a washout marking pencil that works well. My design showed up easily using EZ's white cloth-marker pencil. Very little pressure brings out a fine line that is easy to use and see. The same product in red works well on lighter fabrics and is especially easy to see on fabric prints. An old standby in my studio is the white water erasable Nonce marker. It is easy to see, sharpen, and erase when you finish your hand quilting.

Finally, consider soapstone markers (especially for dark fabrics), which are available in most quilting shops. I like chalk pencils too. Dixon and General make excellent pencils in white chalk that mark easily on dark fabrics. Dixon's red chalk works well on light fabrics, but you must fuss to remove the color after completing the quilting.

Transferring Quilting Designs to Fabric

Your choice of a marking tool also depends on the method you will use to transfer your quilting design to fabric. Your choices are:

- Stencils (which can be traced around or over).
- Transfer pencils.
- Rulers and masking tape.

Stencils

You can buy ready-made stencils in a variety of materials in craft, sewing, and quilt shops or make your own. Stencils of borders, individual motifs, scrolls, feathers, hearts, and more are available in cardboard, plastic, and metal. You can position these stencils exactly where you want the design to appear. Narrow slits cut into the stencil permit special pens or pencils to leave a mark outlining the pattern on your fabric. Lift the stencil and you have a ready-made line to follow as you quilt. More possibilities await if you make your own stencils.

When transferring quilting lines from paper to light-colored fabrics, you may be able to trace a stencil directly by placing the design beneath the fabric. (Darken the lines on the paper with felt pens to make them more visible through the fabric.) If the fabric is not transparent enough, try taping it to a window so you can see through it (impractical for large projects, of course).

Today, portable light tables are practical tools. Modern versions sit on four short legs with a light fixture beneath the table's work

Make Your Quilting Stencils

To make your own cardboard quilting stencils, draw an original design or trace a design from a book or magazine that features quilting designs. Paste the paper copy on cardboard and add perforations yourself.

You can use a craft knife (available in craft shops) to cut slits to outline the design or you can punch small holes to follow. My favorite method when making stencils is to stitch the design by perforating it with a large-eyed chenille needle in hand. I use a thimble, pushing the unthreaded needle along the design line, in and out, leaving behind a trail of little holes.

Choose a large enough needle so the holes will accept a pen or pencil point to leave behind a mark. This is how you will use the floral design shown at the end of chapter 5 to quilt one of your blocks. You may also insert a leather needle (very large size) into your sewing machine and slowly sew around the design with an unthreaded needle. This technique leaves large holes but also dulls your needle, so after using a needle this way, set it aside for sewing only on paper.

surface. Turn on the light and presto! You can trace your design directly from paper sketch to fabric, repositioning as needed.

Transfer Pencils (Permanent Markers)

Special transfer pencils enable you to trace over any design on paper. The paper is placed on the fabric, tracing side down, and transferred to fabric by pressing with a dry iron. The heat from the iron leaves a reverse image of the design on the fabric.

Because transfer pencils leave a permanent mark, most quilters use these pencils only for appliqué shapes that are soon covered with fabrics. Some quilters, however, permit the design to appear on the wrong side of the fabric if they can see the line from the right side.

Rulers and Masking Tape

Perhaps the easiest of all methods, rulers and masking tape, works well when all you want are straight lines to quilt. All you need to do is measure the space between the lines with care. I often just use the width of a ruler itself. Diagonal, vertical, horizontal, or intersecting lines are easy to mark with any marker that leaves lines you can see on the fabric. (You will be using this method on the second block you make in the next chapter.) You can also stick strips of masking tape at regular intervals. Simply quilt beside the tape, and remove it when you finish quilting.

Making and Using Templates

A template is a pattern, mold, or thin plate of wood or metal that serves as a gauge for accurate work. Today's quilters can make their own templates from a variety of materials or choose from a large assortment of ready-made templates.

So, what's the big deal about templates? Everything! Because accuracy is critical in quilting, you need reliable templates. They must retain their exact shape without fraying at the edges with repeated tracing. Accurate templates determine how well patches will fit together during the assembling process.

Does it really matter what materials we use for templates? Yes! We want a material that can be easily cut. It should grip the fabric to avoid slipping and inaccurate cutting. Preferably, the template material will be affordable so we can keep a stock on hand, ever ready to produce new shapes and sizes. Come to think of it, we demand a lot from the humble template!

Templates of many sizes and materials spilled out of my storage box as I prepared to write this book. Let's explore my collection of ready-made and homemade templates. As you read, you will note that each type has plusses and minuses.

Ready-Made Templates

Pre-cut, peel-off art board in various shapes.

Plusses: No tracing, measuring, or cutting; easiest of all to use. Buy only the shape you want, peel it off, and stick it to fabric you're ready to trace. Also works well to cut uniform appliqué shapes. For paper-piecing method, just leave seam allowance of fabric around edges. Press this edge over paper edge, lay on ground fabric, and stitch. Remove after nearly completing blind stitching. Maintains uniform edges through many tracings.

Your Hands and Quilting

Your own two hands holding needle and thread are all you need for the quilting process. But wait! What about thimbles? I marveled at quilters who dutifully placed their thimble on their middle finger. For years, I worked without one. Many assured me I could not achieve fine quality stitching without learning to use a thimble. I tried repeatedly to use one but had no success.

Frustration followed until I made an important discovery. Owing to the shape of my hand and length of my fingers, I found my ring-finger was the one to become sore from stitching too long—not the usual middle finger. Of course! At last I realized that I automatically push my needle with this finger. What a revelation! The distance between my thumb and ring finger is longer than that from the middle finger.

Today, I find it more comfortable to quilt with a thin sewing needle rather than a "between" short, quilting needle and to wear my thimble on the finger that needs it! My ring finger!

Chopin, one of the world's most loved composers and teachers, suggests all pianists should study their hands. His manuscripts state good pianists, at times, should violate traditional hand and finger positions in favor of natural movement. He tells us not to concern ourselves too much with what finger does what. Focusing on using the fingers that achieve the best results shows respect for your own hands. And, so it is with quilting.

Professionals' Template Choices

You may be wondering what kind of templates the quilting experts use. In her book, *Applique 12 Easy Ways,* Elly Sienkiewicz says she favors freezer paper or white poster board to perfect appliqué shapes.

In their book, *Trip Around the World Quilts,* Blanche and Helen Young say "Sandpaper can be glued on the back of poster board templates to reduce slippage. Even pieces of two-sided tape will help the template grab fabric."

In *More Lap Quilting with Georgia Bonesteel,* the author claims, "My alternative to plastic templates are those made from cardboard and covered with transparent contact paper."

Minuses: Limited shapes and sizes; unavailable in many craft and fabric shops, many quilters must order by mail; takes more time than other methods.

Plastic template shapes.

Plusses: Accurate, durable, transparent, and easy to use. Available in nearly all patchwork shapes. Each template provides many size choices. For example, squares can provide 14 square sizes marked every 1/4 inch. Available in most craft and fabric stores. Edges remain smooth though notches on the sides preclude rotary cutting.

Minuses: Not much; only price may be a factor.

Sets of ready-made acrylic interchangeable templates.

Plusses: Sets of templates enable you to interchange shapes for many popular geometric designs. For example, Pandora's Box pattern sets by TV quilting personality Shar Jorgensen will make up to 10 different patchwork designs.

Michael James, in *The Quiltmaker's Handbook,* says, "There are many ways to prepare templates, as many as there are materials out of which to make them." He adds that he prefers designer's illustration board because it is durable, readily available, and easily handled.

Shar Jorgensen, mentioned earlier, not only prefers acrylic templates, but her company manufactures them. So you see, even experts like these differ in their choices. I suggest you try several materials. See which materials produce templates that are easy to cut and use without fraying along the edges with repeated uses. Try a few ready-made shapes. Did they yield better results than your own handmade shapes? The ultimate expert in choosing which template is best for you is . . . you!

Clear plastic makes templates easy to see. Small dots of non-skid material on one side grip fabric.

Minuses: Sets are pricey and unavailable in some shops, but free catalog makes mail ordering easy.

Die-cut templates such as Metal by Ardco.

Plusses: Undoubtedly the most durable of all choices, these last a lifetime! Precision die-cut, each template features a super "grit" backing that makes rotary cutting a breeze. Edges remain perfect forever. Order solid templates such as the hexagon with or without seam allowance. This company's "window" templates also come open in the center with the shape outlined by a perfect 1/4-inch seam allowance.

Minuses: Price is the only possible negative consideration. Ardco produces a free mail order catalog because most local shops do not carry these templates.

Materials for Make-It-Yourself Templates

Ordinary cardboard.

Plusses: Inexpensive, readily available.

Minuses: Good for only a few tracings; you must cut new ones when edges begin to fray from repeated use.

Mat board.

Plusses: Maintains edges much longer than cardboard.

Minuses: Hard to cut (try a mat cutter or craft knife).

Postcards.

Plusses: Inexpensive, readily available, lasts longer than cardboard.

Minuses: Slippery and slick on fabric.

Sandpaper.

Plusses: Often glued to graph and other papers to prevent slipping.

Minuses: Costs a little more than cardboard; frays around edges; only very rough gauges have enough body to use alone.

X-ray film.

Plusses: Transparent, easy to position, retains a sharp edge.

Minuses: Hard to find unless you work in a radiology laboratory.

Freezer paper.

Plusses: One side adheres to fabric for cutting and pressing yet easily peels off; durable, retains cut edges much longer than cardboard.

Minuses: Can be hard to find (but check in the "plastic wrap" section of the grocery store).

Clear quilter's template plastic.

Plusses: Transparent, easy to position on printed fabrics, excellent for applique.

Minuses: A challenge to label or mark with pens and pencils.

Coated quilter's template plastic.

Plusses: The cloudy finish on this plastic's non-skid surface makes it easier to mark than the clear plastic mentioned previously.

Minuses: Can be hard to find.

Quilter's grid template plastic.

Plusses: Wonderful for making geometric shapes, easy to mark on coated side.

Minuses: More expensive than previously listed materials.

Grid Works by The Quiltery, Dritz Co.

Plusses: Coated paper on one side to prevent slippage; temporarily bonds to fabric leaving no residue; peel off and reuse many times; good for both geometric piecing and applique.

Minuses: Initially more expensive than previous materials, but an 18-inch wide, 5-yard roll will provide dozens of templates.

Mastering Squares

Squares appear so simple. Why then, do so many quilters lament that their perfect squares are not perfect? Before expecting your squares to work, you must consider fabric grain. Few geometrically perfect squares will provide trouble-free piecing if they are set off grain.

Following are different techniques for creating perfect squares. Always place the first line or cut exactly on the fabric grain. Try each and choose the method that you are the most comfortable using.

Rotary Cutter and Mat

Cutting precision squares from fabric strips is easy, thanks to rotary cutters and mats. This method begins by creating one straight line along the grain of the fabric from selvage to selvage. One of the easiest ways to do this is to tear a small strip off the edge of the fabric. This ensures that you are truly following the grain line. Next, fold the fabric in half with selvage edges together, lining up the torn edge. Using your iron, press the folded edge. (Some quilters skip the pressing, but this step greatly increases accuracy.) Now fold the fabric in half again (so the first fold and the two selvage edges meet) keeping the torn edges properly lined up. Press the new folded edge.

Because we want perfect squares it is a good idea to now trim off the frayed edge. Lay the fabric (now four layers thick) on the cut-

Going With the Grain

All woven fabrics have three terms that describe the direction of the threads or *grain*.

Cross grain means the woven threads running from selvage to selvage, from one side to the other. Recognize selvage edges as the double-woven, extra heavy edges on all fabric to keep it from fraying. The printed selvage edges also contain fiber and manufacturer information. Never include selvages in any part of a quilt.

Lengthwise grain refers to the threads that run parallel to the selvage edges, which are similar to grain line in wood.

Bias refers to cutting fabric on the diagonal, from one side to the other.

ting mat so the torn edge extends just past one of the vertical grid lines. Line up your quilting ruler along that same grid line, hold it securely, and trim the frayed edge by rolling the rotary cutter blade (away from your body) along the edge of the ruler. Notice that the newly cut edge is perfectly lined up with a grid line on the mat. Now carefully move the ruler (without moving the fabric) however far over to make your desired strip width. For example, if you want 3-inch squares, move the ruler over 3 inches, line up the ruler with that grid line and cut. Voila! You now have a perfect strip.

To cut your strip into perfect squares, open the strip (so it's a single layer) and line it up along one of the horizontal grid lines so the selvage edge extends just past one of the vertical grid lines. Trim the selvage. (Notice the similarity to the previous steps?)

Now carefully move the ruler (without moving the fabric) however far to make your desired square (3 inches in our example), line up the ruler, and cut. Repeat until you have the desired number of squares.

If you are careful with each step and line things up properly, you will be pleased to find perfect squares every time. Spending the time now will save you many headaches later in the quilting process.

Quilters' Rulers

There are many quilters' rulers on the market that simplify the making of perfect squares. Two excellent examples made by EZ International are Is It a Square? and Handi-Square. Both rulers feature 1/8-inch grid marks and a space between marks to see seam lines through the ruler. Is It a Square? helps you create perfect blocks up to 16 square inches. Handi-Square works the same way but limits block sizes to 6 square inches. Both can be used with rotary cutters.

Line up your fabric square under the ruler beside one of the bold lines. Align all four edges with the grid lines. Irregular edges are immediately apparent. Trim fabric to correct.

See-Through Plastic

Another way to cut a square is to use the see-through plastic sheets available in quilting shops and craft stores. Marked with grid lines, these sheets look like plastic graph paper. My favorite is Plastigraph by Leman Publications (available from their Quilts & Other Comforts catalog). Though I have seen gridded plastic with marked lines appearing every inch, I prefer Plastigraph, with its 12 small lines between each single-inch bold line. It truly simulates 12-to-the-inch graph paper.

This plastic allows you to mark fabric with an ordinary pencil. You may erase incorrect lines without disturbing the grid lines. Begin by marking your first line, to the measurement you want, with a ruler. Position your ruler at the end of the line to make the second line at a right angle. You can be sure you will have a 90-degree corner by lining up the second line following the stamped grid lines. Repeat for the final two lines of the square.

Basting—The Critical Step

No matter what blocks you choose for your quilt and which method you use, there is one step that will always apply. Careful basting is essential to good quiltmaking. *Basting* refers to temporarily connecting the quilt sandwich together, in preparation for quilting. Basting prevents the three layers (top, batting, backing) from shifting whether quilting on a traditional frame, a hoop, or in the hand. Efficient basting eliminates not only shifting but puckers and fabric distortion as well. But which method should you choose?

Traditional Basting

Traditional basting uses large, running stitches (in and out) about 1/4 of an inch in length, stitching through all three layers of the quilt.

Use both hands to smooth all three layers from the center toward the edges and tape the layers onto a table top or other hard surface with masking tape. Thread a long needle with scrap threads no longer suitable for sewing or quilting.

Baste layers together while still taped to the table. Begin each basting line from the *center* of each block or quilt working outward toward the corners. (Do *not* baste from one corner to its opposite.) Leave large knots on the right side of the block, when you begin and end each quilting line for easy removal later. Use a back and forth rocking motion, scooping the fabric onto the needle. Don't turn corners as you baste. When you come to within 1/4 of an inch of the edge of the block, tie off and cut the thread. Return to the center and begin with a new basting line.

You will create a grid of basting stitches no farther apart than 4 inches or so in your block. Traditional basting works for large or very small quilts. Basting on a full size quilt stretched on a frame can be a formidable task. That is why you will begin by making smaller, 12-inch blocks. Nevertheless, careful basting such as this goes a long way in assuring the success of a finished quilt, whatever its size.

Safety Pin Basting

Quilters who prefer working on a hoop prefer this method. Using large, medium, or small safety pins, insert and close the pins at regular intervals while the sandwich is still taped to the table or mounted in a frame. When the quilter encounters each pin, she removes it to quilt only one small section at a time by hand or machine. Recently, several notions companies have come up with a new idea—quilter's safety pins. The pin portion comes slightly bent in the center to make insertion without lifting all three layers from the table easier.

Straight Pin Basting

Preferred by some, shunned by others, straight sewing pins or large head quilting pins will also hold the sandwich in place. Take care to place pins close enough together to secure the sandwich and avoid shifting again, while it's still taped to the table or mounted in a frame—no farther than 1 inch apart. If you use this method, take care not to poke yourself with the exposed points.

Using a Basting Gun

Rotary cutters have revolutionized cutting methods for quilters. Basting guns have done the same for the basting process. Resembling a tagging gun used to label garments in retail shops, a basting gun shoots white or red plastic tacks through all three layers of the

Quick Review: Why Bother Basting?

- Think of basting not as a chore but as an essential, preparatory task for good quilting.

- Basting offers an opportunity to use those odd colored threads that make you wonder how they found their way into your sewing room.

- Basting holds appliqués, laces, and trimmings in place.

- Basting first enables you to later make tiny, invisible stitches as you appliqué or quilt.

- Basting coaxes and eases excess fabric from the design area outward to the edges.

quilt sandwich. The 1/4-inch long tacks work equally well on thinner sandwiches or for tying thick comforters.

Plastic tacks neither rust nor corrode. Machine quilters will be happy to know that sewing machines will glide over the tacks easily. Basting guns work well while the sandwich rests in a frame or taped to the floor or table.

Using the basting gun is easy. First, insert the strip of plastic tacks in the notch at the top of the gun. Next, create a little tension by holding the sandwich layers taut. Last, insert the needle of the gun where you want the tack and press the trigger.

Which Method Is for You?

To determine which basting method suits you, why not try a different method on each of the blocks in your quilt top? Observe which method holds most securely with little to no shifting. Consider also the convenience factor as you hand stitch. Sometimes, pins or needles get in the way of hand quilting. Does your quilting thread

- Basting can free your work from puckers and little peaks of excess fabric that announce careless preparation.

- Basting eliminates wrinkles on the back of your quilt. It assures you it will be as lovely as the front without unsightly tucks and pleats to distort fabric grain.

- Basting in the traditional manner can be done on the entire quilt top while mounted on a frame.

- Basting enables you to quilt one block at a time when attached to a special quilt-as-you-go frame or while taped firmly on a table.

- Basting permits you to work without a frame—in the hand.

tangle around them as you stitch? Does this annoyance diminish when hand quilting around the plastic tacks?

A Final Word About Quilting

Always begin quilting in the center-most area, working toward the outer edges. Use the thumb of your non-stitching hand, continuously smoothing and coaxing excess fabric from center toward outer edges as you quilt with your dominant hand. The act of placing small, running stitches through all three layers of the fabric is *quilting,* the verb.

Hand quilting should begin and end without visible knots. Bury your starting knot in the quilt sandwich by tugging it until it "pops" into the batting, hidden from view.

For beginners, hand quilting requires even stitches rather than small ones. Once you can quilt evenly, you can practice making smaller stitches.

Hand quilting looks best when the spaces between stitches equal the length of the stitch itself.

Hand quilting takes time but enjoy the process. Careful stitches will outlive you. Witness the antique quilts we still admire today. The fabric may fray away but the hand quilting endures.

Now, on to chapter 5, where you'll learn how to make six different quilt blocks and four different projects.

chapter

5

Creating Your Quilting Projects

▼▼▼

IN THIS CHAPTER YOU WILL learn how to make six different quilt blocks and how to turn those blocks into finished projects. The blocks (in order from easiest to most challenging) are:

- Rail Fence
- Irish Chain
- Pinwheel
- Hearts Appliqué
- The Fan
- Ohio Star

The Projects (again, in order from easiest to most challenging) are:

- Wall Hanging
- Table Mat
- Pillow
- Sampler Quilt

The instructions will refer to the specific colors and patterns used in the final projects, but of course you are encouraged to be

creative in your own selections. Within the world of quilting, there are probably as many techniques as there are styles of finished quilts. When you select the blocks and projects for this book, choose a variety so you might experience as many techniques as possible. Unifying everything is that each block is the same size, has the same width lattice strips, and is sandwiched with the quilt-as-you-go (QAYG) method.

When you finish these projects, your experience will help you determine whether you prefer to quilt by hand or machine. Most modern stitchers confidently say that grandmothers would have used machines if they had them. You need to try it both ways to learn which method you prefer.

I recommend that you quickly read through the entire chapter to see all the possibilities. Then decide which finished project you would like to make and which block(s) you will need. Once these decisions are made, you are ready to select your fabrics.

Block #1: *Rail Fence*

Rail Fence is one of the blocks used in the sampler quilt example. This age-old pattern belongs to the 4-patch family of blocks because you will construct four separate, 6 1/2-inch square units before assembling the complete block, which will measure 12 inches when completely finished. It will introduce you to easy strip piecing where you will sew long strips of different fabrics together, cut them into sections, and reposition the sections to create your quilt block. *Rail Fence* will also introduce you to a quilting technique known as "stitch-in-the-ditch."

Before you begin, it would be a good idea to review the "how to" section in chapter 4 for detailed instructions on fabric grain, cutting, and sewing. Precise prep work pays off in the finished product.

Cutting the Fabric

Make sure you start with a perfectly straight edge along the fabric grain line running from selvage to selvage. Use a rotary cutter and mat or quality fabric shears to cut a strip from each fabric B, C, D, and E exactly 2 inches wide by at least 26 inches long. (I usually add an extra inch or so. Better to have a bit extra to trim off than to end up with not enough.) Don't worry about fabric A right now. We'll use it later for the lattice strips.

Piecing

Refer to figure 1 to get an idea of what we're about to do. Lay your first two strips (fabrics B and C) right sides together with fabric B on top. Pin and stitch the strips together by hand or machine using a 1/4-inch seam allowance. Experienced quilters recognize the importance of making seams that measure *exactly* 1/4 inch.

Fabric Key

A = Light blue

B = Red

C = White

D = Dark blue

E = Yellow

Open the pieced B/C unit and position fabric E on top of B. Pin and stitch. Repeat this, stitching fabric D onto E. Now you have a pieced unit, four strips wide.

Press seam allowances toward darker colors. The joined strip unit should measure 6 1/2 inches wide.

If you have a cutting mat, quilting ruler, and rotary cutter, cut the joined strip into 6 1/2-inch squares. (See figure 1.)

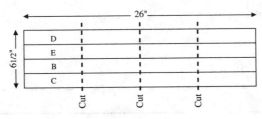

Figure 1. Piecing your fabric.

6 1/2"

6 1/2"

Figure 2. Making a template for exact measurements.

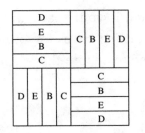

Figure 3. Positioning your squares.

If you will be using templates, choose your template material from those discussed in chapter 4. Make a template to measure exactly 6 1/2 inches square (see figure 2). Lay the template on one end of your strip unit and mark with a thin pencil line across all four joined strips as shown by the dotted lines in figure 1. Cut across the strips on the marked lines. Trim if needed so each patch measures exactly 6 1/2 inches.

Refer to figure 3 and position the four patches (squares) as shown. Pin and stitch the top two patches together, then pin and stitch the bottom together. Now you have two halves of your quilt block. Press seam allowances toward fabric C.

Pin the top and bottom sections together, being careful to match the center vertical seams. Double check to be sure the center seams match, then sew the two halves together.

Press the completed block, but do not press seam allowances open as you do when making garments. Press the center seam to one side, whenever possible onto darker colored fabric. Note that the same color (fabric C) of all four patches will come together in the center of the block.

Remember my description in a previous chapter of making a small, mini-ironing board for pressing small patches and blocks at your sewing table? Think of this also as a 12 1/2-inch master template for making 12-inch blocks when finished. Lay your completed block on the master template (or on your cutting mat if you have one). The extra 1/2 inch is your seam allowance and will be consumed when you add lattice strips to your block. Trim, re-sew, or adjust whenever needed to ensure that each block measures 12 1/2 inches *exactly*.

Adding Lattice Strips

Now, it's time to make lattice strips for your block. Cut 2 1/2-inch strips out of your background fabric (fabric A). You will need two strips at least 12 1/2 inches long for the top and bottom, and two strips at least 16 1/2 inches long for the sides. (See figure 4.)

Pin and stitch the lattice to the top and bottom of the block. Press the seam allowances toward the lattice strip. Then trim any excess lattice so the side edges are perfectly straight.

Next, pin and stitch lattice strips to the sides of the block. **Note:** They will include the top and bottom lattice strips, completely framing your block. Press seam allowances toward the lattice strips.

Congratulate yourself. You have just completed your "block."

Basting

To prepare your block for basting, cut a piece of batting slightly larger than your *Rail Fence* block. Then cut a piece of your backing fabric (Fabric A) slightly larger than your batting. Place the backing fabric (right side down) on your table. Center the batting on the backing, then center your *Rail Fence* block (right side up) over the batting. Quilters call this the "quilt sandwich." Notice that you can see the edges of the lower layers. This will help you "see" what's happening to them as you baste. Also, the extra batting and backing will be helpful when it comes time to join your blocks together.

In chapter 4 we discussed many techniques for basting. Whichever method you choose, be sure to keep all layers of the quilt flat and smooth to avoid puckering. *Always* begin basting from

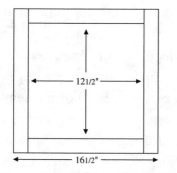

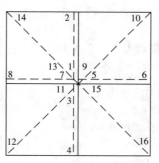

Figure 4. Measurements for cutting lattice strips.   **Figure 5.** Basting steps.

the center of the block and work your way outward. If you are basting using the traditional needle and thread method, refer to figure 5. Start in the center (#1) and baste to the top edge (#2). Then start in the center (#3) and baste to the bottom edge (#4). Continue for the rest of the pattern.

Quilting

The next decision is how to do the quilting. Just as in basting, whichever method you choose, *always* begin quilting in the center-most area, working toward the outer edges. The act of placing small, running stitches through all three layers of the fabric is *quilting,* the verb.

For our *Rail Fence* we will use the "stitch-in-the-ditch" quilting pattern. Because the quilting is not very visible, it gives you a chance to practice without worrying about how your stitches look if this is your first time.

For handquilting, use quilting thread to match either the backing fabric or the lattice strips. Quilting thread is thicker than sewing thread and comes with a waxed coating to make hand quilting easier.

Machine quilters should use regular sewing thread and larger machine stitching than you would use for garments. A quilting foot, also known as a walking foot, will make your machine quilting much more even and eliminate puckers at the back that occur when the quilt sandwich shifts as it passes beneath the machine needle.

Stitch single rows of hand or machine quilting directly over all of the seam lines of each strip, gently pulling them apart as you sew. This causes a "ditch" to appear between strips, which raises the strips into log-like shapes. Do *not* quilt onto the lattice strip area for now. We'll do that later. (If hand quilting, you do not need to cut and knot excess threads as you reach the lattice strips. Just leave them dangling in place where you can rethread them later, after your blocks are joined.)

Congratulate yourself again, you have just completed your first QAYG quilt block. Are you ready for another?

Block #2: *Irish Chain*

The *Irish Chain* block also belongs to the four-patch family. You will see it in the sampler quilt. Compare the photograph of the completed project in the color insert to figure 6. Notice that patches #2 and #3 are solid pieces of fabric, and that patches #1 and #4 are

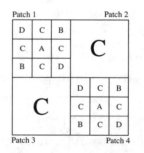

Figure 6. The four-patch block.

made from nine smaller pieces, called "nine-patches." Actually, the Irish Chain is a four-patch block that includes smaller nine-patch blocks. So it goes in the world of quilting. Patterns within patterns to make up new patterns.

Traditional *Irish Chain* patterns use two fabrics, one white or cream color and one contrasting fabric. Because the Irish Chain is part of the sampler, white is used for the background (fabric C) and three different fabrics are used for the chain. The following instructions are for the block as it appears in the sampler. Your desired finished project will help determine your fabric choices.

Fabric Key

A = Light blue

B = Red

C = White

D = Dark blue

Cutting the Fabric

If you are using templates, begin by making a new template, 2 1/2 inches square (figure 7). You will also reuse the 6 1/2-inch template from the *Rail Fence*.

Cut two 6 1/2-inch fabric squares from fabric C. Set aside.

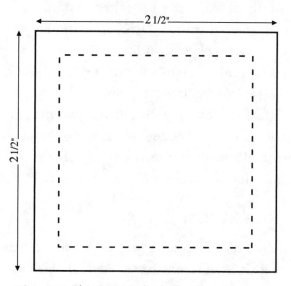

Figure 7. The 2 1/2-inch square template.

Next, cut out the 2 1/2-inch squares, eight from fabric C, two from fabric A, four from fabric B, and four from fabric D. *(If you are making a traditional two-fabric block, cut eight background squares and ten from the second color.)*

Piecing

Pin and sew the top row of 2 1/2-inch squares as you saw in figure 7. Note that you will have a white square in the center. Press seam allowances always toward the darker fabrics. Pin and sew the three squares for the middle row (but now the white squares are on the outside). Press seams toward the darker fabrics. Notice that the top and bottom rows are the same, just rotated. Repeat the sequence for the top row to complete the bottom row, and press seam allowances.

When you have completed three rows of squares, pin the top row to the middle row, making sure your intersections match. Sew the rows together. Add the third row to the first two.

Make your second nine-patch the same way.

Take up your 6 1/2-inch plastic template again, or go to your cutting mat. Both of your nine-patches should be *exactly* 6 1/2 inches square. Re-sew or trim to correct any imperfections now.

Lay out the five patches as in figure 6. Pin and sew patches #1 and #2. Press seam allowances toward the nine-patch. Repeat for patches #3 and #4. Pin the two half blocks together, again making sure that the intersections match perfectly. Sew, press, and trim center seam allowances, if needed, to make the block lie flat.

Measure the block. Trim, re-sew, or adjust whenever needed to ensure that each block measures 12 1/2 inches *exactly*.

Adding Lattice Strips

Using 2 1/2-inch strips of fabric A, pin and stitch strips to the top and bottom of the block. Add strips to the sides. (Please see the "Adding Lattice Strips" section of the *Rail Fence* block for more details.)

Marking Quilting Lines

Because it's much easier to draw lines when your quilt block is directly on a table top or hard surface, it's better do it before you add the batting and backing.

We'll start with the decorative pattern on the two solid patches. Using one of the marking implements discussed in chapter 4, trace quilting lines from figure 8. Next, mark a line 1/4 of an inch from the seam line, as in figure 7, for the "outline quilting."

Look at the "grid quilting" across the nine-patches for *Irish Chain* in figure 6. Mark lines diagonally with a ruler. It's remarkable how much simple, diagonal lines of quilting can transform your block, isn't it?

Basting

Begin by cutting a piece of batting slightly larger than your block. Then cut a piece of your backing fabric (fabric A) slightly larger than your batting. Place the backing fabric (right side down) on your table. Center the batting on the backing, then center your block (right side up) over the batting. Notice that you can see the edges of the lower layers. This will help you "see" what's happening to them as you baste. Also, the extra batting and backing will be helpful when it comes time to join your blocks together.

Begin basting in the center of the block and work your way outward.

Quilting

Last, the fun part. Complete the quilting by hand or machine. On this single block you have learned decorative quilting (the floral design), outline quilting (the two large squares), and grid quilting (the diagonal lines running through the nine-patches).

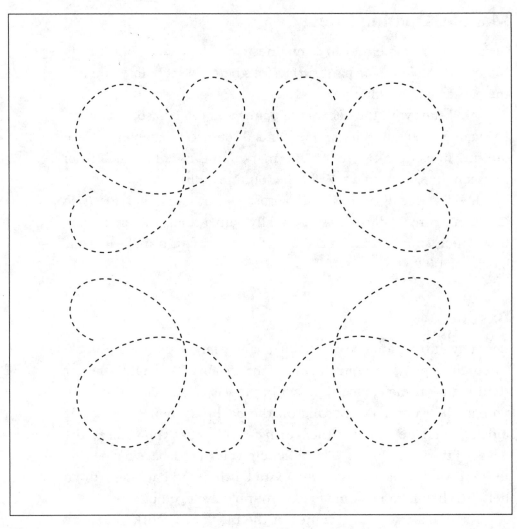

Figure 8. Quilting lines to trace.

Block #3: *Pinwheel*

Any time you use triangles, you will encounter one of the major challenges in quilting—working on the bias. But do not fear using blocks with triangles. Learn how to tame those bias, wavy edges as you make *Pinwheel* (figure 9), an easy, four-patch block made en-

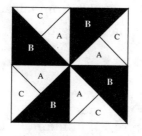

Figure 9. Pinwheel.

tirely of triangles. Follow the upcoming steps and you need never fear stitching triangles together again.

This block was first made for the Sampler Quilt in red, white, and blue and it looked so nice the same theme was repeated for the Wall Hanging. Wouldn't it look darling in a little boy's room? Compare the finished projects and figure 9. See the four patches? Did you notice that each patch is identical? Well they are, just rotated to give the illusion of a child's pinwheel. Notice also the lattice strips. The color used in the Sampler Quilt was dictated by the rest of the project, but on the Wall Hanging the background is white for both triangle C and the lattice. Which do you prefer?

Fabric Key

A = Light blue

B = Red

C = White

Here are a few tricks to help avoid stretching. Spritz a little spray-starch on the fabrics, *before* cutting out the triangles, to help stabilize them. Handle the triangles as little as possible. And press only along the grain, never on the bias edges.

Shall we begin?

Cutting the Fabric

Make two new templates, both triangles from the patterns provided (figures 10 and 11). Be sure to note the directional arrow on the templates. It is very important that the arrow lines up along the straight of the grain. (See figure 12.)

Cut four large triangles from fabric B and set aside.

Next, cut four small triangles from fabric A.

Repeat for the four small background triangles from
fabric C.

Piecing

Begin by examining figure 13. Remember that this is a four-patch
block and that all four-patches are exactly the same. This should
make it easier to see how the pieces fit together.

Referring to figure 13, pin and stitch the two smaller triangles
together. I find it is easier to stitch when I begin with the right angle
(square) corner and end with the sharp pointed angle.

Press seams to one side, *carefully*. Do *not* drag the iron back and
forth. Press with the grain. Avoid letting the iron press the bias
edge. Press up and down gently to avoid stretching the longer bias
seams.

Next, join the large triangle B to unit A/C. If machine stitching,
reduce stretching further by sewing with the larger triangle on the
bottom. This will ease the bias edge of the larger triangle to the
more stable straight-grain edges of the other triangles.

Press seams toward the smaller triangles just as carefully as before. See what you've done? The long, bias edge is stabilized by joining it to the two short, straight-grain edges.

This completes one-quarter of your block. Repeat to make all
four-patches.

Each square should measure exactly 6 1/2 inches and line up
with your larger template used for the last two blocks. If not, adjust
seams now.

Lay out the four-patches according to the design in figure 9. Notice how the straight edge of triangle B will stabilize the bias edge of
triangle A.

Pin and stitch the top two patches together. Again, if you are
machine stitching, sew the seam with the bias-edged fabric on the

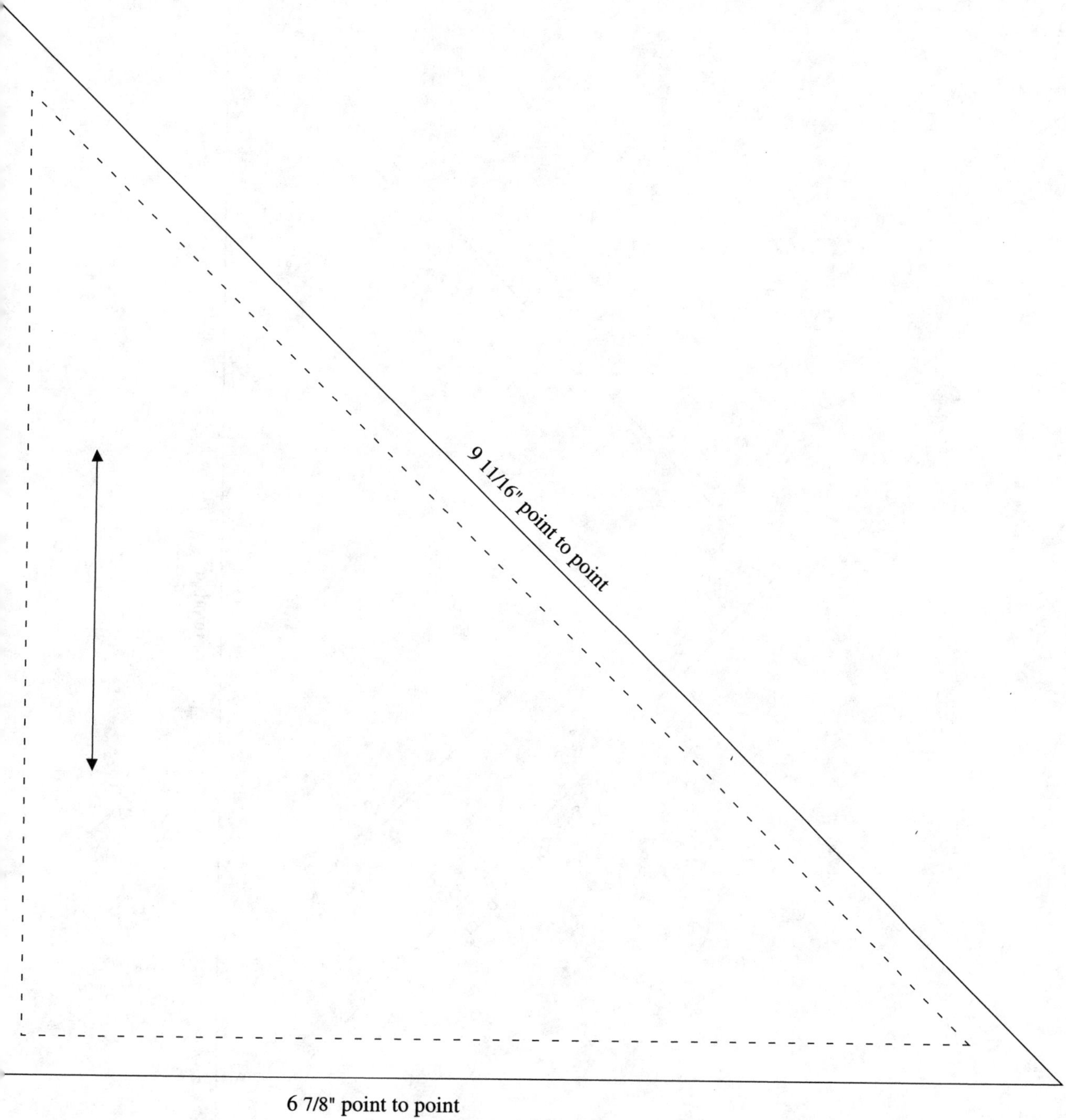

9 11/16" point to point

6 7/8" point to point

Figure 10. Triangle template pattern (showing directional arrow).

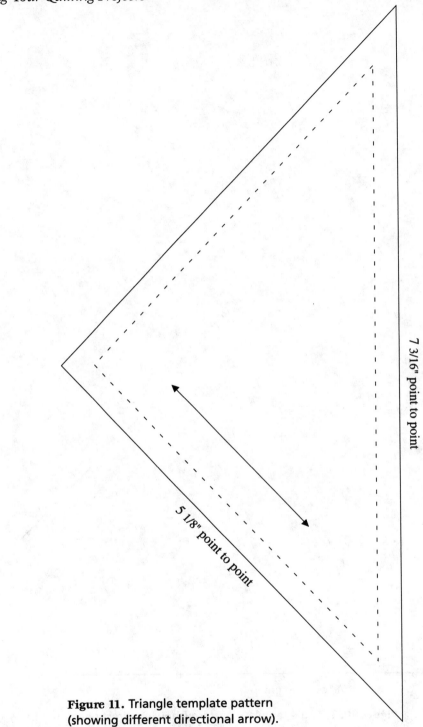

7 3/16" point to point

5 1/8" point to point

Figure 11. Triangle template pattern
(showing different directional arrow).

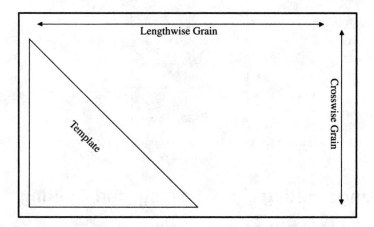

Figure 12. Placement of triangles along the straight of the grain.

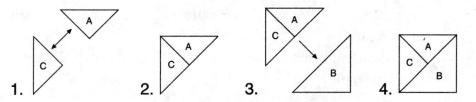

Figure 13. Pieces of four-patch block.

bottom and the straight-edged fabric on top. Press the seam toward the straight edge of triangle B.

Repeat with the two bottom patches.

All that remains is to join the two halves together to complete the block. Take care to have center seams match in the middle of *Pinwheel*. Press gently as before.

Measure the block. Trim, re-sew, or adjust whenever needed to ensure that each block measures 12 1/2 inches exactly.

Adding Lattice Strips

Add lattice strips along each side edge as before. Refer to *Rail Fence* block for details.

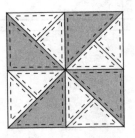

Figure 14. Example of outline quilting triangles.

Marking Quilting Lines, Basting, and Quilting

Pinwheel usually features outline quilting, as shown on the Sampler Quilt. But for variety, the Wall Hanging was quilted using the stitch-in-the-ditch method described in the *Rail Fence* instructions.

For outline quilting, mark triangles 1/4 inch inside all seam lines as in figure 14.

Form quilt sandwich as usual. Baste and quilt through all layers as before, and quilt.

Block #4: *Hearts Appliqué*

This block is a little more challenging than the previous because heart shapes have both inside and outside curves. Ready for a little challenge? It also introduces a new technique called appliqué. Rather than piecing different fabrics together to make our block, appliqué blocks start with a solid piece of fabric (called the "ground") and then we stitch different fabric shapes onto the ground fabric to make up the design.

The *Hearts Appliqué* block is used to make the Table Mat. Notice how things are done differently here. The other blocks in this book are all 12 inches and then lattice strips are added to make them into 16-inch squares. The Table Mat is full sized without the lattice so more hearts can be included. Because *Hearts Appliqué* is such a versatile block, you are free to be as creative and expressive as you wish. The following paragraphs include instructions for 16-inch blocks made with or without lattice.

You may use any fabric you please. Use one fabric only for all the hearts or make each one different. Notice the interesting visual effect created by centering the template over the leaves that were scattered throughout a red print fabric. Using clear plastic makes it easy for you to choose exactly what part of a print will show up where on your finished heart.

Cutting the Fabric

Select a light-colored fabric for your ground fabric. Cut a 16 1/2-inch square (12 1/2 inches if you will add lattice strips.) Set aside.

Make two heart-shaped templates. (Trace carefully for this will determine the final outline of the heart.) The larger (figure 15) should be made from clear plastic. The smaller (figure 16) should be made out of heavy paper or cardboard.

Lay out your fabric right side up, and position the plastic template over your desired section of fabric. Trace around the outside of the template. Note that there is a 1/2-inch seam so your finished heart will be significantly smaller than the template. For the solid 16-inch block, cut a total of 14 hearts. (You will need about eight to ten hearts if you're using lattice strips, depending on how you choose to lay them out.)

You will use the paper/cardboard template to help you press the 1/2-inch seam allowance over to the wrong side of your fabric hearts. Center this smaller template over each fabric heart. You will need to cut a small slit in the top "V" to allow it to turn, but be careful not to cut all the way to the seam line. Press the seam allowances over the paper edges, then remove the paper. See what you have? Perfectly made fabric hearts with soft curved seam allowances pressed to the back. You may reuse the paper until the edges are too

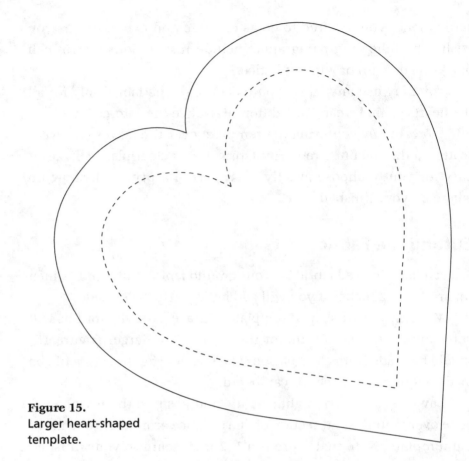

Figure 15.
Larger heart-shaped
template.

frayed. Using paper to shape appliqué is one of the best ways to get precise shapes and curves as it guides your seam allowances to the back of the fabric.

Arrange your hearts onto the ground fabric as you please, up to (and no closer than) 1/2 inch from the outer edges of the ground fabric. You may place them in a circle or in rows or turn some upside down. When the arrangement pleases you, pin the hearts in place onto the ground fabric.

Blind stitch the first heart in place beginning at the top, inside the "V," taking tiny stitches on this inside curve. Continue stitching toward the bottom point. As you go, check to make sure the heart is still flat, neat, and well shaped. Continue making invisible stitches

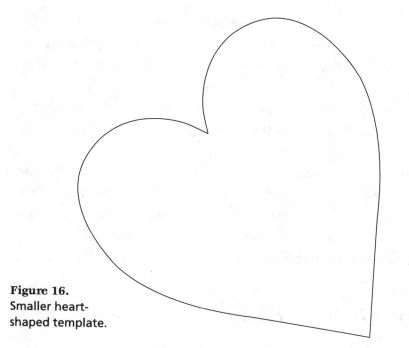

Figure 16.
Smaller heart-
shaped template.

around the heart until you reach your starting point. Tie off your thread invisibly on the wrong side of the ground fabric. Appliqué all the hearts the same way to your ground fabric.

Marking Quilting Lines, Basting, and Quilting

Hearts Appliqué gives you the opportunity to learn a new quilting motif. Most appliqués feature a line of quilting worked 1/4 of an inch away from all appliqué shapes. Because it repeats or "echoes" the basic appliqué shape, it is known as *echo quilting*. This is the design I recommend for beginner quilters. Mark the lines using your choice of implements as previously described.

If your design includes lattice strips, add them now. Sandwich, baste, and quilt as usual.

Did you know???

"Old" fabrics are quite popular now. Fabric manufacturers are copying the designs and colors of older quilts, calling them "reproduction" fabrics. Quilters snatch them up quickly, but for those who cannot get their hands on them, you can "fade" newer fabrics with tea staining or bleach to achieve the "antique" look.

Those of you who are intermediate or advanced quilters might want to tackle "stippling" as done in the Table Mat. Stippling, by definition, is stitching small, random, puzzle-piece shapes keeping all stitch lines no farther apart than 1/4 of an inch. Stipple stitches should form convoluted, interlocking shapes that never cross over one another. Check with quilting supply stores for pre-cut stipple patterned stencils.

Hearts Appliqué was quilted by machine. If you can drop or lower the feed-dogs of your machine and have practiced free-motion stitching with a special foot for that purpose, you can stipple quilt the background as done here. Stippling requires practice while you learn to move your block in any direction without distorting it.

Block #6: *The Fan*

This popular design, used in the Sampler Quilt, combines skills and techniques from the previous blocks, piecing, and appliqué. *The Fan*, one of the most popular, endearing, traditional designs falls into the one-patch piecing design and only one single template is needed (figure 17). Eleven rays of the fan are individually cut out and pieced together. Then the entire fan is appliqued as a unit onto the background. We call this technique "pieced appliqué."

Fabric Key

A = Light blue

B = Red

C = White

D = Dark blue

E = Yellow

Cutting the Fabric

Cut a 12 1/2-inch square of a plain fabric on which the pieced appliqué will rest. We call this, the "ground" fabric. Make sure it is a quiet color so the *Fan* stands out. Press it well.

Make a template from the pattern shown in figure 17. When marking the fabric, be sure you follow the grain line arrow. You want each of the rays to have the right side on the straight of the grain and the left side on the bias.

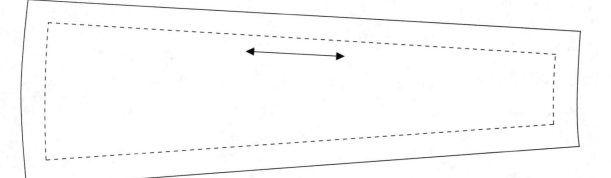

Figure 17. Fan template.

(Then each seam will have one fabric cut on the grain to stabilize the one cut on the bias.)

You will need a total of 11 rays for this block, and balancing the colors can be a challenge. The Sampler Quilt was designed with four colors and a white background, with four rays in red, three in dark blue, two in light blue, and two in yellow (figure 18). You may choose any number of fabrics from two to eleven for your *Fan*, but whatever colors you choose, keep good design principles in mind. Use contrast to enhance each segment from its neighbors. Play with your choices on your flannel board. Be sure the fabric or color of one segment does not overwhelm the others.

Piecing

When your choice of colors and fabrics pleases you, pin and stitch the first segment to the second, always maintaining that important 1/4-inch seam allowance. Add the third to the second. Continue stitching the segments this way until you have joined all 11 sections. Press all seam allowances of your pieced appliqué in one direction.

Prepare your pieced fan for appliqué. First make a template from the pattern in figure 19. With the template on the wrong side of the fan unit, turn and press the raw edges of the fan over the template.

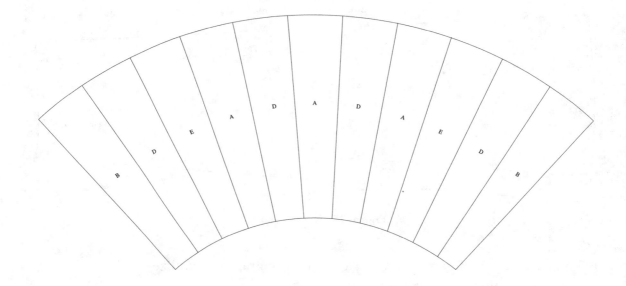

Figure 18. Colors of fan rays in the Sampler Quilt project.

Remove the template and position the fan unit (right side up) on the ground fabric. Look it over until the final positioning pleases you. Pin in place.

Blind stitch your fan in place, beginning with the smaller curve at the bottom. Next, blind stitch the sides, and last, blind stitch along the top of the *Fan*. Press your appliqué lightly.

Adding Lattice Strips

Cut and add 2 1/2-inch lattice strips. Please see the instructions for the *Rail Fence* block if you have questions.

Marking Quilting Lines

For the Sampler Quilt, the stitch-in-the-ditch method is used around each of the fabric pieces, so these lines are already marked. But notice how lines of quilting are added to become the spokes of the *Fan*. Mark the spokes using a ruler and a quilters' pencil or erasable felt

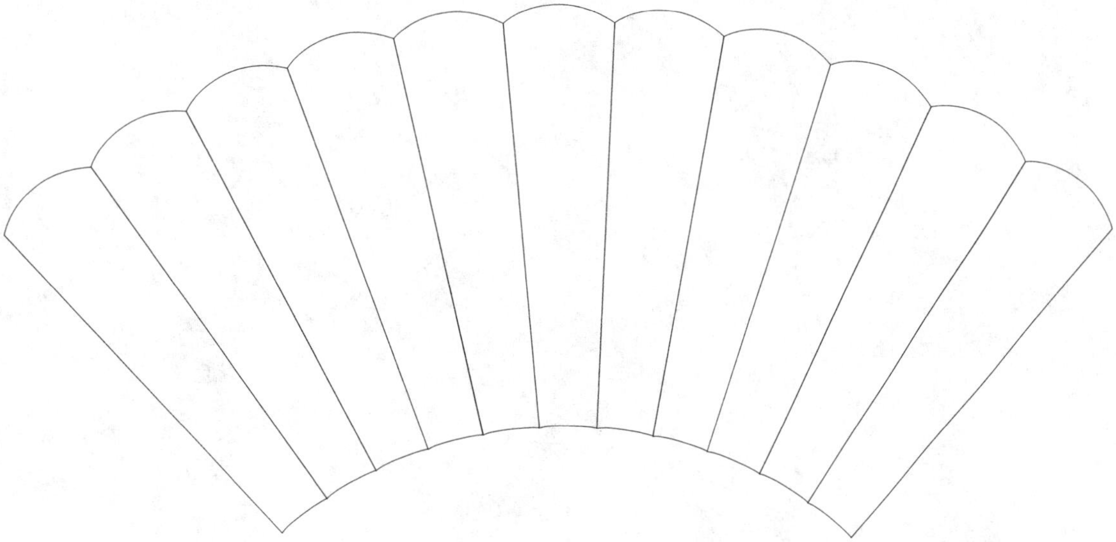

Figure 19. Fan pattern template.

pen according to figure 20. Begin with the two outside spokes first. Once you know the intersection spot where these two lines connect, the rest is easy. Line up the ruler along each of the pieced seams and the intersection spot. Mark the line. Eventually all your lines will intersect on the same spot.

Basting and Quilting

Now, you are ready to quilt your *Fan* block. Prepare the batting and backing fabric as before, and baste with your preferred basting method.

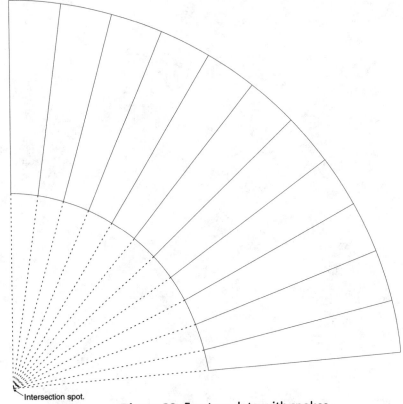

Intersection spot.

Figure 20. Fan template with spokes.

Thread color is not so much of a consideration for the stitch-in-the-ditch, but the spokes are quilted using colors from the fan itself in alternating red and blue. Here is a tip when quilting the spokes. As you near the point where all lines converge, you will find you cannot extend all the lines without a pileup of thread in the corner. Stop quilting some of the diagonal lines just before they connect with the others. It will appear that these spoke lines end behind the complete lines.

Block #6: *Ohio Star*

Ohio Star, the last block in this book, belongs in the nine-patch family. Compare the two pillows in the color insert to figure 25. Similar to *Pinwheel*, this block uses triangles to make squares. But this time we'll use four smaller triangles all the same size. In fact, *Ohio Star* requires only two templates: one triangle and one square. Five of the patches are solid squares, and the other four patches are pieced exactly the same, just rotated differently.

Handy Hint

A = Green

B = Yellow

C = Red

Look again at the two pillows. One obvious difference is that the purple pillow has a ruffle instead of lattice strips. But notice the difference in the stars. The center square in the yellow star is the green background fabric from the corners, while the center of the purple star uses the light fabric from the star itself.

There are no right and wrong ways to color an Ohio Star. Though the squares and triangles measure the same and are constructed alike, using different colors in different combinations will give you strikingly different results. Have fun and experiment with color and positioning. Consider making photocopies of figure 25 and color them with crayons or felt-pens to test your color preference.

For the sake of clarity and simplicity, I will refer to the yellow, red, and green star in the instructions.

Cutting the Fabric

Begin by making templates from the patterns in figure 21 and figure 22.

Cut five squares from color A (green in my example).

Cut 12 triangles from color B (yellow), and four from color C (red). Lay the template so the *short* edges line up with the grain of the fabric. The long side of the triangle will be on the bias (see figure 23).

Did you know???

Basting has been around for centuries. Traditionally, it's done with needle and thread; however, in the last few years, several fabric sprays have appeared on the market to hold the layers temporarily until hand or machine quilting is completed.

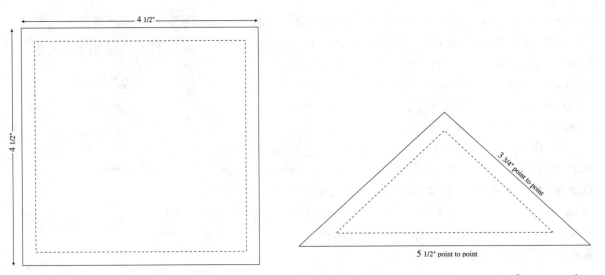

Figure 21. Template pattern for Ohio Star.   **Figure 5-22.** Diagram showing placement of your patches.

Piecing

Before beginning the piecing process, lay out all patches in place. This is your last opportunity to change or reposition colors so make sure you like the arrangement.

See figure 24 for the sewing order for the triangles. Pin and sew the first two B triangles. Keep all seams to 1/4 of an inch. Pin and sew triangle B and C. Each of these units makes up what quilters call *half squares.*

Press seam allowances of each half square to *opposite* sides carefully. Do not drag the iron back and forth. Press with the grain. Avoid letting the iron press the bias edge. Press up and down gently to avoid stretching the longer, bias seams.

Pin and stitch both half squares carefully so intersections match. Press. Check the size of your patch against the square template. It should measure exactly 4 1/2 inches. If not, adjust seams now.

Complete the remaining pieced patches in the same way.

Handy Hint

Spritz a little spray starch on the fabric before you cut the shapes. This will help stabilize the bias and reduce the risk of stretching. Handle as little as possible.

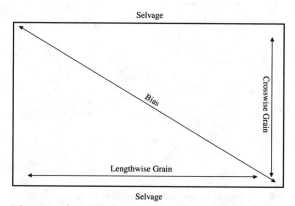

Figure 23. Diagram showing how to position your triangles.

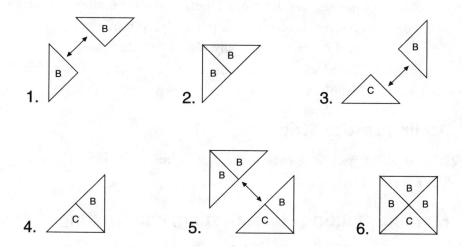

Figure 24. Sewing order of triangles.

You're most of the way there, but don't skimp now. The next few steps are critical to ensure that the color C (red) triangles line up properly creating the "square with a square" effect.

Lay out all nine patches according to the diagram in figure 25. Carefully pin and stitch the top row of squares together keeping that ever-critical 1/4-inch seam allowance. Press seams toward the solid patches.

Repeat the process for second and third rows.

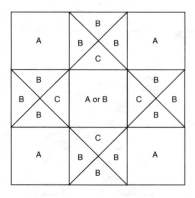

Figure 25. Diagram showing placement of your patches.

Pin the top and middle rows together. Double check to make sure you match seam intersections perfectly. Stitch.

Add the third row the same way. Press the block well.

Measure the block. Trim, re-sew, or adjust whenever needed to ensure that each block measures 12 1/2 inches exactly.

Adding Lattice Strips

Add lattice strips along each side edge as before. Refer to *Rail Fence* block for details.

Marking Quilting Lines, Basting, and Quilting

Ohio Star usually features outline quilting, as done on the purple pillow. But for variety the yellow star pillow is quilted using the stitch-in-the-ditch method described in the *Rail Fence* instructions.

For outline quilting, mark each section as shown on figure 26. You can use a quilter's marker described previously or consider buying quilter's tape (1/4-inch-wide masking tape) and using it as previously described.

Outline quilting is used on the purple pillow, but the stitch-in-the-ditch method is used for the yellow, green, and red pillow.

Form quilt sandwich as usual. Baste and quilt through all layers as before.

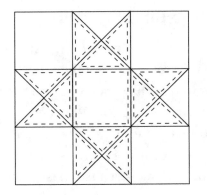

Figure 26. Marking your outline quilting.

Finishing Your Blocks: The Projects

Now is the time to make something to show off! Take your time and use what you've learned, and the result will be something you're proud of. Take a look at the color insert in the center of the book to see what these projects look like when they're finished.

Wall Hanging

Single block quilts may be used as Wall Hangings as in the *Pinwheel* example. Because we used the quilt-as-you-go method, your wall hanging is almost completed. All that is left to do is add a binding and hang it on the wall. "Binding" a quilt means to enclose the raw edges on all four sides with a strip of fabric—front and back. You may purchase rolls or packages of ready-made bias binding in sewing or craft shops or make your binding from one of the fabrics used in your project. Most quilters prefer to match the fabrics in their quilt by making the binding themselves, so that's what I'll describe in the following.

> ## Handy Hint
>
> I find it easier to stitch when I begin with the right angled (square) corner and end up with the sharp pointed angle.

▼▼▼▼▼▼▼▼▼▼▼▼▼▼▼▼▼▼

Handy Hint

Careful when folding
your quilts to store
them. Folding a quilt
the same way all the
time will crease the
fabric permanently
and "cracking" will re-
sult. Refold each quilt
in your chest or closet
two or three times a
year to avoid this.

▲▲▲▲▲▲▲▲▲▲▲▲▲▲▲▲▲▲▲▲▲

Prepare the Binding Strip

The length of your binding strip should be a few inches longer than the total edges of the project, as it takes extra fabric to go around each corner. Because each side of your block (with lattice) measures 16 1/2 inches, we would simply multiply this times the four sides to get 66 inches total. Adding four extra inches for the corners means we'll need a total of 70 inches of binding. Because most quilting fabrics come in the 44–45 inch width, we'll need a total of two strips.

Cut two strips of fabric 1 1/2 inches wide. Sew them together into one continuous strip. Press the seams open (not to one side like we usually do in quilting.)

Next, create your seam allowance. Lay the strip (right side down) on the ironing board. Fold and press one long edge of the binding 1/4 of an inch to wrong side of the strip.

Take up your sandwiched quilt. It is okay that the batting and backing are slightly larger than the top. We will trim these later. Working on the top side of the quilt, pin the unfolded raw edge of the binding to the quilt's edges (right sides together and edges matching) beginning in the middle of one side of the block—not in the corner. Ease extra binding-strip into the corners as you make the turns. Before you do any stitching, look at the backside of the quilt to make sure everything is laying flat. Fix any problems now.

Using a 1/4-inch seam allowance, stitch through the binding and all layers of the quilt. Stop stitching when you are 2 inches away from where you began. Trim the binding strip so the ends will overlap by about 1 inch. Turn the end with our usual 1/4-inch seam allowance and pin the remaining binding strip into place. Now, go back and continue stitching to complete. The binding is now completely attached to the front of the quilt.

Now, trim the batting, and the backing so they are even with the top and binding. You should now have a smooth edge (four layers thick) of binding, top, batting, and backing.

Turn and pull the binding to the wrong side of the block. Pin the folded edge of the binding over just enough to cover the previous line of stitching holding the binding to the quilt block. Use plenty of pins, especially is you will finish stitching by machine. Ease the two ends of the binding together so they will lay flat.

If you are hand stitching, sew the binding along its fold to the quilt block with small invisible stitches and matching thread.

If you are machine stitching, you will work from the front side of the quilt. I know this seems strange, but the front side is what everyone will see and we want it to look its best. We will stitch-in-the-ditch where the binding meets the lattice strips. But before you stitch, look at the back. Is the binding really covering all of the previous stitching line? Adjust any areas where it's not. When you're satisfied, turn the quilt top side up and stitch-in-the-ditch. Look at the back. See how the binding was caught by the bobbin thread. If by chance the binding shifted during stitching and missed a spot or two, don't worry. Just hand stitch these to the backing. Look for the end of the binding strip. You might also want to hand stitch the two pieces together. Sometimes I do, sometimes I don't. It's totally up to you.

Now you've completed your Wall Hanging quilt. Have you decided what you want to start working on next?

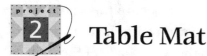

Table Mat

Any blocks you enjoy making can be made into place- or table mats. These also sell very well in small fairs and boutiques. For this project, we'll use the block design using heart-shaped appliqué.

The *Hearts Appliqué* Table Mat is finished with butted corners, a slightly different binding method than continuous binding used on the *Pinwheel* Wall Hanging.

Butted corners mean that you will neither miter (diagonal line of stitching on border) nor use continuous strips. Butted borders are the easiest to make for beginners though many quilters will rely on making mitered corners only when their skill level rises.

Unlike the single-strip continuous binding, butted corners bindings are made from four separate strips of fabric and will end up a bit wider than the borders on the *Pinwheel* Wall Hanging.

This project uses a contrasting fabric not found on the quilt top. It features a dark green in the same color family as the background fabric.

Prepare the Binding

Cut four pieces of fabric 1 1/2 inches wide and a little longer than the edge of the quilt top (18 inches would be about right). Press each piece in half along the long, narrow edge. Along one edge, also press a 1/4-inch seam allowance as you did on the Wall Hanging.

For this method, we will bind one side at a time. With right sides together and edges even, pin a strip to the top edge of the quilt so that the extra length of binding is more or less evenly distributed on either side. Turn the binding fabric back at the ends so the binding has nice folded edges that line up with the sides of the quilt. (The folded length with the seam allowance should be laying free upon the quilt for later turning.)

Using a 1/4-inch seam allowance, sew the binding to the quilt, backstitching a few stitches at both ends to secure the seam. Next, trim the batting and backing so they are even with the top and binding edges. Turn and pull the binding to the wrong side of the quilt so it covers the previous seam. Pin to hold in place. Hand stitch with invisible stitches from the back side or machine stitch-in-the-ditch from the front side.

Next, bind the opposite edge of the quilt in the same way. Then bind the last two edges.

Your corners will have small openings where the binding loops around the edges. Hand stitch these closed with small stitches and you are done.

Pillow

If you wish to make a pillow, you have several choices, depending on how big you want your finished pillow to be. The yellow, green, and red *Ohio Star* was made from the block with red lattice strips and a green binding. The purple *Ohio Star* uses just the block without any lattice, and an added ruffle. You may add additional ruffles or lace or any other trim that strikes your fancy. The secret to quilted pillows is to use a completed quilt sandwich (minus the binding) for the front of the pillow. You'll add a second backing, stuff, and seal. Voila! You have a quilted pillow.

Directions for the Yellow, Green, and Red Pillow

Begin with your completed quilt sandwich and a piece of backing fabric cut a little larger than the quilt top.

Create the continuous binding strip as we did for the Wall Hanging. (Please review the instructions in the Wall Hanging section if you need a more detailed explanation.) Cut two strips of fabric 1 1/2 inches wide. Sew them together into one continuous strip. Press the seams open (not to one side like we usually do in quilting). Next, fold and press your 1/4-inch seam allowance along one edge.

Lay the quilt sandwich on top of the new backing (wrong sides together, right sides facing out). Pin the binding strip to the quilt top, starting in the middle of one side. Make sure there is enough binding to overlap itself by at least 1 inch.

Examine figure 27 to see where you will stitch the binding. Notice which side of the project includes the ends of the binding strip. Leave the middle of this side open for stuffing. Attach the binding by sewing through all layers. Now trim the excess batting and backings so all edges are even.

Turn the binding around to the back, pin and stitch just like you did for the Wall Hanging, but do not bind the opening. Leave the two ends of the binding strip loose for now.

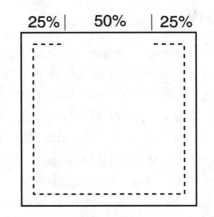

Figure 27. Diagram showing where to stitch the binding.

Stuffing the Pillow

You can purchase ready-made pillow forms in a variety of sizes, but I prefer to make my own. You can start by making a "pillowcase" just a tad smaller than the pillow. Usually I use old pillowcases or even sheeting for this. Sew it around three sides, leaving the last side open and fill the pillowcase with polyester fiber-stuffing (sold in craft and quilt shops) or shred leftover pieces of quilt batting to stuff the pillowcase. You can make "fat" or slimmer pillows, as you prefer. When you feel satisfied with the amount of stuffing, stitch the opening of the pillowcase together.

Whether your pillow form is homemade or store bought, insert it into the opening and fluff the pillow until you are satisfied with the shape. Now you are ready to seal up the opening.

Pin one of the binding strips in place on the front side of the pillow. Starting from where the original seam left off, hand stitch the one edge of the strip to the front of your pillow using invisible stitches. Pull the other edge around to the back and hand stitch into place. Repeat for the other end of the binding strip, but turn under the end to give you a finished edge. Once you've finished the binding, the pillow is complete and ready for display.

Directions for the Purple Pillow

Begin with the 12-inch block without lattice strips, and choose your background floral fabric for the ruffle.

To allow for adequate gathers, the rule of thumb is that you will need the ruffling to be about two and a half times the length of the distance around. For a 12-inch block you need 120 inches (48 + 48 + 24 = 120). Because fabric comes in 44-inch widths, three strips equals 132 inches. Close enough. Better to have a little bit too much than not enough.

For a completed 2-inch ruffle (as shown) cut three strips 4 1/2 inches wide. Join them together to make one long strip, then join the two ends to make a large ring. Fold and press in half, wrong sides together.

Gather the strip along its raw edges with a basting stitch by machine or by hand. Use strong or doubled thread so when you pull the threads to gather the ruffle around the 48 inches around your block, it will not break.

Pin the ruffle to the pillow front making sure you distribute the fullness evenly around. Machine or hand baste the ruffle to the very edge of the pillow.

Cut a square of fabric for the back of your pillow.

Take the pillow front, which includes the basted ruffled edge. Place it on a table right side up. Smooth the ruffle so it lies over the *Ohio Star* design and all raw edges are even. Place the backing of the pillow on top, right sides facing. Your ruffle will be sandwiched between the pillow top and its backing. (If you place your ruffle to the outside of the pillow top and the backing, it will end up inside the pillow where you will never see it again.) Pin carefully, smoothing the ruffle to the inside so it will not get caught in the stitching line. You want only the raw edges of the ruffle to become part of the seam.

Look at the diagram in figure 27. Notice the stitching line and how much of the one side is not stitched. This leaves an opening for you to later insert fiberfill or a pillow form.

Begin stitching 1/4 of an inch from all raw edges, through all layers. Be sure to backstitch at the beginning and end on the seam. If you stitch inside the basting line of stitches holding the ruffle, no stitches will show when you turn the pillow right side out. Trim the excess batting and backings so all edges are even.

Turn the pillow right side out. Tug on the ruffles a bit to make sure they are even and firmly stitched in place. Check the corners. You may need to go back inside and trim the corners to reduce excess bulk.

Stuff the pillow with your choice of materials (see the other pillow instructions for details). Now all that is left is to close the opening. I recommend hand stitching using invisible stitches.

 ## Sampler Quilt

The magic moment has arrived! Let's turn those four individual quilt blocks into one lovely, unforgettable quilt! You will join the blocks together as if they were a giant four-patch block. You will have two rows of two blocks each. Begin by arranging your completed blocks on a bed or floor so you can see them all at once. Create a pleasing and balanced arrangement of your sampler blocks. Take time moving blocks around, adjusting until you feel positive with the final arrangement.

Step 1: Join the Top Row

Refer to figure 28. You are about to join blocks #1 and #2.

Start by pinning the two lattice strip edges together where you will soon stitch. Now we'll have to move the batting and backing out of the way. To do this, fold and pin the batting and backing away from the soon-to-be-stitched edge. Do this on both blocks. Stitch the seam with a backstitch at the beginning and ending to secure seam. (Do not loosen the batting and backing yet.)

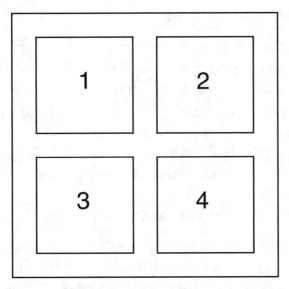

Figure 28. Blocks 1, 2, 3, and 4 of the four-patch block.

Open the blocks up on a table so both blocks lie face up and side-by-side. Check the area between joined lattice strips and make sure it measures 4 inches. If needed, adjust the seam and measure again from the front. If you do this with every pair of blocks, QAYG quilts will always go together easily. Don't fudge here!

Step 2: Mark Your Quilting Lines

Once your joined lattices measure 4 inches wide, mark your quilting design on it while it is easily assessable. Quilt shops sell a variety of narrow stencils intended for use on borders and lattice strips. To facilitate marking, cut a piece of cardboard exactly 4 inches wide by 12 inches long and slide it beneath the joined lattices.

Using your favorite marking pencil or pen, mark your design on the combined width of the lattice strips. Make sure to center it so the space remaining at the top and bottom of the area is even. (Do not mark any lines beyond the quilt block length. You will cover this area with horizontal quilting once all four blocks have been joined.)

Step 3: Trim the Batting

Turn the marked blocks back over, wrong sides up, remove the cardboard piece, and unpin the batting. For now, keep the backing flaps folded to the sides. Notice the excess of batting between the blocks. Carefully trim the batting so it fits together to form a single layer. Better to trim twice then to cut away too much leaving a gap between the batting edges. If this should happen, you can mend the area by basting in batting scraps.

Handy Hint

If you have fabric in colors you like, but seem too strong to use in a quilt, turn the fabric over and use it wrong-side up where the lighter color is showing. This will soften the original print and colors.

Step 4: Join the Backing Pieces

Once the batting lies evenly, smooth a single layer of backing fabric from the block on the left toward the right side. Do not turn under the raw edge. Just smooth it over. Next, fold over the raw edge from the block on the right side. Lay the finished fold over the first backing fabric. Pin in place along the fold line.

Before stitching, make sure to center the folded edge of backing over the seam joining the quilt blocks on the front. Adjust the folded edge if needed so both seams line up. You can check this by inserting pins directly into the seam from the right side. Then, bring the folded edge of the backing fabric to meet the inserted pin. This helps make QAYG quilts look indistinguishable from traditional quilting methods. Blind stitch the folded edge from top to bottom. Machine stitching does not work here. You must stitch by hand so you only catch the batting and the backing fabric. (You do not want your stitching to come through and show on the right side of your quilt.)

Step 5: Quilt the Lattice Strip

Now, quilt the 12-inch length lattice area between blocks #1 and #2. You see it is much easier than expected isn't it? You have joined two finished blocks!

Step 6: Join the Bottom Row

Repeat the process, joining blocks #3 and #4 in the same way.

Step 7: Join the Two Rows

Now, you can join both halves together along the center seam. Follow the same process as before, and don't forget to mark your lattice design horizontally from one side to the other. (But stop the design when you reach the outside edge of the blocks. You will mark the outside lattice strips later along with the borders.)

Step 8: Add Outside Lattice Strip

Notice that the four outer edges of your quilt are short a width of lattice. They have no partner block to bring the area to 4 inches. Thus, you must add another strip of lattice to each edge, adding both to the top and to the backing.

For the top, you could use the same fabric you used for the other lattice, or use a different fabric from your quilt top. Whichever fabric you choose, cut four strips 2 1/2 inches wide. Also, cut four strips 3 /12 inches wide from your backing fabric. (I like to have extra backing sticking out when I'm pinning the binding. It helps me "see" what is going on back there, and alerts me to problems when they occur.)

You will now, with one seam, add both the top and backing strips at the same time. Working along one of the side edges, trim the excess batting and backing so they line up with the top. Pin both the top strip and the backing to the quilt. Double check to make sure all the edges line up together, and sew through all the layers: the top lattice strip and the quilt (right sides together), and the backing lattice (right sides together with the quilt backing). Press all seams toward the outer edges.

Repeat this process for the other side edge.

Repeat the same process for the top and bottom, extending the strips to include the new side lattice. Press toward outer edges.

Mark additional quilting designs along outer borders on all four sides.

Naturally, this area has no batting yet. Here's my favorite trick to finish up. Before binding, "stuff" your outer border with strips of leftover batting. You will have a fuller edge if the batting is slightly wider than the borders. Allow excess batting to extend to the outer edge of the quilt on all four sides.

You now have a completed quilt ready to bind as is or one to which you may add additional borders if you wish. Consider adding one or more borders of varying widths and fabrics to make your QAYG quilt larger.

Quilting literature is rich with wonderful, imaginative books for finishing quilts. I leave it to you to follow through if your QAYG quilt is calling out for borders. One of my favorite books on the subject is *Finishing the Edges of Your Quilt*, by Mimi Dietrich, published by That Patchwork Place.

I hope you have enjoyed learning this method of quiltmaking as much as I have enjoyed sharing it with you. May there be many more QAYG quilts in exhibits and shops. Done properly, only a true expert can discern their structure from the traditional methods. But you know you did it the easy QAYG way.

Your Craft Vision

▼▼

NOW THAT WE HAVE COVERED quilting for fun, does the idea
of quilting for profit appeal to you? Have you begun to think about
the possibilities for turning your love of quilting into a small, home-
based business?

Consider your present schedule to determine whether you
must rearrange your calendar to accommodate your quilting-for-
profit activities. How many weekly hours do you want to devote to
quilting for profit, and how much do you want to set aside for your
own quilting fun?

Working for profit only when you feel like it will give you a
chance to determine whether you like being a "craft professional,"
while at the same time letting you gather a little business experience. Even more important, you will have the chance to test the
market to learn whether a demand exists for the type of quilting
you want to make and sell.

Starting your business on a full-time basis means being able to
work a full day without interruptions. If you still have small children, childcare, even in your home, may become a consideration.
To make sure you can accomplish what you want to do, make up a
well-organized but flexible work schedule. When starting out, you

should test the waters and try part-time work, rather than jumping in full time.

Check off the possible scenarios that most closely describe you and why you want to quilt to earn money:

☐ You have a full-time job outside your home but want to work on your quilting business three evenings per week and most of each weekend to make a steady, part-time income.

☐ You have a part-time job outside your home and want to set aside two whole days for quilting for profit to supplement the income of your outside job.

☐ You have a part-time, home-based job. Consider reorganizing your time by setting aside a specific period, for example, mornings for your present job and afternoons for your new quilting endeavors. Maybe reversing this plan will work for you, as it does for me. You will find me writing from early morning until mid-afternoon when I leave my home office for my sewing studio at the other end of the house. Not much commuting here! My schedule allows me to write while also leaving me time to design, sew, and create new projects to sell to magazines.

☐ You are retired, are a stay-at-home mom, or presently are not working for pay. If this describes you, do not assume you do not need to plan. On the contrary, if you have an open schedule, you must learn to organize your time carefully in order to avoid misusing it. If you have not needed to organize your time for a while, you may find it takes time to train yourself to maintain a work schedule.

☐ You have minor to major health constraints and feel that working outside your home is no longer possible. Setting up your own work schedule to accommodate your needs and limitations can be the perfect solution if you want part-time income, while reserving time for the rest you need. If this is the case, perhaps you can work the first four hours of the day, then lie down to read, study, or rest for an hour or two before returning to your quilting tasks. In this case, perhaps all you want to earn from your quilting is enough money to make your quilting pay for itself.

What Do You Want to Make for Sale?

Quilting reminds me of playing musical instruments. That is, no one can live long enough to play them all perfectly. As a serious pianist, I asked one of my teachers when I should stop practicing a piece before leaving it. "Never," he replied firmly. And so it is with quilting. It offers so many techniques, skills, and variations that we can never know everything. Narrow the field and consider starting your for-profit quilting with what you already know. What do you do best? What do you enjoy making most? Do you know your weak points? Believe me, I still have them. Certain quilting techniques make my work look like a beginner did them. I prepare myself to take extra care, work slowly, and check every step where I know my skills are weak. Why not start with what you do best? Here's a list to get you thinking:

- Full bed-sized quilts
- Wall hangings
- Traditional, contemporary, or "art" quilts
- Pillows
- Accessories, such as tote bags, wallets, place mats, pot holders, and so on.
- Art to wear
- Quilted and stuffed toys and animals
- Appliqué

What Are Your Goals?

Before proceeding to the business section of this book, consider your goals specifically. Check the ones that describe what you want to do:

☐ I just want to make a few quilted items to give as gifts to friends and family.

☐ I want to make a few items each year to donate to my church and other favorite charitable organizations.

☐ I want to make several small items per year and sell them at local flea markets, street fairs, and local craft events.

☐ I want to make enough items to rent a booth at several local and regional quilt shows.

☐ I would like to work from home, making custom quilts for individual customers.

☐ I would enjoy quilting completed tops for others, either by hand or machine.

☐ I would like to try selling quilted items by mail.

☐ I would like to design and sell my quilting patterns to shops or by mail.

☐ The Internet fascinates me. I would like to sell my quilted items online, and perhaps even design my own Web site.

☐ I would like to teach simple quilting classes at local shops and guilds.

☐ I have thought about writing about quilts and other quilters in books or magazines.

☐ I don't want to sell my quilts, but I would like to sell my original quilt designs in a leisurely way to quilting and craft magazines.

☐ I have always dreamed of traveling to major quilt and craft events to sell my quilted items, patterns, and designs.

☐ When I retire, I'd like to eventually work at different quilting activities on a full-time basis.

- Scrap quilts
- Pattern design
- Fabric printing, dyeing, and marbling
- Teaching
- Quilt restoration
- Quilt appraisal
- Quilt judging

When your vision, goals, and dreams of being a professional quilter have become clear in your mind, you will be ready for the second part of this book. It will tell you, step by step, how to make them a reality.

Part Two

For Profit

▼▼▼

Profiting from Your Talent

▼▼

AS YOU CONSIDER BEGINNING a craft business, you should keep in mind that you can retain your quilting activities as a hobby some of the time while also working at it part time for profit. You alone can decide how far you want to go. Some part-time quilters are satisfied to earn a small amount of cash for spending money, while others want to pay for their "habit" by earning enough to buy fabric, supplies, and books. Still others want to earn a regular, but small, income. It's up to you. If you feel ready to pursue earning money, whatever the amount, this chapter will explain how to get started.

Everyone who wants to start a small, part-time business wants a foolproof, easy system that will guarantee the most profit with minimum wasted resources. So will you. Sadly, no magical formula exists. But if you wish to sell your products, here are five important things you need to do:

1. Offer only products of high quality and excellent workmanship.
2. Produce what people want to buy, not just what you want to sell.

3. Find a niche in the quilting world.
4. Develop a professional image.
5. Minimize your expenses.

Success in business also demands that you never stop marketing yourself and your business, a topic discussed at length in chapter 10.

Creating High Quality Products for Sale

If you want to maintain quilting as a hobby, you can continue to make whatever pleases you or the family and friends to whom you give your quilted gifts. To turn your hobby into cash, however, you must produce a high-quality product that people want to buy.

When I say "high quality," I mean that your quilting must pass muster as professional work. You must produce a well-made product, exhibit good workmanship, and make good use of color, design, and finishing details. If you are not sure whether your skills have reached a professional level, consider entering a quilt show or two. Quilting judges not only award ribbons to winners, they also provide written notes for entries that do not win, commenting on what they found lacking.

As a quilt judge myself, I grant awards to people who submit their work to shows and also suggest ways they can improve their work. Other judges with whom I have worked agree that, to determine whether we will grant an award or provide written suggestions for improvement, the following must be considered:

- Use of color
- Use of design elements
- Quality of hand or machine work
- Consistency in workmanship

■ Finishing (framing, lining, binding, and borders on quilts and quilted items)

Exhibiting your work to receive such valuable feedback can be an education in itself. The experience will help you evaluate your skills and determine whether your work will stand public scrutiny. However, although winning one or more ribbons can indicate your readiness to enter the quilting marketplace, you should not let failing to win discourage you from participating. Where else can you find a qualified, objective critique of what you need to practice and perfect? Keep and study judges' comments after you have entered a show, then follow up on their suggestions by studying quilting books and magazines. After you have polished your skills, try again.

Producing What People Want to Buy

Read current quilting and craft magazines to learn what people want to buy. Visit quilt shows and exhibits to observe what other quilters are making. Shop in quilting stores and make note of displays and classes and what you find for sale. Surf the Internet if you have access. Excellent quilting Web sites that offer items for sale show you from the comfort of your home what other quilters are selling and what consumers are buying. Regularly conducting such research will keep you up-to-date about what the public wants. To make a profit, you must fill the needs and desires of your customers.

Sometimes, you may find that what sells well differs a bit from your personal taste. Although I am not suggesting that you make

Handy Hint

You can add to your market research by visiting several quilt shows and exhibits. By studying quilts that have won ribbons and awards, you can learn a lot about what people want to buy. Quilts that merit awards receive them because of workmanship, color use, design quality, and how they compare with other entries. In particular, look for quilts that have received "Viewer's Choice Awards." This means that everyone who attended the show voted for a particular quilt without necessarily considering the criteria used by judges.

things you really dislike (though I have occasionally done this my-self), I am saying that you must remain sensitive to the external marketplace if you want to sell what you make. That means staying aware of color trends as well as the fibers, styles, and designs that are currently popular.

Color Considerations

My favorite colors have not changed since I was a little girl. I still reach for anything in yellow, gold, orange, and especially red-orange. (My house is easy to find. It's the only pale orange house in the neighborhood, and it's trimmed with rust, a disguise for dark orange). However, I always read and study articles and announcements about current color trends in trade journals. Marketing experts find that most people choose blue as their favorite color, fol-lowed by its variations such as turquoise, aqua, and, recently, rich purple, which is made by mixing blue and red together.

> ## Did you know???
>
> According to the National Craft Association, blue is the most popular color in the world.

Purple may not be in vogue a year from now, but its current popularity cannot be denied. There was a time when you couldn't find purple shoes unless you dyed them yourself. Today, even in-fant clothing comes in shades of purple, to say nothing of shoes and a certain stuffed dinosaur children love. My point is that I can choose to make most of my quilts in my favorite warm, tropical col-ors for myself, but to successfully sell what I make, I must yield to current color trends. You must be willing to do the same.

Fibers, Styles, and Designs

Consider the above principle not only when you choose colors, but fibers, styles, and designs, as well. For example, cotton is hot now;

Sources of Design Ideas

- **Design Books.** I love the coloring books published by Dover and other publishers meant for doodling and coloring with felt pens. I have countless such books showing flowers and birds in all sizes, as well as books filled with stained-glass windows that I use for designing quilts. Note that designs in Dover's "Pictorial Archive" series of books are copyright free, so you may use them in any way you wish on your quilts or other items.

  From one of my butterfly coloring books, I got the idea for an elaborate jacket covered with appliqué butterflies in painted silk and outlined in gold and silver threads. I also perched a few dimensional ones, where the butterfly wings stand away from the fabric as if in flight.

- **Quilting Books.** Buy them or borrow from the library but study them, ever watchful for interesting design ideas. Did you know that several nationally known American publishing companies publish nothing but quilting books? (See Resources.)

- **Color Wheels.** I don't have one, I have six, and I use them all when designing projects.

polyester is not. Victorian designs have regained popularity, while country and folk designs have declined. Embellishments on quilting items have shown no sign of slowing down and seem more outrageous than ever. People today also favor dimensional work like floating petals, stuffed areas on quilts, metallic threads, and lots of strong texture. Nostalgia is more popular than ever, and new methods in photosensitive materials allow you to make quilts based on treasured photographs of family members.

Trends in fibers, styles, and designs will change in the future, so stay alert to the need to make necessary adjustments in your for-sale products. (For ideas on how to find inspiration for new designs, see sidebar, "Sources of Design Ideas.")

Finding Your Niche in the Quilting World

Naturally, you will want to make things within your own skill level, moving to more sophisticated designs and use of color as you gain experience. As you continue to study the market, begin to choose the aspects of quilting that appeal to you most. Once you have singled out one or more specialties, study and practice until you reach a level of proficiency and expertise in making the items you want to sell. Assess how your specialty fits into the existing marketplace. Because you cannot serve the entire quilting industry, you should identify what part of the market your niche seems best suited for.

Begin by buying at least a dozen magazines. Choose a few quilting magazines, two or three sewing magazines, and several craft magazines. What patterns, designs, and projects do you find? Magazines are market driven, which means publishers and editors continually conduct surveys to find out what their readers want to make or read about. They know if they offer information readers find of little interest, subscriptions and magazines sales will decline. They publish the designs people want and focus on current trends and fads.

Analyze current trends, and read letters and questions to the editor by readers who want to learn more. Study the classified ads to learn what people are buying and what others are offering for sale. Request copies of quilt catalogs to see what they offer. Catalogs are expensive, so most are market driven. This means the pages contain only what consumers want to buy as opposed to what the seller wants to sell. (See Resources for a list of magazines and catalogs.)

Attend as many local, regional, and national quilting events as possible. Note which classes fill to overflowing and which attract only small numbers of students. Learn what topics popular teachers offer and which seminars and lectures keep the audience's attention. This will help you know "what's hot and what's not." After completing your market research, you will be in a better position to create a market-driven product yourself—one that will satisfy a recognized need.

To find your niche in the marketplace and learn how to stand out from the crowd, you need to answer the following questions, each of which is discussed in the following section:

- What do you do best?
- What can you do that few others are doing?
- What quilted items are most in demand?
- What benefits will people see in your products?

What Do You Do Best?

Many quilters do not like to design a quilt, cut out fabric, mark it, and piece it all together, while others love this process. Would you prefer to make the quilt top and have someone else quilt it for you, or would you prefer to quilt the tops made by others? I prefer hand appliqué, while others will do appliqué only by machine. Specializing in something you enjoy most and do best is a good way to build a business.

What Can You Do That Few Others Are Doing?

Have you heard about successful quilting-related services in other parts of the country that don't exist in your community? I know quilters who machine quilt for others who live out of state because customers wanting this service cannot always find someone locally to help them.

Linda Moran, who you met in the first chapter of this book, marbles fabric for sewers and quilters. Few artists can do this, but they know that quilt lovers literally gobble up the fabric they paint.

In one of my previous books, I told Millie Becker's story. Millie suffers from mysthenia gravis and must use a wheelchair. However, this did not stop her from making something no other quilter was making, then or now. Millie knows that no one can reach every American consumer who loves quilts, but she has identified her market—the most likely buyers of her products—to be individuals who are confined to wheelchairs. Millie makes and quilts colorful tote bags that hang from the backs of wheelchairs because she found that many people like herself hated the plain, black bags sold for the disabled.

"Why can't those in wheelchairs have beautiful bags to hold their supplies as they wheel themselves around?" she asked. Many wheelchair-bound people agree with her. Today, she successfully sells these special bags by mail and on the Internet.

What Quilted Items Are Most in Demand?

Be aware of changing trends. Dinosaur quilts have passed in popularity, but dimensional art quilts continue to win most ribbons at quilt shows. You'll recall my mention of watercolor quilts in a previous chapter. Today, people are not only making them, but other enterprising quilt lovers are meeting the needs of watercolor quilt enthusiasts by selling packets of hundreds of the 2-inch squares required for this method of quilting. Many sellers promise duplicates will not be found in their packets (a marketing benefit; see following).

How well do you design and make garments? Art-to-wear garments continue to be very popular, so much so that some quilting professionals make only garments and no longer make quilts.

What types of design do you make well? Maybe you don't want to design at all. Perhaps you prefer to make traditional quilts that will be handed down for generations to come. Look for patterns in catalogs. Which traditional patterns or quilts continue to sell from one catalog to the next? This tells you what people want to own and, thus, what you should make if you favor traditional quilts.

What Benefits Will People See in Your Products?

Successful marketers know that consumers buy products that offer a perceived benefit. Take Millie, for example. She states that her tote bags are made to fit around the handles of standard wheelchairs, clearly a benefit to her wheelchair-bound buyers who love quilts and colorful accessories. To sell well, the benefits from your products must be clear to buyers. Perhaps you want to stress that you use 100% cotton materials. You can advertise that you use only 100% wool, too. Can you reassure customers that all your materials are colorfast? You might emphasize that the entire quilting process is done by hand. Customers who recognize such added benefits in your products are more likely to pay more for them.

The Importance of Defining Your Niche

Once you have defined your niche in the marketplace, you will be better able to:

- Know what to read and where to find help and information

- Focus your effort and energy in the direction most likely to be profitable

- Avoid becoming too scattered and diversified to maximize your success

- Locate the most likely customers for your product or service

- Advertise and promote your business where it will do the most good

- Let customers know what benefits your products provide

In my marketing classes, I always remind people to buy frozen dinners for convenience, which is the real benefit. People don't expect gourmet, fresh, or culinary delights when they buy frozen dinners. Why buy perfume? It does nothing for your body. Perfume's benefits include making you smell more desirable so others want to come even closer to you. This logic also applies to quilting. Think about tote bags. Would you prefer one with deep, convenient pockets inside? Inside pockets offer a benefit over tote bags without pockets. I enjoy making art-to-wear garments that are fully lined. In fact, many are completely reversible. These become benefits, too. Got the idea?

Developing a Professional Image

Giving your work as a gift does not require a special identity, but selling it does. To present yourself as a professional businessperson, you must develop a professional image on paper. When you feel ready to announce to the world that you take your business seriously, you should create an image on paper of who you are and what you do.

Without the various printed materials discussed in the following, your quilting endeavor will be stalled in the "hobbyist mode." Once you have them, however, you will be perceived as a professional, no matter how small your business may actually be. Here are some tips on how to create and use the specific printed materials you need: business cards and stationery, a brochure, a resumé, and a portfolio.

Business Cards and Stationery

These printed materials announce that you're a professional who owns a business. A business letterhead is particularly important when communicating with manufacturers from whom you want to buy at wholesale. You will not be taken seriously if you request a catalog written on personal stationery or note paper.

Your business cards and stationery should match in design, style, color, and information. Include your business name, logo (if you have one), your name, address, phone and fax numbers, and Web site and e-mail addresses if you have them. If you have unlimited funds, you can pay a graphic artist to design both your business cards and stationery. If you have access to a computer, you can design your own printed materials using desktop software programs, printing copies as needed. If you have a tight budget, standard designs can be ordered by mail from a variety of office supply catalogs.

Brochures

Brochures enable you to tell more about yourself and your business than what will fit on a business card or stationery. When designing your brochure, choose paper heavier than standard 20 lb. bond. Simple is better, so consider a bifold brochure, an 8 1/2 × 11–inch sheet

Choosing a Business Name

Be careful when choosing a business name. For example, "M & B Enterprises" sounds vague. People will have no idea about your business from that. "Jane's Quilts," however, offers more specific identification. To say even more about your business, include a line in a smaller font beneath your business name, such as "Each a handmade treasure." Together, the words *handmade* and *treasure* say you make quilts of high quality that are precious enough to keep for a long time—two marketing benefits. (See chapter 11 for more tips on how to pick a good business name.)

of paper folded in thirds. Hold it vertically and you will see you have six distinct panels on which to organize your information. Following you will find suggestions on how to fill these panels:

- Panel 1: The front cover should contain the same contact information included on your business cards and stationery.

- Panel 2: Use the left inside panel to describe your product or service and its benefits.

- Panel 3: Use the center inside panel for some biographical information about yourself (called a "bio"). In writing this statement, try to answer questions others often ask such as when, where, and why you began to quilt. State when and where you became a professional and close with recent achievements. If you can afford it, you might consider a photo of yourself at the top of this section.

- Panel 4: Use the right inside panel to describe the typical customers you serve (your target market).

- Panel 5: Use the right outside panel to list endorsements and testimonials from satisfied customers. (Ask satisfied buyers for permission to use their comments here.)

- Panel 6: Use the center outside panel for a mission statement that describes why you care about what you do; or, leave it blank if you want to use the brochure as a self-mailer, in which case this space would be used for address information.

Get printing estimates from a few printers, because price can vary dramatically from one to another, depending on the type of printing equipment they use. (Don't print a large quantity of brochures thinking you'll save money because you will probably want to make changes to it after a few months' time.)

Take your printed brochures and business cards to professional functions, conferences, and seminars. Hand them to those who ask questions about your business. Let your brochure tell your story to the recipient when he or she has more time to study your information.

Resumé

A resumé is a summary of your experience and references. New quilters often worry that they do not have much professional experience to include. If you are just beginning, list your education, any awards you may have won for your quilting, and past work experience that relates to your present professional quilting activity, such as a degree in art or working in a quilting or sewing shop.

Experts suggest that resumés be limited to one or two pages. Bookstores carry many books on how to write a resumé and some software packages actually offer templates with resumé styles from which you can choose and simply fill in the blanks.

Portfolio

A well-arranged and compelling portfolio provides a professional, pictorial story about you and your business. It should include (1) your business card (placed in the small window on the inside cover); (2) your brochure; (3) a short biography (typed on your business stationery); (4) your resumé; and (5) any tear sheets, published articles, or photographs you may have (see nearby sidebars on this topic).

Buyers, editors, and publishers study portfolios at shows, seminars, and conferences to choose quilters and crafters for their publications. I have had local shop owners ask to see my portfolio before hiring me to teach or exhibit my work.

Tear Sheets and Published Articles

When designs of established quilters appear in magazines, publishers send designers one or more complimentary issues in which the work appeared. These pages, when removed from the magazine, are called "tear sheets." Trim ragged edges and ads or other text not related to your work and place one tear sheet per portfolio page.

If you have not had your work published yet, don't give up. Write a letter to the editor of a magazine or newspaper offering your opinion on a pertinent quilt-related issue. You might also write articles for newsletters of local quilt guilds. Though you may not receive payment for these, copies of these in your portfolio will project professional credibility. My professional writing career began just this way.

A needlework teacher for many years, I had not yet considered writing as a serious business activity. But after I delivered a speech on color, design, and textiles, a newsletter publisher approached me and asked if she could have permission to print my hand-out sheet in her publication. Payment: $0. Later, a magazine publisher saw the article in the newsletter and offered me $20 for permission to reprint it. I didn't know it then, but this experience began my writing portfolio!

Writing about yourself and your work is not as effective as when someone else writes about you. The publicity adds credibility to your professional status. Include in your portfolio such articles, showing the date and issue number of the magazine or newspaper. Periodically, when I feel the need for a little publicity or a boost in my career, I send a letter to the editor of one of our local newspapers. Either I tell them what is new and unusual in the quilting world, or mention my recent quilting activities. When the editor calls, I follow up with more details. Make your news or opinion sound as interesting to them as it is to you, and publication often follows.

Quilters often confuse a scrapbook with a professional portfolio. Padding the cover of a binder and adding a patchwork design framed by a ruffle shouts "scrapbook." A proper, zippered portfolio portrays your business image far more professionally. Available in stationery or art supply shops, portfolios enable you to position photographs of your work and tear sheets from magazines if you have had your designs and articles published. Avoid crowding the pages of your portfolio by placing too many small items on one page in the manner of a collage.

Minimizing Your Expenses

This chapter would not be complete without some tips on how to increase profits by minimizing expenses. To make money selling quilted items you must control your costs like all other businesses.

Shop around before you buy supplies that do not qualify for wholesale purchasing, things not used in the production of products for sale, such as office supplies, tools, and equipment. Look for the lowest possible prices by checking discount stores, chain office supply stores, and mail-order catalogs.

Once you've established a business, you can increase your profits by buying at wholesale everything you use in the creation of products for sale. (Buying quilting supplies on sale, while appropriate for hobbyists, is not as profitable as what you can make by gaining the difference between the retail and wholesale costs of raw materials. See sidebar on how to save money on fabric purchases.)

Photographs for Your Portfolio

Color photos of completed projects form the heart of your portfolio, so make them as professional as possible. Do not use Polaroid snapshots as they fade in time and often are out of focus. Good photos can range from 3 × 5-inch snapshots to full-page, 8 × 10-inch professional shots.

Include photographs of completed quilts and related items, grouping pictures of items for sale with an identifying label of "Available Designs" to separate them from things that are no longer available. (Pieces you no longer have because you gave them as gifts still help tell your story.)

You will find a list of mail-order catalogs specializing in sewing and quilting supplies in the Resources at the back of this book. On-line buying in all craft areas continues to grow, too. Surfing the Web is today's shopping experience, so many quilting/sewing Web sites have also been included in Resources.

When soliciting wholesalers, don't use scented stationery or note paper with smiley faces at the bottom. Approach companies in a professional manner, writing on your business stationery. Do not use cute or folksy language or in any way create the impression that you are a hobbyist seeking wholesale buying power for personal use, for they will surely refuse to sell to you. Make your letter brief. In three paragraphs, state the following:

1. **Inform the company that you are familiar with their product line and have used it before.**

2. **Tell them how you will use the product in your retail business activity (quilt batting to stuff teddy bears, thread to make quilts for sale, and so on).**

3. **Ask the company about its "terms of sale." This means you are requesting prepackaged literature that will explain to you the company's minimum order amounts, shipping locations, shipping details, supply catalogs, brochures, and credit information.**

Prepare for a few inevitable refusals by contacting more suppliers than you need. This way, you can still choose from those that offer to deal with you. Study their terms of sale carefully. Select companies that sell what you want to use in your quilting business.

Once you establish a buying record and good credit with a few wholesalers, you will find it easier to add others. When you wish to increase the number of companies you deal with and are writing to a new wholesaler, be sure to include the names and addresses of other companies with whom you have established good relations. These become your "business references" and will help in acquiring even more wholesalers to expand your business. Wholesalers can become valued friends and the lifeblood of a business that sells merchandise to the public. I count many of my suppliers as important connections in my quilting business, and so will you. Honor your commitments to them and treat them fairly, and you will find that they, too, are eager for you to succeed.

Saving Money on Fabric Purchases

To find fabric wholesalers, look through trade journals such as *The Professional Quilter, The Crafts Report, Craft & Needlework Age, Craftrends,* and *Craft Supply Magazine* (all available by subscription only; see Resources). The latter two magazines publish annual directories specific to the craft and quilting industry each year. Information is listed both by supply categories and alphabetically by company name, with contact names, toll-free phone numbers, and Internet addresses.

Looking for something very specific? When I needed plain silk for painting, I looked in my copy of *Craft Supply Directory* and found Qualin International, Inc. How about something more general but essential? In the section, "Crafts/Home Sewing Products" listed in *Craftrends,* I looked up "quilt batting." I found 25 companies in the United States that sell quilt batting, and chose a company called Hobbs Bonded Fibers. You will find contact information for these and many other suppliers in the Resources.

Also study *Quilting Quarterly Journal,* published by the National Quilting Association, and *American Quilter Magazine,* the quarterly magazine of the American Quilter's Society. Most sellers of wholesale quilt supplies advertise in these special magazines for devoted quilters. Note ads that say "Dealer Inquiries Welcome." That means you!

Wait until you see *The Thomas Register!* This set of encyclopedia-like books in libraries lists all wholesale companies in the United States by company and/or by specific items. If you know the name of the company you want to buy from, simply look in the alphabetical section to find contact information. If you don't know which company sells silk-pins, for example, look under "sewing notions," then under "pins." Don't be overwhelmed when you see how many are listed.

The best news I've heard about *The Thomas Register* is that they now make their invaluable information available on CD-ROM for your computer and on their Web site.

Pricing Your Quilts

▼▼

WHAT SHOULD I CHARGE for my quilts?" is the first question most quilters ask when preparing to sell their quilts for the first time. They assume the question can be answered in a line or two, but the truth is that there are as many systems for pricing quilts as there are quilters who sell them.

Recently, two quilters chatting on the Internet had a good laugh after they figured out what it would cost to make a queen-sized, pieced, and hand-quilted quilt. They came up with a materials cost of between $205 and $260, and between 512 and 950 hours for piecing, laying out the design for assembly, and hand quilting. Then, with tongue-in-cheek, they played around with different hourly rates to see what the customer's price should be.

At a dollar an hour, the quilt's price worked out to between $717 and $1,210. (A buyer might be willing to pay this price, but would you be willing for do this much work for a dollar an hour?) At $5.15 an hour, the theoretical quilt would have cost between $3,897 and $5,152; at $20 an hour (quite reasonable for skilled labor), the price jumped to between $10,545 and $19,260. Now you know why these quilters were laughing!

Okay, back to reality. Let's go to the other extreme. I have heard from new quilters that, though they may consume the same amount in materials and time as the previous example, they do not consider their labor at all. Often, they explain that because they quilt at home while watching television and do not have to pay for child care, they price their quilts and quilted items to cover materials only.

One person told me that it didn't matter that she charged only enough to cover actual expenses because she loved the work so much. If you feel this way, why not remain a hobbyist? Then you can choose to whom you will give your beautiful work because if you sell your work for the cost of materials only, you are literally giving away your labor. You might as well give it to friends and family rather than to strangers.

Pricing Elements

Let's get practical now and examine the middle ground, starting with a discussion of pricing elements to make sure we all define them in the same way:

- **Labor** does not mean how much money you will accept to make a quilt when you sell it. Labor must be equivalent to the value you place on the time it takes not only for you to make the quilt but also what you must pay an employee to duplicate it when you need help. You may be happy to charge $3 per hour to make your quilted items, but what will you do if you become ill or need to pay someone to help if you receive an order too large to fill by yourself? Will you find others willing to work for $3 an hour? Consider this as you build labor costs into your pricing structure.

- How much do you want to earn? How many hours must you devote to your work to earn this amount? Have your skills reached a professional level? All these questions need to be considered as you calculate your labor.

- Raw materials include all the supplies required to make your product. Fabric, thread, ribbons, and beads seem obvious, but don't overlook small items such as glue, pins, freezer paper, fusible interfacing, and textile paints.

- Overhead includes all other costs related to the operation of your business, including rent, utilities, postage, insurance, wear and tear on your equipment, travel, repairs and maintenance, telephone costs, packaging and shipping supplies, delivery and freight charges, cleaning, insurance, and office supplies.

- Retail price is paid by the consumer who buys your product and takes it home. People who buy handmade items rarely concern themselves with how much time it took to make them. This is why the final price you choose for each item you sell must conform to what the market will bear where you live. Do not be surprised if you rent booth space at a show only to find that buyers want to negotiate your prices as if they were visiting a flea market. Once you settle on a price, stick to it during a show or boutique unless you've had the item for a while and want to get rid of it to recover material expenses.

- Wholesale price is what you charge when you sell your quilts or other products to someone else who, in turn, will resell them to the ultimate consumer. Shop owners and catalog buyers are but two examples.

- Wages refer to the sum you pay someone else who works for you. Although this is a business expense, some new business owners confuse the term with "owner's draw." The latter

Handy Hint

You can learn a lot about pricing just by keeping your eyes and ears open. Visit quilt shops and learn what they charge for services and products comparable to yours. To find out what other teachers, designers, and quilters in your community are charging for their services, read their classified ads in local newspapers. You may request their brochure or call for a quote on a quilt project, but don't expect professional quilters to give you free lessons in how to price your own work or services. Instead, study the pricing examples and formulas in this chapter to find a method that works well for you.

refers to the amount you, the owner of the quilt business, take from your business account to pay yourself.

■ Profit refers to the money that remains after you sell merchandise for more than it cost you to make it, which includes your labor. New business owners often fail to add profit into their price structure, but profit is why we work! It's an expensive mistake to calculate wholesale and retail prices based only on the cost of materials, labor, and overhead. After all I have said, you really do not want to give your work away, do you? If not, let's talk about how to set profitable prices for everything you make.

A Pricing Example

Let's say that you have been commissioned to design and make a quilted wall hanging that measures 3 feet square. The client does not know about the time or skill required but has specifically asked for a floral design in appliqué with a hand-quilted, all-over grid pattern for the background. How would you calculate the fee? Begin by listing the raw materials, as indicated in the following example:

2 yards of fabric for a quilt top in several colors: $14.00
1 1/2 yards of fabric for backing ($6 per yard): $9.00
1 bag of batting, crib-size: $2.49
1 spool of quilting thread: $2.00
3 spools of sewing threads: $4.00
New pencil to mark design: $1.29
Stencil chosen by customer: $2.99
Total cost for materials: $35.77

Now, let's say you want to charge $8 per hour for labor. To make the quilt top, you have calculated that it will take you about 18 hours to make an easy appliqué design with a few large shapes; 22 hours to make one a little more complex; and 25 hours for more intricate appliqué shapes. Rounding off labor costs, your fee schedule could look like this:

	Simple Design	Medium Design	Intricate Design
Labor @ $8/hr.	$150	$175	$200
Hand Quilting	$50	$85	$125
Drafting Design	$25	$40	$60
Totals	$225	$300	$385

In addition to the labor costs shown, you must factor in the cost of materials, overhead expenses, and the time needed to draft the design (also at $8/hour). This would then give you the final price of the quilt.

Study this price schedule and compare it with what the market will bear in your area. If you live near an artists' colony where handwork is highly valued, you may have no trouble charging these amounts. However, if you live in a small farming community where many people quilt and there are frequent shows with quilts for sale, you may need to lower your price to compete with the current, local market.

Different Pricing Methods

As I said earlier, there are as many systems for pricing quilts as there are quilters who sell them. Following is a discussion of how various quilters charge

- **By the hour**
- **By amount of yardage used**
- **By the square foot**

■ By the square inch
■ By using a pricing range

Charging by the Hour

To use this pricing method, you would set your minimum hourly fee and multiply by the units needed. For example, if it takes you three hours to cut, piece, stitch, and baste one 14-inch block and you charge $6 per hour, then you would charge $18 per block.

If your customer ordered the same block on a king-sized quilt composed of 24 blocks, you would charge $432 for everything except the quilting ($18 × 24 = $432 for 72 hours of work @ $6/hour). To do the quilting, you can negotiate whether the buyer wants it done by hand or by machine and charge accordingly. (See sidebar, "A Hand Quilting Pricing Formula" below.)

Charging by Amount of Yardage Used

Some quilters simplify their pricing by charging according to the amount of yardage consumed in their labor. For example, if a quilt consumes eight yards of fabric for the top alone, and you charge $35

A Hand Quilting Pricing Formula

Nonprofit quilt guilds, church groups, and others set their prices for hand quilting a quilt top by charging by the number of spools of thread being used. The concept is simple: It takes the same amount of time and thread to make a given amount of stitches, be they widely spaced or close together. (Currently, the price in California is $100 per spool, but call within your state to determine current prices.) When a client wants a quilt top hand quilted, the price depends on the amount of thread consumed. Thus, large quilts with minimal hand quilting may cost the same as small wall hangings with profuse, close quilting lines.

per yard (which would include your labor), you would charge a total of $360, a reasonable amount for a smallish, double-size bed quilt. Of course, the customer must pay for the fabric, either buying it herself or reimbursing you for its cost.

Charging by the Square Foot

One well-known quilter sticks by a basic hourly formula that works well for her: she simply charges $50 per square foot plus materials.

Another quilter in California uses varying hourly prices depending on the complexity of the design being used. She determines the square foot measurement and multiplies it by $20 for easy design work, $25 for medium design work, and $30 for complex designs:

Easy Design Work	Medium Design Work	Complex Designs
$20/hour	$25/hour	$30/hour

To test this pricing method, I applied it to a quilt I made recently. It measured 36 × 42 inches, or 1,512 square inches. I divided this by 144 inches (the equivalent of 1 square foot) for a total of 10 1/2 feet. Because my quilt featured intricate appliqué and hand quilting, I multiplied $30 by 10 1/2 feet to get a total of $315 for this work (plus raw materials).

Out of curiosity, I researched past records and found I had made a quilt with approximately the same measurements four years ago. The design featured fabric painting, piecing, and hand quilting. The publisher of a nationally known craft magazine had paid me $300 for my work. Because publishers customarily return quilts and other projects after photography, I had the option of keeping or reselling my quilt to increase my profit even more. (This is why I prefer to sell my original designs to magazines before offering them in any other way.) Although I had not heard about the square-foot system described previously, it proved to me that the publisher had paid me a fair price.

Charging by the Square Inch

Merry May, owner of School House Enterprises, has devised a clever way to price her quilts. "I determine the square-inch measurement of a quilt, then multiply that by $20 for a simple design, or $25 if I find it more complex and detailed," she says. "This provides me with a starting place." Here is how her system works:

To calculate the price on making a wall quilt that measures 40 inches square, first determine the total square inches by multiplying 40 by 40, which equals 1,600 square inches. Divide this by 144 (the equivalent of 1 square foot) and you have 11.11. Then multiply by $20. The resulting amount is $222.20, which can be rounded to $220 or $225 to make the quilt. If you use the $25 factor, the asking price of the quilt would be $277.75. After all of this, check market prices to be sure your labor as a quiltmaker can compete. If necessary, raise or lower the price so it fits within market demand.

Using a Pricing Range

Making quilts for sale is the sole occupation of a quilter I spoke to recently. Though she uses a different system to arrive at her prices, the results are surprisingly similar to the example given previously. Note that in making a similar wall quilt, she too would charge from $100 to $175, depending on the degree of difficulty. Each price bracket includes a range based on whether the piecing is simple or intricate. Here is the system she uses to charge for labor only:

	Simple Project	Intricate Project
Miniatures	$125	$150
Wall quilts	$100	$175
Full-size bed quilts	$350	$500

Denise Schultz's Pricing Method

I thank quiltmaker and colleague Denise Schultz for sharing the following comments about her pricing principles:

"To price a quilt, I first figure the number of square feet in it. Then I estimate the cost of materials (top, batting, and backing), with a little extra thrown in for thread and incidentals. I deduct this material cost from the price I charge for the quilt, allocating the balance to labor.

"Then I divide the money I am planning to charge for labor based upon federal minimum hourly wages. If a quilter receives only minimum wage (not skilled labor), in many cases she would have had only 30 hours or so to make a queen-size quilt! Not really possible even using a sewing machine for the quilting in place of hand quilting. My estimate for materials was modest, but I'm sure if I counted every cent, there would be even fewer hours at minimum wage allocated to each quilt.

"I want this to be an eye opener for people, to harden their resolve not to underprice their work, and to make buyers understand why current pricing structures fall short. I see this as a necessary part of the maturing of the quilt industry. Superstar quiltmakers should not be the only ones who command a living wage for their work. I want others to know that not only do we undervalue ourselves in the marketplace, but at times we pay someone else to take our quilts away from us! When you realize that the federal government does not allow us to pay an employee less than minimum wage, then multiply the actual number of quiltmaking hours by that wage, plus the cost of materials, that would become the legally based minimum we should charge for a quilt.

"Currently, the oppressor (in terms of pricing exploitation) is not just the buyer, but the quiltmaker, when she sets her prices too low. We cannot possibly expect the marketplace to change

A Common Pricing Formula

In her book, *Creative Cash: How to Profit from Your Special Artistry, Creativity, Hand Skills, and Related Know-How* (Prima Publishing), Barbara Brabec discusses a shortcut pricing formula used by many craftspeople, including quilters. Figures for labor, raw materials, and overhead are added to get the wholesale price, which is then doubled to arrive at the full retail price.

Let's take an example of an elaborately quilted pillow you have made, which totals $36 including labor, raw materials, overhead, and a built-in amount for profit. Using the method just discussed, $36 would be the wholesale price. Doubling this amount to $72 provides the retail price.

Bear in mind that when you sell at wholesale, you should set a minimum amount for vendors who buy pillows or other products from you. Though you make less than you would selling individual items at full retail, you make up the difference by selling several items at once. (You may also cut your labor time by using assembly-line sewing methods to produce them.)

Prices do vary from one geographical area to another, so regardless of the pricing method you choose, you must remain sensitive to what your local market will bear. How do your prices compare? You must always consider the prices charged by other quilters nearby and adjust your final price to accommodate your market.

voluntarily. We must also work on our side of the equation. It's partly a self-worth issue, too. People are not doing us a favor when they buy our quilts. Rather we sell to them something of high intrinsic value in terms of materials plus labor plus durability, not to mention artistic value, which the marketplace often does not recognize or acknowledge.

"Quiltmakers, particularly older quilters I know, often say they aren't artists (even though the content of their work clearly disproves this). They continue to hold the view that buyers do them a favor in buying their work. I want quiltmakers to learn to see the bigger picture and value themselves and their work more highly in the future. All quilters should tackle the issue of sustainable pricing."

Choosing Your Own Pricing Method

To find a price-setting formula that is perfect for you, try the following exercise. Choose a quilt project you might undertake in your business. Price fabrics and other needed materials in your area. Set up a mock materials cost list like the one shown earlier.

Now, price your quilt project using each method described in this chapter. Take the resulting prices from each method and add them together. Divide by the number of pricing methods you used to get an average price. Then, visit quilting events and shops in your community. How does the resulting price fit in your geographical area? Is it higher or lower than the market will bear? Is it competitive with other quilters nearby? Perhaps this pricing exercise will provide you with a practical fee schedule you can live with for quite some time.

Handy Hint

There is a unique way to display the prices of items during a show. Just paint the price on decoratively painted wood blocks and place them among your quilts.

Selling Your Quilts

IF YOU STILL WANT TO SELL some of your quilted items, close your eyes for a few moments before reading further. Think about how you would approach the water at the seashore. First, you must decide if you want to go. Second, you must determine how to find the nearest beach. You may need a map so you don't get lost. Third, you will want to know if the shore that interests you is shark infested or safe. You decide to go.

Once you arrive, you prepare to meet the water by taking off your shoes and changing into beachwear. Then, step by step, you make your way through the sand, mentally preparing yourself as you near the water. You may feel anxious for a few minutes. Maybe the water will be too cold or the currents too swift. You think it over.

Like most people, you do not want to plunge into the deepest areas without testing the water first. So, you walk to the water's edge, and ever so gingerly let a few splashes go over your toe. As you gather confidence—if the water feels good—you step in up to your ankles. Picture yourself standing in the ocean and finding the experience wonderful. You walk forward until the water reaches your knees. Maybe you are the conservative type who, although still standing there a while longer, actually scoops up water in your hands. You splash it on your upper body for a final test. Finally, convinced your efforts are worth the risk, you may walk forward up to your neck and, at last, plunge in and begin to swim.

Am I suggesting you go to the seashore before you begin to sell your quilts? No. But I am suggesting you approach the selling process in much the same way. Why jump in with no preparation when you can take your time, test the situation, gather confidence and experience, and then dive forward when you feel sure of yourself?

As you begin to think about how and where to sell your quilts, you may be surprised to learn that you have many options. Selling your quilts at a craft or quilt show may come first to mind, but this is only one of many ways you can sell what you make. Why not start the easiest way and work your way up to more challenging methods where a greater investment of time, money, and experience comes into play?

Following is a discussion of several different selling methods and types of outlets where you can gradually get your feet wet as you sell your quilts or other products (see nearby sidebar for a summary list of them). Later in the chapter, you will find ideas on how to dip into new waters by learning how to teach, sell special services, or sell how-to projects to magazines.

Strut Your Stuff at a Fundraiser!

When you feel ready to choose the first place to sell your quilts or quilt-related items, why not play it safe? Choose a local fundraiser. Where I live, the Senior Center sponsors a fundraiser every Christmas. For $35, you get a card table, folding chair, and a space to strut your quilting stuff. A percentage of each sale goes to the center to advance programs for seniors. Local residents are the primary buy-

Table Mat

Sampler Quilt

A Summary Checklist of Your Selling Opportunities

- Fundraisers: Have fun while you strut your stuff!

- Bazaars: Use them to gain local selling experience.

- Craft Festivals: Test your prices at festivals outside your immediate area.

- Garage Sales: Earn extra profits over a weekend.

- Craft Fairs: Gain selling experience while you check out the competition.

- Holiday Boutiques: Consider selling out of your home during the holiday season.

- Consignment Shops: Give them a try, but get selling details in writing.

- Quilt Shows: Connect with appreciative quilt buyers here.

- Craft Malls: Check them out, but research carefully before signing a contract.

- Mail Order: Diversify your business by selling products by mail.

- The Internet: Broaden your work by taking your business online.

- Commission Sales: Many opportunities await the professional quilter!

- Wholesaling: Something you may wish to consider in the future.

ers. Usually, there is no gate fee. Buyers come to support a local cause they care about and to look for gifts that catch their eye.

Consider fundraisers sponsored by churches, girl or boy scouts, community centers, and service groups such as Kiwanis, Lions, Veterans, and Rotary clubs. Nearly all hold annual fundraisers to keep worthy programs going. Also look into small shows sponsored by local art, craft, or quilt guilds to raise money to support their groups. All these nonprofit events are easy to find in your community. Look for event names, places, and dates in your local newspaper and at your local Chamber of Commerce office. Call to see if they rent booth or table space, or write show sponsors to request application forms.

Gain Experience at a Local Bazaar

Spontaneous in nature, bazaars are informal gatherings where local residents meet to buy, sell, and even to barter. They may be

- A market consisting of a street lined with shops and stalls

- A shop or a part of a store in which miscellaneous articles are for sale

- A fair or sale where miscellaneous articles are for sale, often for charitable purposes

Rent space at a local bazaar to become familiar with meeting the public while you do a bit of marketing, listening, observing other sellers, and asking questions. Table and booth fees are minimal and travel expenses are low. After you work a few such shows, you will have a realistic picture of the market for your products. Street fairs and privately sponsored craft shows are also worth considering to get you started. Look for such events listed in your local newspapers.

Visit bazaars in which you are considering participating, looking at them through the eyes of a buyer and a seller. Listen to the comments of those who buy and those who do not. What do they say about the goods they see? Too high priced? Maybe they wonder why prices seem so low. Would they have preferred other colors, styles, or sizes in the items they found of interest?

After you have sold a few items at local fundraisers and bazaars, look over your pricing structure. Did you sell enough to feel motivated to participate in larger events? Did you find you needed more or different supplies at your table? Could you make change easily? What about your display? Can you improve and spiff it up now before you try a larger event, such as a craft festival?

Test Your Prices at a Craft Festival

After you sell at a few craft festivals, you may be more certain of your pricing structure, what's hot and what's not, and which of your quilting items people snatch up first.

People come to festivals to celebrate something and to enjoy a party atmosphere. They come to find entertainment, good food, and interesting things to buy. What festivals go on where you live? Visit them first. Talk to the vendors at each show. How do they like it? Do they come back year after year? Ask where else they sell.

Peruse newspapers for events throughout your county. Your county courthouse and chamber of commerce may supply a list of local events with contact names. Also consider visiting a few cities nearby that offer craft, art, or quilt events. As you go farther from home, you will encounter fewer familiar faces and more serious buyers. Request literature from groups sponsoring countywide events and check out what they require from vendors setting up in a small space.

In Marin County, where I live, an annual outdoor festival sponsored by county restaurant owners offers music, arts, and crafts. Each summer, food vendors from all over the county set up booths while people wander about, eating and drinking and enjoying live music. Around the perimeter, people from the community set up small booths with crafts of all kinds, including quilts.

In nearby Sausalito, people come from all over the state to attend a well-known yearly art festival. This festival is for artists, by artists, to celebrate arts of every kind. Musicians and magicians come to entertain. Food and drink vendors come to sell and, of course, crafters and artisans of all types come and set up little tables lining the main street.

Profit from a Weekend Garage Sale

Want to have fun while selling inexpensive items? Think about committing an entire weekend to a garage sale. Many people like me have garage sales, but no garages, so we hold a "driveway sale" instead. Together with our neighbors, we hold a large group garage sale each Labor Day weekend. Some of these sellers are more serious than you might expect. One couple who sells linens from a store in San Francisco offers discounted items, end-of-year sales, and damaged goods at our group event. Another couple makes and sells marketing items such as pens, ashtrays, glasses, and clocks to businesses. Leftovers appear at our group event.

Others sell ordinary household items they have tired of and that others buy with relish. Buyers come to our annual event with a list in hand. They travel from one garage sale to another during the weekend but they come to ours early in the morning because they can visit several homes in our neighborhood at once.

I often sell items that were made on commission for magazines for which I write. Publishers return my goods to me after publication, then I offer these one-of-a-kind items during our group driveway sale. I also sell leftover supplies to make way for new purchases. Buyers always snatch these up first!

Investing in our neighborhood sale costs each of us about $9, a percentage of the total cost to place an ad in our local newspaper. If you don't have such sales in your neighborhood, consider starting your own. Consider participating in an informal setting like this by making a few small things throughout the year. Remember the pot holders I mentioned in the introduction? This is your chance. How about making a few pillows, tote bags, and similar items? If they disappear before your garage sale ends, you may be ready for a crafts fair.

Find New Buyers at a Fair

If you enjoy meeting the public and talking to potential buyers personally, you may enjoy working a fair where many types of crafts are represented. This is a good place to check out the competition to see what type of quilted products others are offering for sale, and how they are priced.

In addition to exhibiting in regular state, regional, and county fairs are also a good choice if you offer quilted items with broad, general appeal. Here, too, you will make direct sales. Finished products such as bed quilts, wall hangings, toys, clothing, and accessories appeal to the buying public shopping at state and county fairs. However, you may be surprised to learn that although customers prefer exclusive, one-of-a-kind, handmade items, they often expect to pay the same prices they pay for ready-made items found in chain or department stores. It's up to you to educate your buyers and explain the differences between handmade and mass-produced items. Being able to process credit card purchases is important because fairgoers typically make impulse purchases. (See chapter 11 for details on how to obtain merchant status for your business.)

Regardless of which type of consumer fair you choose, start small and work up to larger events, for you will need to gather practical experience. You must learn to:

- Build up an adequate inventory of goods available for sale well before an event.

- Set prices appropriate for your geographical area.

- Set up appealing displays to showcase your products. (Make sure your display information and brochures include details about your creative process. Photos of you at work, and those that show works-in-progress, will help tell potential buyers your story at a fair.

- Greet the public warmly and explain your wares. (Prepare to answer the question, "How long does it take you to make this?" many times a day.)

Generate Holiday Sales at Home

Once you have some selling experience, consider selling out of your home. Home boutiques held around Christmas or other holidays provide another opportunity to sell directly to consumers. However, this requires a good deal of advance time to prepare.

Two sisters I know illustrate how simple, yet effective, home boutiques can be. Both work all year making quilts, knitting and crocheting sweaters, and making wreaths, floral arrangements, dolls, and home decor crafts. During the first weekend of December, they decorate one of their homes with their collection. They advertise simply by placing ads in local newspapers and distributing colorful fliers at nearby schools and churches. Shoppers come looking for one-of-a-kind handcrafted items for holiday gift giving.

The sisters spend a week before the event arranging an appealing display in two rooms in one of their homes. They mark and price each item. During one weekend, they generate enough income to buy craft supplies to make new items for the following year, pay expenses, and add to their bank accounts during the holiday season.

A friend of mind works all year making small, quilted items for Christmas. She decorates her living room with satin angel dolls, Santas, stuffed animals, patchwork placemats and table runners, tree skirts, and more. During one weekend, she opens her living room to the public after distributing fliers and placing an ad in the local paper. She sells so well that she always makes a profit in addition to earning enough money to buy new materials for the next year.

If you decide to sell this way, plan ahead. Collect names and addresses of customers who might visit your home show or boutique. Make a sign-up sheet readily available. Each year, you can mail invitations to those who have supported you in the past.

Give Consignment Shops a Try

Consignment selling requires that you design, make, and complete a quilt or quilted item, then look for a buyer. People who own consignment shops display the goods from many artisans and crafters and keep a percentage of each sale to help maintain their business, pay the rent, and advertise. You do not pay them up front to display your goods. Rather, when someone buys your item, the shop owner keeps her portion and gives you the balance of the money as previously agreed upon (see following).

Handy Hint

When selecting display equipment for craft fairs, choose the best equipment you can afford because you will be competing with established craft professionals who are on a higher level than you would usually find at local and neighborhood events. Manufacturers of show display equipment advertise in craft trade journals such as *The Crafts Report*. This publication also runs frequent articles about how to prepare and set up show displays of all sizes and where to buy display equipment such as tents, lighting, shelves, tables, and so forth. (See Resources.)

To begin your research, visit local consignment shops, malls, and galleries. Carefully survey each shop you are considering as an outlet for your work. Ask yourself the following questions:

- **What items fill the shop?**

- **Does your work fit in?**

- **Does your style fit the shop's mood, theme, and price range?**

- **Does the staff respect the work of its consignors, protecting it from customer handling?**

- **Do you find most items tastefully displayed?**

Once you find a shop where you would like to place your work, express interest and ask to see its consignment contract. Shop owners always protect their own interests in such contracts, but they do not always protect the interests of the individual consignor—you. Following are a few key areas you should investigate.

Display

How will the shop display your work? If you submit a full-size quilt, for example, will it hang on a wall or rest on a bed? If it is the latter, will customers be able to sit on the quilt or handle it? Does the shop allow customers to bring food and drinks into the shop? Quilts fade in direct sunlight. Request that your work be protected from sunlight as well as from handling by many caressing hands, which will make it look secondhand in no time.

Percentage Agreement

What percentage of the selling price goes to the shop owner and how much to you? Amounts vary from one shop to another, but in the last few years, a 50-50 split has become the normal percentage, though you will still find some that take only 40 percent, giving 60 percent to the crafter. Never settle for an oral agreement here. Get it in writing!

Pricing

Do you mind if the shop owner lowers your retail price if your products do not sell in a given time? If you don't want this to happen, say so in writing. You may prefer to come and pick up your merchandise rather than have it marked down.

At times, experienced shop owners realize you have underpriced your work and know it would bring in more money if the price were higher than the one you set. If you disapprove of this, say so in your contract, but remember that this could also work to your advantage. Wouldn't you be elated if you priced a quilt at $150 and agreed to a 50-50 split and later learned the shop owner had sold it for $500 and given you half?

If you are just starting out consigning, consider the advice of an experienced shop or gallery owner and talk to others who sell quilts locally, in quilt guilds, or at shows you have attended. If you find you continually undervalue your work, your pricing schedule needs your attention immediately.

Notification and Payment Terms

How long will you wait for the owner to notify you that you have a buyer for your quilt? Disappointment and frustration may occur if you find a quilt sold immediately upon display and you didn't receive notification for 90 days. Besides, if your items are selling quickly, you want the opportunity to take in more for sale.

Your contract with a consignment shop should clearly spell out when you are to be paid for merchandise that has sold. Generally, payments are made to consignors on a monthly basis. If you don't receive timely payments, follow up immediately. Don't let shop owners operate on your money interest-free, which is just what happens if your item sells right away and the shop owner fails to notify you on time that a sale has been made. Make it your business to remain in touch with the shop regularly.

Once your quilts or other handmade items saturate nearby consignment stores and continue to sell well, it may be time to expand. *The Crafts Report* and other trade journals provide monthly lists of consignment shops throughout the United States that seek textiles and quilted items. Contact them with persuasive cover letters and

What's the Market for Quilts in your Area?

As you begin to think about selling a few of your quilted items, continue your market research by visiting the following types of shops and stores:

- Quilt, Sewing, and Craft Shops. Visit as many as possible, not to buy, but to research the quilting market in your geographical area. Notice what types of quilts grace the walls in quilt shops. Inquire about the most popular classes. Find out what people want to learn, make, or buy for themselves.

- Sewing Shops. Check to see if local shops have a small quilting supply section in addition to patterns and fabric for garmentmaking. Shops that add a limited selection of quilting supplies to enhance fabric sales choose merchandise carefully. To compete with quilting shops, sewing shops will select only those products that turn over quickly. Does the sewing shop offer essentials such as batting and quilting notions? If it has quilts on display, what type are they? Appliqué, pieced geometric quilts, or art quilts?

- General Craft Shops or Chain Stores. Do such shops in your area have a quilting section? If so, what have they chosen to offer quilters? Because quilting is not their specialty, they, too, will carry only what they find easy to sell.

Do any of these shops sell patterns for quilted wearables? Make a note of what they offer for sale to improve your research. Shops do not stock patterns that do not sell. They take the time to learn what customers want, and you must, too.

quality photos of your work. Nurturing your relationship with a few consignment shops across the country can keep you in business for years.

Meet Your Target
Market at a Quilt Show

Quilt shows, fairs, and exhibits differ from events mentioned previously because at these shows, the buyers have already expressed an interest in quilting merely by attending a show. Recognize people who attend these shows as your target market.

Quilt shows attract quilters at all levels and can be wonderful for you if you have products specifically directed to them such as tools, books, and patterns in addition to quilts. Quilt shows allow you to make direct sales to quilt-oriented consumers. Competition may be stiff because most booth vendors will have products similar to yours. Presenting yourself as a professional in your field counts even more when dealing with knowledgeable buyers. Answer questions briefly but completely because quilt fairgoers usually come to learn the latest about new materials, tools, and techniques.

Information about your products and demonstrations on how to use them are vital. Successful vendors at quilt shows are often those who attract attention with interesting activity such as speed-cutting fabric, making templates, using tools, and so on. Pointing out the benefits of your product to potential buyers must remain your primary goal.

Finding quilt shows is easy. Nearly all quilt magazines provide monthly listings of shows throughout the country. *Quilter's Newsletter Magazine* provides the most comprehensive list, state by state. If you belong to quilt and craft guilds, you will receive advance notice about upcoming quilt shows.

Exploring Craft Malls

Craft malls are a fairly recent phenomenon. Cropping up everywhere, they attract the buying public to a single location. Originally, when craft malls first began, crafters and quilters sold their wares from small push-carts in the open areas of shopping malls. Now, enterprising craft lovers have come to the rescue of crafters and quilters who want a secure place to sell their goods. Presto the craft mall! Think of it as a combination of commission selling (you may be asked to make something in a different color), and consignment. (Although you are in total control of your merchandise, the craft mall is in control of sales, and you will receive no payment until something sells.)

When selling in craft malls, you're in deeper water, financially speaking. This method is the first I've discussed so far where a regular monthly payment may be required of you whether or not you sell anything. Risk factors now come into play. What if you don't sell anything for a three-month period? If you signed to lease the spot for three months, you still owe rent for the space. Rent varies considerably from one mall to another, so shop around for a good craft mall before you commit.

Perhaps my craft mall experience will give you some perspective. Three years ago, I decided to place my one-of-a-kind quilted, crocheted, and knitted items in a craft mall. Since then, I have heard that many people have had an unsatisfactory experience similar to mine.

I had only one craft mall to choose from within a 35-mile radius and knew enough that I wanted to keep my eye on the shop and visit regularly. The shop owner showed me the individual stalls in the shop, which contained shelves and a pegboard. Renting the space on a monthly basis cost $75 (with three months payable in advance) whether I sold anything or not. The contract stated that the shop would keep 20 percent of the retail price, and I would receive 80 percent. I decided to try it and took several items I had made to the shop and arranged them.

During the first three months, I sold only one item, a hand-painted shirt embellished with stones and ribbons. I had already decided to remove my things at the end of the three-month period when I began to read comments from crafters and quilters on the Internet. Many had also found that some craft malls will take literally anything that is handmade and professional looking. They do not plan to earn their income from making a percentage of sales but rather from the regular rent crafters pay for space. They do not advertise as much as they would if they had money invested because many find that the payment they receive from crafters each month pays their own monthly rent and expenses plus extra profit.

The craft mall I used had more than 45 stalls, bringing in $3,375 per month to start but their rent was less than $1,000 per month. The few items that sold quickly added to their income by 20 percent and became "gravy." If I were to do this again, I would walk around the shop with a tablet, write down the names and phone numbers from tags on items for sale, call the artisans and ask them about their sale success. I suggest you do the same.

Some craft malls require you to sell your wares in person. Others have a co-op system where someone else sells your items directly to the consumer. Still others may require that you work in the shop once a week or so. Visit those nearby and check out the competition. If you cannot find a craft mall nearby, lists of them across the country appear in trade journals and on the Internet. Write to ask if you can deal with them at a distance as you do with out-of-state consignment shops. (Be sure to check the popular craft malls operated by Coomers and American Craft Malls. Both are listed in Resources.)

Moving into Mail Order

This method of selling requires careful investigation. Many ads exaggerate the money-making potential of a mail order business and myths appear everywhere. As one who sells this way, I can assure you that my mail box does not overflow with dollar bills that drift onto the porch. I tell students in my college mail order classes that they should reconsider selling in more conventional ways unless they love detail and a lot of paperwork, are well organized, are not procrastinators, and are willing to take financial risks. Still, the very words *mail order* sound exciting to most people, so I am including a realistic discussion of the topic here.

Even if you already have a profitable quilting business, consider mail order selling as an additional form of retail sales and a way to offer your quilted items and services directly to the customer without a middle man. Items not readily available in retail stores such as hand-embellished wearables and unusual, original designs sell best. Sell not only handmade quilted items, but consider patterns, kits, and booklets, too.

There are two ways to sell by mail. You can place ads in magazines or start a direct mail advertising program. In mail order advertising, potential customers read your ad and send you a check with their order. In direct mail advertising, you solicit orders by sending customers and prospective buyers your brochure, catalog, or other information that describes your product line. Many famous catalog houses specializing in quilting supplies began their businesses by using direct mail. Working from home, they mailed only two- or three-page catalogs at first, and so can you.

If you find the idea of selling by mail interesting, begin by creating a "house list," of your present buyers and potential customers (names of friends, neighbors, and business associates). Take care to use current addresses and avoid duplications. Computer software will allow you to organize the list alphabetically and by zip code and will purge duplicate names. Continue to expand your house list by adding the name and address of everyone who sends you an order or makes an inquiry by mail. Also consider trading customer lists with other non-competing, quilt-related business contacts you may have. This, too, will expand your house list.

Direct mail advertising is an effective way to get new business, but it is also one of the most costly forms of advertising. Therefore, it is always prudent to make a small test mailing to a portion of your mailing list to make sure order results will offset your costs of printing and postage. Producing a mail order catalog of your own can be expensive when you consider photography, production, printing, binding, and postage, to mention a few prime expenses. If your funds are limited, perhaps you can share expenses and work with quilting friends or members of a quilt guild who have something to sell by mail. How about a co-op catalog featuring the designs of several people? Several quilters pooling resources can make this idea practical.

To effectively sell by mail, you must have a good understanding of how to advertise through classified and display ads, topics discussed at length in the next chapter. Also see Resources for Erwin J. Keup's excellent book, *Mail Order Legal Guide,* which will help you prepare to sell by mail order and to understand the legalities of selling by mail.

Selling on the Internet

Every day, we see new sites on the World Wide Web offering everything from apples to zippers! Today, so many quilters sell directly

> **Handy Hint**
>
> Because this is the computer age and Internet selling continues to grow quickly, think about buying computer software to facilitate bookkeeping if you plan to become serious about selling by mail order. Maintaining data about a mail order business is one of the tasks best suited to computers. Choose from many programs advertised on the Web, in discount stores, and in computer or office shops, or post a request on craft and quilting bulletin boards and ask who is using what program and how they feel about their systems.

from their Web sites that one person cannot possibly check out every one, but you will find a list of quilting Web sites in Resources to whet your appetite.

If you think you'd like to sell this way, prepare to do a lot of research. For a large investment of your time and a small investment of cash, you can offer your goods to people around the world. Having your own Web site means you can combine the advantages of selling on consignment, on commission, and by mail, all in one place for a low monthly fee.

I began my Web site nearly five years ago, jumping in early as the system was still developing. I expect you know that you need regular access to a computer, basic computer skills, and an Internet Service Provider to gain access to the World Wide Web. If computers fascinate you, start with one of the "dummy" books such as *Hypertext for Dummies*. You can do it all yourself with enough time and patience, or pay someone else to create and maintain your site for you.

My husband and I chose to create my site ourselves. It features my books, business reports, article reprints, and audio tapes. Soon I will be teaching quilting and craft business management through correspondence courses from my Web site. No doubt about it, this is the wave of the future!

Initially, selling directly from my Web site or to other members of online craft and quilting groups I belong to seemed a marvel to me, but it is beginning to feel like "old hat" now. World Wide Web auction sites, such as E-bay and others that are springing up, allow anyone to sell anything over the Internet. Crafts, collectibles, and handmade items are among the biggest sellers using this unique method. Watching the progress of these online auction groups is an education in itself. Such groups tout that you need no middle man. Sellers who want to buy from you contact you directly, and you personally ship them what they have paid for. The cost is as little as 2 to 5 percent of the selling price. No wonder this concept is taking off!

Quilting on Commission

Change into your professional clothes, this is serious! Working on commission comes to those with experience and a proven track record. People who place custom orders with you must feel confident that you will produce good work and deliver it on time. Commission work on a professional level is much more serious than a relative simply asking you to make a quilt in their favorite colors and designs.

Did you know???

That Internet sales are projected to reach more than $220 billion by the year 2001?

The advantage of quilting on commission is that you have a sure sale before you begin a new project. It means you will create a project made to order, following a customer's preferences. "Customers" may include individuals who pay you to make something for them as well as magazine publishers, manufacturers, or others who commission you to make a specific quilted project to order.

A disadvantage of quilting on commission is that customers occasionally change their mind after you have begun a project or, perhaps, when you are nearly finished with it. Many people who hire others to make things for them do not know how complicated it is to "make a few changes before you're done," as they usually put it. This question frequently comes up on quilters' chat groups on the Internet. Recently, a quilter requested that others in the group give her suggestions about a problem she had experienced. Someone had commissioned her to make a quilt and, when it was nearly completed, called the quilter asking her to make "minor" changes that added many hours to the work as originally described. The quilter wondered if she should add these extra costs onto the original price or take a loss on her labor.

Karen, a helpful quilter who prefers to remain anonymous, says she learned an important lesson the first time this happened to her. She gave me permission to pass along her feelings on this topic, originally shared online in a chat room for quilters.

"Sorry, but I must advise you to take the loss and stick to the original estimate," she says, "unless when you gave your customer your price quote, you specifically mentioned that should the job take longer, you would bill extra. I've learned you can't always predict what the customer will bring you or want. Today, I get all the particulars of a job in advance and in writing. I list everything as specifically as possible."

Karen suggests that quilters make a checklist of all the variables that could happen and include this information on their order form. Assign each task a specific price per hour, and counter Murphy's law by adding at least 25 percent extra to the hourly time you expect a project to take. Following is Karen's list of special tasks you should consider adding to your price list:

- **Sewing on the bias**

- **Buttons, cording, and other embellishments requiring hand sewing or basting**

- **Hand quilting, by the hour**

- **Hand washing**

- **Ironing and preparing fabric**

- **Fabric supplied by customer. (Will extra be supplied for errors or miscalculations? If not, who buys additional fabric?)**

- **Challenging fabrics with special patterns (such as stripes, checks, and plaids)**

- Fabric requiring special handling. (Silks, organza, and other fine materials may not work easily by machine and need hand sewing instead.)

- Alteration of patterns supplied by the customer

- Layering and basting of the quilt sandwich. (Will you or the customer do this work?)

- Quality of batting. (Has the customer provided a low-quality batting? If so, explain that you do not guarantee the finished project if the product is inferior.)

"I list all of this on the back of my laser-printed order form and list the basic prices added up on the front," says Karen. "Then I ask the customer to sign it." (Make sure your customer reads and understands what he or she is signing. That way, you have the list handy and can add to it if needed.) When working on commission, never release a completed item until the customer has paid you in full. Pleading for payment you have already earned creates uncomfortable confrontations and undermines your self-esteem. Surrendering the completed item before receiving final payment also causes you to lose a valuable negotiating position.

"If I don't get what I feel is fair," Karen concludes, "I prefer not to make a particular item rather than undercut myself. To feel good about my work, I will refuse an order rather than feel someone has taken advantage of me. Better to give such items as outright gifts than to give myself the message that my work isn't worth much."

Wading into Wholesale Waters

Like commission selling, wholesaling is serious business. To consider this method of selling, you must first be able to produce goods in quantity at wholesale prices. Though you sell your quilted

How to Find Quilting Commissions

Use the following promotional methods to find commission clients:

■ On your business stationery, write to fabric and craft shops and quilting magazines. Many keep a file of dressmakers and quilters who will work on commission. (Quilt shops often have their own staff to work for customers, thus they may not be your best bet.)

■ Place want ads in the "Services Available" section of your local newspaper or in the classified sections of quilting magazines.

■ Contact local community groups and offer to give programs, exhibitions, or demonstrations of what you can do.

■ Show your work at exhibits and fairs so others can see it. Onlookers at fairs or those who attend programs you present can become potential clients, so engage them in conversation. Educate them about the value of handwork, and distribute fliers and brochures describing your services whenever possible.

products for less when selling to wholesalers, remember that when you act as a wholesaler you can require minimum orders to encourage larger sales. In other words, these buyers do not buy one-of-a-kind items. Because they buy to resell, they buy in quantity. This means you can set your minimum order at six of one pattern, for example or three pillows or a dozen pot holders.

Also, bear in mind that, unlike consumer sales, payment is not immediate. Even though your invoice may stipulate payment in 30 days, it is common for retailers to stall payment for 60 to 90 days.

Following is a brief discussion of two ways that professional quilters might wholesale their products: through wholesale trade shows and mail order catalog companies.

Selling Through Trade Shows

Wholesale shows, also known as "trade shows" (so named because they specialize in offering products directed to a specific trade), require more preparation and professional status than the other shows discussed in this chapter. Here you will be selling to buyers who own gift shops, boutiques, and catalogs, or others who have retail connections. They will help you create new markets for your products. (See nearby sidebar for the names of the three largest quilt shows in the country.)

Trade shows are fewer in number than retail, consumer-oriented shows. When applying to attend or participate in these shows, expect to prove you are part of the sewing or quilting trade. Because they do not admit consumers, professionals must prove they qualify by producing any or all of the following:

- A letter requesting show information written on letterhead stationery

- A business license from the city where you live

- A copy of your seller's permit (if you plan to sell at the show)

- A voided business check

- A business card

Selling to Mail Order Catalog Companies

Have you ever thumbed through a beautiful color catalog and seen products in it that you could have made? Once you are in a position to wholesale your products, you may be able to get your items listed in such catalogs.

Study many craft, sewing, and quilting catalogs before choosing the one most suited to your products and style. (See Resources for a list of them.) Write to companies whose product line complements your products and express your interest in having them carry your product(s). Include brochures and other literature describing your items and send photos of professional quality.

You may need to negotiate if interested catalogers contact you. Clearly state your terms to the buyer. Make it clear you are willing to compromise but not surrender wholly to the catalog buyer's business preferences. You must also make your production schedule clear. No established cataloger will want to continue working with you if they advertise and receive orders for your product only to find you cannot meet their customers' demands. If you can only make two dozen patchwork pillows per month, for example, explain this to the catalog buyer early. Later, if your pillows sell well, they have the opportunity to ask for a greater quantity while giving you sufficient time to find someone to help you produce more in less time.

If you decide to work with a mail order company, learn how it works. New quilters often assume that quilting catalogs will do everything to promote their items. Do not expect them to take the time to create, lay out, and write your sales copy, for example. Make it easy for them to work with you by doing a good job of this yourself. Send high-quality sketches or photographs that clearly illustrate your item and include details about prices, sizes, and colors.

Creative people often have introverted personalities and dislike asserting themselves this way. I understand this because it describes me, too. However, to profit from your quilting skill, you must create your own business image and niche in the quilting marketplace. This means that you must learn assertive marketing and sales techniques and must speak and write in a confident manner if you want to expand your business by selling to mail order catalog companies. You are playing with the "big boys" here.

Selling to Magazines

Quilters often think the only way to earn extra money from quilting is to sell the quilt itself or to become a teacher. Not so! You can sell every quilt you make and still get paid to write about its design for a magazine before you sell it to consumers. As a professional designer, quilter, and crafter myself, I now make most of my income from commission sales not to individuals, but to magazines.

Important Shows for Quilters

See Resources to obtain descriptive brochures on the following shows of importance to quilters:

- The International Quilt Market and Quilt Festival Held annually in the fall in Houston, Texas, is the largest show in the country devoted exclusively to quilting. (The Market is a trade show for professionals, but all sewers, dollmakers, and quiltmakers are invited to attend the Quilt Festival, a consumer show held in conjunction with the Market a day or two later in the same location.)

- The National Quilting Association (NQA). This annual quilt show for consumers moves around the country to a different state each year.

- The American Quilter's Society (AQS). This quilt show for consumers is held annually in Paducah, Kentucky.

- The Hobby Industry Association (HIA) Show. Held annually in January in different cities each year, this trade show—the largest of all annual craft trade shows in the world—has much to offer professional quilters. Quilt vendors sell at this show, which may have as many as 3,000 exhibitors. Professional quilters attend the show to make connections with important editors and publishers and receive free samples of the latest quilting tools and supplies from manufacturers.

Publication of your designs establishes credibility. Magazine editors need writers and designers to satisfy the never-ending demand for new ideas for their publications. Readers and hobbyists need writers to inspire and motivate them. If you have perfected your quilting technique, consider combining your skill with words.

Dozens of quilt and other craft magazines buy designs from freelance designers and writers, but you have more to sell to a magazine than a set of how-to instructions for reproducing one of your creations. Many magazines want articles about the process of designing, color use, special tips, and the latest trends, tools, books, and techniques. Polish your writing and quilting skills and pair them up. Together, they can more than double your income as you market and sell your creative quilting skills. Here are a few tips to help you get started:

- Become an expert. Subscribe to the leading quilting and sewing magazines to remain informed of current market trends such as style, color, fabrics, notions, and methods. Research continually. Digest the important quilt and craft magazines.

- Write at a professional level. Beautiful quilt designs mean little if the writing and instructions are unclear. Describe each step of what you make with your hands. You must also be able to put into words what your hands do "automatically." Readers usually do not have your skill level. Leave nothing unsaid.

- Develop priority-setting skills. Deadlines will become routine. Maintain a monthly action list with time lines. Hang a blackboard in your office or studio to keep current obligations and deadlines ranked by priority easily visible.

- Get organized. (See sidebar, "Filing and Retrieving Information.")

Working with Editors

When you feel ready to sell your designs, select several magazines you think are appropriate. Remember that magazines other than quilting publications buy quilt designs. Make sure the magazine suits your style and collect as many issues as possible. Keep them filed alphabetically by magazine title so when you have a quilted item to sell, you can shop for the best market among your collection.

Editors from all types of magazines complain regularly about their frustration with articles or designs entirely unsuited to their particular publication. (Example: Do not send traditional designs to a contemporary quilt art magazine or clothing to a magazine that features only quilts.)

Before submitting an idea, request the free writer's guidelines offered by magazines and study several back issues. The guidelines will tell you what type of articles the editor seeks as well as length, format, styling, and other details. Many guidelines will tell you the best months to submit seasonal designs.

Using your business stationery, prepare the best query letter possible. Query letters attempt to interest an editor in your idea and should be only one page. Make your letter crisp, businesslike, brief, and grammatically perfect. After completing your letter, enter the information about the design and publication in your records to simplify tracking outstanding designs. Keep a design file, listing the project, to whom it was sent, date, and whether it was accepted, rejected, and/or resubmitted.

With my query letters, I always include a single project fact sheet that provides descriptive details about the project. Good-quality snapshots count. Learn to photograph your quilted products to best show what they look like. Send an overall shot plus one or two close-ups to show details.

Send your informational package with your business card, resume, and copies of previous articles (if you have them) in a presentable folder. Include a self-addressed, stamped envelope so editors can return your package to you if they decide not to use it.

When a design or project has been accepted for publication, you will receive a contract. Read it carefully, as it will explain how much and when you will be paid (on publication or on acceptance) and what rights the magazine is buying. (See "Selling How-To Projects to Magazines" in chapter 11.)

Manufacturers' Endorsement Programs

Many manufacturers have endorsement programs. This means they may provide complimentary supplies to qualified designers. Some, but not all, companies pay an endorsement fee whenever one of your designs appears in print along with a materials list that mentions their product by name. Therefore, keep a list of manufacturers of products you use. Each time you plan a new design, contact a few of them. See if they will supply you with materials to make the project at no cost to you.

From batting to fabric and notions to thread, manufacturers recognize qualified designers as their target market. They know that if we support their products, use them, and endorse them, everyone wins. Designers benefit from the year-round product information mailings each company provides. Consumers feel confident when they shop from a materials list prepared by a competent designer, and shop owners find it easier to satisfy customers who know what they want.

The Society of Craft Designers (SCD)

This is the most important organization to belong to if you wish to sell your designs for publication. SCD's annual seminars and newsletter prepare you to deal with both manufacturers and editors. Here you will meet dozens of magazine editors who will examine your work and portfolio, and buy from you directly. SCD also provides workshops to help you learn to write proper design instructions. SCD's Certified Craft Designer program is an added bonus, helping designers of all types achieve a truly professional level. Many doors in the industry opened to me once I had earned this certification, and I urge you to consider it if and when you decide to expand your business.

Filing and Retrieving Information

Researching, filing, and retrieving information is not possible without an efficiently organized filing system. You will need file folders, cabinets, and file boxes to track:

- Patterns, articles, and graphs

- Quilting and sewing catalogs

- Idea files and magazine articles used for reference

- Samples of trade/consumer/quilting/sewing magazines, alphabetically arranged

- Writer's guidelines from the different magazines you want to write for

- List of magazines that buy quilting, patchwork, applique, and wearables (preferably on computer)

- List of editors, addresses, and phone numbers (preferably on computer)

- File of your published articles/designs (tear sheets)

PATRICIA'S STORY

Quilting came into my life nearly 16 years ago," says Patricia Hammond of Hearthstone Designs. "For several years, quilting served as a hobby while I worked my way through college and, later, during my years as an inside sales coordinator for a tool company.

"In late 1989, a small quilting guild, The Flying Geese of Harford County, was formed, and I became one of the original 12 members. The guild grew quickly and friendships strengthened. Because of our small treasury at the time, I received an invitation to lecture and demonstrate hand quilting at one of our monthly meetings. I prepared for several weeks, creating handouts and hand-quilted samples. The lecture was a success, and a spark ignited in my heart for teaching and speaking about quilting.

"After the birth of my daughter in late 1991, I became a stay-at-home mother and began to focus more upon ways to spend time raising my daughter while I created a home business. The time seemed right and a "pattern company" idea began to take form.

"I began creating several mixed-technique mini-quilts and soon realized my passion soared with hand appliqué. My self-confidence wasn't quite there yet, so, secretly, I designed and constructed my very first original pattern, "Sunflower Burst." I completed the quilt and quietly brought the project to a weekly meeting to hem the binding. Someone sitting across from me asked to see what I was working on. Throwing caution to the wind, I stood up and proudly exclaimed that it was an original design and that I had decided to go into the pattern business. I went home knowing that I had turned a big corner in my career.

"One pattern soon became five. With my husband's help, we created cover sheets, photos of the quilts (he's a professional photographer. Convenient, right?), the templates, and written instructions on our home computer. With help from the local printer and a $500 start up investment, Hearthstone Designs was born.

"Friends in the quilting guild were my strongest supporters, and several hosted workshops in their homes. As my confidence in my designs grew, I made phone calls and established myself as a vendor in several local quilt shows. After vending at a show, a quilting guild from Pennsylvania called and asked me to be a guest speaker for their group. I felt overwhelmed and didn't even know what to say when they asked for my fee schedule. We agreed on $50, and the lecture was a great success.

"With a new bounce in my step after the lecture, I approached two quilt shop owners and brought my patterns and lined up a few classes. In its newsletter, one shop featured a "press release" article about me and my pattern company, complete with my photo. When the newsletter was released, I received more invitations to vend and lecture. Inspired by my success and the unending support of my family and friends, I began designing and quilting much more seriously.

"On April 1, 1999, Hearthstone Designs premiered its first "electronic newsletter," the *Hearthstone Herald*. The quarterly newsletter features articles, a block of the month/mystery quilt, special coupons for new designs, a quilt show calendar, featured quilt artist interview, charitable ideas for guilds, book reviews, retreat information, and so on. In July 1999, my company celebrated three years in business. My pattern line now has 35

(continues)

dynamic appliqué and mixed-technique designs, ranging from simple beginner wall quilts to elegant, sophisticated projects for the advanced applique enthusiast.

"I spend at least six to eight hours per day working on some aspect of my company, and I have established a strategy for staying focused and creative that works quite well for me. I truly believe that the changes I have made and the daily schedule I have created allow me to focus on my company without losing precious time with my daughter, Caitlyn. Some days, my time is spent on paperwork, taxes, and bills. Each day, I read my e-mail and return or follow up on any notes I receive. I review my Web site each week and see if the highlighted designs need to be updated or whether I need to add or change some information. I spend lots of time in my studio,

Other Ways to Profit from Your Quilting

In addition to selling their designs and how-to projects, many professional quilters add to their income by offering special services, such as:

- Cutting, sewing, or hand quilting for teachers and busy professionals who need another pair of hands

- Providing services to other quilters who may not wish to complete their own quilted projects or who need help

- Doing hand or machine quilting for customers, or quilting to order either making additional samples of popular designs for trunk shows or classes or constructing new projects. I also spend time each week reading quilting journals and magazines trying to learn something new, gather advice, or just follow the new quilting styles and trends.

"Recently, I completed the program to become an NQA Certified Teacher. Many people have asked why I wanted to become certified because I have been lecturing and teaching nationally for some time at guilds, shows, shops, retreats, and conferences. It's because I felt this quilt "boot camp" would make me a better teacher and also will serve as a professional, credential challenge and self-confidence booster. Like many other professionals, I take classes whenever possible to keep my skills and techniques fresh.

- **Completing the unfinished projects of others, or mending, restoring, or embellishing them. (One quilter I know will visit a home and mount and baste a quilt top to a frame, leaving the remaining hand quilting process to the owner.)**

In addition to offering special services, you may eventually be able to earn money as a speaker who talks about quilting. Think of public speaking not as a fearsome experience but as an opportunity to share what you know and love about quilting. Professional speakers and expert quilters have a wealth of information to share! Recall a few of the interesting quilting speakers you have heard in the past and consider where you might fit in. Remember that popular, in-demand quilting speakers started small once upon a time. They were not born and labeled "famous quilters" from childhood. They worked hard, learned, and persisted, and so must you.

Finally, consider teaching. Several organizations offer important certification programs to train you as a certified craft or quilt teacher. If you prefer specific accreditation in quilting, contact the National Quilting Association. Its year-long correspondence program trains and prepares quilting teachers all over the country.

If you plan to make and sell original designs, the Society of Craft Designers offers certification in your choice of craft arenas, one of which is quilting. Look around and you will find several other national and regional organizations to acquire teacher's certification. Of course, if you have credentials for teaching at the primary, secondary, or college levels, you have a great advantage.

A mere six weeks after my first exposure to quilts, I found myself on a plane for Houston to attend the International Quilt Festival. Two years and many workshops later, I decided to propose a new class in addition to my needlework classes at our local community college where I had been teaching for two decades. September brought not one but three classes for me to teach. I was on my way, but must confess I learned even more about quilting by teaching. Thank goodness for enthusiastic students!

The following year, I signed up for NQA's correspondence course (mentioned earlier). I began to make all the required quilts in all shapes, sizes, and techniques, and categorized my books and patterns as required. I temporarily put aside all other needlework to immerse myself totally in my new obsession. Finally, the day arrived when back in Houston I would have an interview with three accredited quilting teachers. After a personal interview, the judges asked me to leave the room while they reviewed my large trunk of quilted homework, which I had made over the last year. I was dismissed. Butterflies (my favorite motif) fluttered in my stomach as well as on two of my quilts.

Later in the day, I was called back and asked to present a sample class on how to hand quilt. After just four years of quilting experience, I passed the test and received a diploma saying I was now an accredited quilting instructor. It was an exciting moment for me.

Marketing Your Quilts

▼▼▼

IF YOU DO NOT INFORM the public about what you have to sell, they can't buy it. Thus it is up to you to make your products or services publicly known, recognized, and observed, either by advertising or other promotional means. This chapter explains the difference between classified and display advertising, and offers suggestions on how you can promote and publicize your quilting business for little or no money at all.

Advertising vs. Publicity

Advertising can be costly but still not guarantee sales. If you feel apprehensive about spending money without being sure of the results, you are in good company. Many quilters and crafters I know (including me) place ads infrequently, if at all. Other alternatives exist, but before I discuss them, keep this thought in mind: Good advertising can build sales and remind customers about the benefits of your product, but it cannot create steady, sharp increases in sales, solve cash flow problems, or substitute for low-quality merchandise or indifferent service.

Whereas some small businesses feel they cannot afford to advertise, even the smallest can publicize, or promote, their businesses for little or no cost. You can bring yourself, your business, and your individual products and services to the attention of the public in the following ways:

- Through your printed materials or Web site
- Exhibiting or demonstrating in your community
- Sending news releases to local papers
- Networking with others who share your interests

Remember, there is no product so good that it will sell itself. Advertising is how most business owners begin, but if your budget won't allow for paid advertising right now, try any of the previously mentioned promotional strategies, which are discussed in detail later in this chapter.

Important Questions to Answer

Before you spend your well-earned money on advertising, answer the following questions:

- What do you want to sell?
- Have you found a strong demand for your product or service?
- How do you know your product or service is in demand?
- Can you prove it with research?
- Why do you think your product or service will sell?
- Identify its principal benefits. Beauty? Warmth? Clothing? Art?
- How will you prove your product's benefits are real? Testimonials? Guarantees?

Now give some thought to all the other quilters who will be vying for the same customers as you. Profile your competition by answering the following questions:

- Who is your competition?
- Where are they?
- What is better about your product or service?
- What is better about their product or service?
- Where do they advertise?
- What is their position in the marketplace?
- What benefits do they offer?
- Where else is your product available? Mail order? Retail? Wholesale? Out of your regional area or country?
- If there is no competition, why not? Is your idea sound?
- How much does your competition charge?

One-Step vs. Two-Step Advertising

To introduce our products in print, we can choose either a one- or two-step process when we buy classified or display advertising in magazines or newspapers. One-step advertising means that you sell your item directly to the buyer from an ad. Customers read your ad, then send you their order with payment. You send the ordered product. Each of you had to take only one step to complete the sale.

If your product description requires more than what you can express in an ad, try two-step advertising. In this case, you would advertise the availability of a catalog or brochure that offers detailed information about your product or service. The customer responds to this type of ad by requesting your advertising information (which may either be offered free or for a small price to cover postage and printing costs). You send a package of information that includes a brochure or catalog describing your products, a persuasive sales letter, and an order form. The customer returns your order form with payment. You fill and send the order. Both of you had two steps to follow to complete the sale.

- What kind of customers do they have?
- Who are their vendors, distributors, wholesalers?

When you know the answers to all of these questions, you may feel knowledgeable enough to spend money on paid advertising, and confident you are placing it in the right place.

Classified Advertising

Paying by the word describes classified ads, a popular and easy way to advertise. There is more to writing a persuasive ad, however, than first meets the eye. Professional writers strive to "write tight." This means using fewer words to present a strong written message. Because classified ads charge you by the word, you want to say as much as possible in the fewest possible words for your budget. Study the following two sample ads. Which do you find most persuasive and easiest to read and understand?

Sample Ad #1:

Every fabric lover longs to make her own quilt. Why shouldn't you? There are thousands of beautiful, exciting fabrics on the market today. Wouldn't it be nice to learn how to make use of them in making your own beautiful quilts and quilted clothing and accessories? We are proud of our new booklet telling you how, step by step. Send in your check in the amount of $12.95 for our new publication telling all about how to make your own quilts. Why not make your own quilt today? (88 words)

Sample Ad #2:

Make beautiful quilts and accessories yourself. Tips from 10 quilt pros help you make a quilt quickly and easily. Order *Make Your Own Quilted Treasures,* $12.95 ppd. (26 words)

If a magazine in which you have chosen to advertise sells classified ads for $1 per word, these two ads would have a price difference of $62 ($88 − $26 = $62). In addition, because print ads must appear several times before achieving results, repeating the more costly advertisement six times would make a $372 difference in your advertising budget!

Interestingly, even if you could place both ads for the same amount, the second one would be more effective. Because people tend to scan ads rather than read every word, the shorter ad is more likely to catch their eye. In fact, more people will actually read all the words in a tightly written ad. The word *Treasures* added to the booklet title in the second ad also signals a marketing strategy. *Treasured quilt* sounds more valuable and worthwhile than *quilt* alone.

Display Advertising

Newspapers, magazines, and phone directories all feature display ads, which charge by the inch rather than the word. Write to request press kits from publications in which you would like to advertise. You will receive ad rates for both classified and display ads, along with readership information and publishing frequency. Display ad rates for craft and needlework magazines are costly, yet affordable to the serious business owner, but you may go into shock when you learn that general consumer magazines charge thousands of dollars for a single-color display ad.

Once you have a business telephone number, your phone company will automatically list your number in both the white and yellow pages in your local phone directory. However, you may wish to consider broadening this coverage by placing a display ad in the yellow section. You must pay an extra monthly charge for this, so check the back pages of your telephone directory for ad information. Most have different size boxes in which you can place a display ad if you think your product needs sketches, line drawings, or graphics to help it sell better. You place your information in the chosen space and pay by the total number of inches the space consumes. A display ad will definitely enhance your credibility as a professional, but you will have to weigh the value of this against the regular monthly charges.

Media Selection

Whether you are placing classified or display ads, you must be concerned about media selection and the number of times you will repeat an ad. (See sidebar, "The Importance of Repeating Ads.") Once you find an appropriate magazine (that is, one that your target customers read), and an ad you place brings in more sales than it costs, make no changes! Why tamper with success?

Many years ago, I placed an inexpensive ad in a magazine targeted to my ideal customer. I offered challenging pattern booklets to advanced needleworkers. I began to make sales after four months, and once they began, they kept coming. Thus, I left the ad virtually unchanged except to add new booklet titles as I published them. The ad ran for nearly 11 years!

I'd like to be able to say that my sales were steady only because my booklets and designs were so marvelous, but that was not the

The Importance of Repeating Ads

Mary-Jo McCarthy, an expert in marketing quilts and other crafts throughout the United States, offers this wise advice to beginning advertisers:

"When a quilter decides to start advertising, she needs to plan a minimum of four ads a year in the same publication. She needs to have the funds to invest and not expect her mailbox to be stuffed with orders when the first ad appears. The ad needs to reflect the product and should always be simple and to the point. Include ordering information in the ad. A new businessperson can consider the first ad successful if it recoups only the ad cost. Usually, it's the publication of the second or third ad that begins to generate profit."

prime reason for my success. Selecting the appropriate magazine contributed the most to generating such regular sales.

I did not have much money to spend on advertising, so I chose a magazine with a very limited readership—only 2,200 subscribers at the time. Few subscribers mean that smaller magazines charge less because ad costs are based on the size of the subscription list. In this case, I paid $24 per issue, but the critical point is that this particular magazine was targeted to readers longing for challenging designs and bored with larger magazines that focused on beginning stitchers.

In selecting magazines for a classified ad, scan the ads in several back issues to see if items similar to yours are being advertised there. Remember to match your ads to the interests of each publication's readers. For example, if you want to sell patterns using variations of time-honored quilt designs, you might place an inexpensive ad in *Traditional Quilter* because it specializes in these. If you want to sell handmade cloth dolls wearing quilted outfits, choose a doll magazine. If you have quilting designs that combine textile paint with beads, choose a general craft magazine.

Though many people think that consumer magazines such as *Better Homes & Gardens* or *Sunset* are ideal places to advertise because so many people subscribe to them, think again. Magazines that focus on home issues and activities are not only too general for a one-person quilting business, but cost prohibitive.

Narrow your search instead and look for magazines such as *Quilt* or *Quilting Today,* which have smaller readerships but ones that are tightly focused on your market. They charge less than large, glossy publications while reaching your most likely buyers.

Writer's Market, an annual directory published by F&W Publications, is my favorite source for locating specialty magazines. In fact, this directory is where I found the obscure magazine in which I first advertised. Until then, I had never heard of that publication. Although this directory (available in libraries) is aimed at writers looking for magazines where they can submit articles, over the years I have found its information equally suitable for advertising research.

Identify one or two magazines whose readership matches your target market, and you've won half the battle of deciding where to place your ads. Write to quilt and craft magazines to request their free press or media kits. These publications will send you every-thing you need to know about advertising in their pages and de-scribe their typical readers for you. When you receive the material, compare it to your customer profile (see sidebar, "Identifyng Your Target Market.")

Remember Millie Becker from an earlier chapter? Placing ads in magazines and newsletters for the disabled, while appropriate for her, may not be for you. However, if you plan to finish quilts for oth-ers, advertising in the classified sections of quilt magazines may be a better idea. Their readers are primarily quilters, some of whom may prefer to have their quilts finished for them.

Inexpensive Promotional Methods

"Promotion" is the act of placing your products and services, your name, and your business before the public. Unlike paid advertising, many promotional efforts cost little or nothing at all, yet some can generate hundreds or thousands of dollars worth of business. Here are several ways you can promote your quilting business or get publicity:

■ Present quilting demonstrations at street fairs and quilt shows.

■ Offer to give presentations and programs for local community groups. They need not be quilt related. (I have given programs to PTA groups, 4-H groups, Rotary

Identifying Your Target Market

Your "target market"—your best potential customers—is where you should aim your advertising and publicity efforts. Write a profile of your best imaginary customer by answering the following questions:

- Is gender important? Will your item appeal more to men, women, or both?

- Does age matter? Are your customers children, young adults, middle-aged people, or seniors?

- Do they need special skills to benefit from your product? (No, if they are buying a quilt. Yes, if they are buying your quilt patterns.)

- What about income? Can everyone afford your item or must they be affluent? People of average income buy quilted sweatshirts. Wealthier art lovers buy large wall hangings.

- Where are your customers located?

- How will you reach your target customers? Through trade journals, consumer publications, direct mail, the telephone book, television or radio, or promotional activity?

meetings, church groups, junior and senior high schools, art clubs, and business and entrepreneurial groups, to name a few.)

- Place fliers and posters about your product, service, or special event (home boutique, for example) in local shops, stores, and community centers. (If you plan to design and make quilts for consumers, consider leaving fliers and brochures at local sewing centers. Customers who admire such items but cannot make them or do not have the time to quilt often seek referrals from shops where fabric is available for sale.)

- Write letters to the editor in magazines, commenting or asking questions.

- Consider writing short articles for newsletters, journals, and other publications. (Nothing provides professional credibility like being published!)

- If you have a product, introduce it to the quilting/crafting community by listing it in trade journals, which usually do not charge for one-time announcements.

- Consider making TV or radio appearances. Many craft and quilt shows invite quilters to demonstrate or exhibit their work.

- Send news releases to local newspapers. Make them interesting, as mundane news simply will not do.

Networking to Advance Your Business

Networking means the informal sharing of information among individuals or groups linked together by a common interest. Today, it has become critical to everyone who wants to get ahead in any business large or small, part time or full time.

Quilt hobbyists enjoy getting together to share techniques and to admire each other's work. After all, this is the primary function of quilt guilds. Quilt professionals, however, must go beyond quilting on a social level to networking with others in the field, developing professional contacts, and sharing manufacturer and product information (such as wholesale sources, marketing trends, teaching opportunities, and upcoming trade shows).

Networking regularly takes place at guild meetings, shops, classes, and conventions. At first it may sound like conversation, but listen carefully. Rather than hearing small talk that shifts from one subject to another, you will notice that networking remains focused on a specific topic. Participate by asking questions and listening attentively. When someone needs information you have, share. Networking invites an even more avid discussion of common goals, ideas, and problems.

Participants introduce themselves and then respond to previously agreed upon issues common to them. Think of networking as playing two roles simultaneously—that of teacher and student. Take pains to avoid a common networking pitfall. It is not fair to drain others of information and provide none yourself. Exchanging freely and equally characterizes proper networking protocol.

So, how do you start? Join local, regional, and national organizations where quilters and other crafters gather. Quilting organizations address quilting issues and provide continuing education in the field. Groups such as the Hobby Industry Association, National Quilting Association, American Quilting Society, and Society of Craft Designers will help you see the business of quilting in craft context. All of these groups, along with many others, provide regular conferences and seminars giving professionals the opportunity to exchange ideas and to meet others in their field to discuss common concerns.

Let's discuss the two primary organizations for quilters, the National Quilting Association and the American Quilting Society (whose addresses are in Resources). Both groups publish quarterly magazines to keep serious quilters updated on the status of quilting. The National Quilting Association maintains a directory of members they have certified as teachers. Join one or both of these organizations to learn about:

- **What respected teachers have to say**
- **Which quilt styles and designs are in vogue**
- **The latest quilt books and newsletters**

MARILYN'S STORY

Marilyn Maddalena began her working life as a businesswoman with an interest in law and journalism. She spent nearly 30 years as a legal transcriber for Court Reporters and went on to become a legal secretary for a number of law firms. From 1977 to 1988 she owned and operated her own secretarial service, I'm Your Type, in the Mt. Shasta area of Northern California. Teaching business skills for Shasta Community College, she also wrote a weekly column for the local newspaper, *The Trinity Journal,* for three years.

Marilyn's quilting passion began as a hobby in 1958 when she made her first three quilts. These were simple, tied flannel baby quilts—one for each of her sons. Eventually, she completed 23 more quilts. Working evenings and weekends, she turned her quilting hobby into a part-time, home-based business, called Sew Special, in 1996.

No, she does not sew one quilt after another. Her quilting obsession lies not in making more quilts but in their history and traditions. Wanting to see as many quilts in her lifetime as possible, Marilyn is working on a certification program in quilt appraisal, restoration, and renova-

- The latest quilt tools and other related products
- The locations of shows, exhibits, and workshops across the country

Next, join regional or national craft organizations. Their seminars and publications will help keep you informed about the entire craft market, of which quilting is a part. You need to know how quilting fits into the craft world, paying particular attention to the areas of needlework and sewing. A list of these organizations and their addresses appears in Resources.

tion. To examine and scruti-
nize as many quilts as she can,
she is also working on her
judge certification from the
National Quilting Association.

Retiring from her "day
job" in the summer of 1999,
she began presenting pro-
grams to quilt groups regarding the identification and
history of antique quilts, as well as fabric preservation and proper care. She
also regularly appraises for the quilting public at the Folsom History Museum, where the public is invited to bring both old and new quilts for appraisal. Marilyn continues to put her business and writing skills to work in
her unending research and identification of more quilts, following their
history back to every state in the union.

Also consider joining non-quilting/non-craft organizations in
your own community. This will give you a good opportunity to publicize your business locally. Wear or display your work to attract
added attention. (For many years I was known as "The Needlework
Lady" in my community because people became so used to seeing
me always stitching on something at meetings of every kind.)

Finally, consider joining your local chamber of commerce. Exchanging business cards and brochures at meetings is a good way to
generate new business locally.

Promoting Your Business on the Internet

In the previous chapter, I mentioned the value of selling from a Web site on the Internet. Here, I'd like to focus on the incredible promotional power you will have once you're online. I am not a computer consultant or programmer but I can tell you that the wave of the future has arrived via the Internet.

Hundreds of books are available to explain how the Internet works and how you can benefit from it. Avoiding technical jargon, I will simply tell you how I use it. E-mail fascinates me most. Mailing messages and receiving responses in seconds astounds me. I can communicate instantly with other quilters, authors, designers, teachers, and sellers of products (not to mention my family in Central America), all for a small monthly fee. My telephone toll calls are practically nonexistent as communicating this way is inexpensive and fast.

How Networking Builds a Business

A magazine that polled women entrepreneurs reported that the average business owner spends 25 percent of her time creating a product, and the remaining 75 percent marketing and promoting it. Patricia Hammond of Hearthstone Designs, would agree.

"My designs may take up to six months to construct the sample, create original templates and written instructions, and actually print and fold the patterns," she says, "but I spend far more time on promotion."

You'll recall meeting Patricia in the last chapter. She credits her success to these simple practices: She always does research before making decisions, listens carefully, and never hesitates to ask for what she wants.

Perhaps the best aspect of this technology is the feature that lets quilters join electronic mailing lists specializing in every topic imaginable. Sticking just to quilting Web sites and mailing lists, you can ask questions to like-minded people around the world and receive answers not only from them but from authors, manufacturers, and retailers who read your questions too.

Rather than read a daily newspaper that contains a lot of information that does not interest me, reading posting from quilters and crafters around the world keeps me up-to-date and well informed about the industry. Many such lists are free to join, but when you post a question or provide an answer, basic information about you and your business can appear in your signature line at the bottom of your message, a free promotional activity if ever there was one! Why settle for "Sincerely, Betsy Webb" when you can sign every message with your name, business name, address, telephone and fax numbers, and even your Web site address. You can literally blow your own horn simply by signing every posting this way.

"Part of my research for any marketing activity begins with networking with pattern reps, shop owners, other pattern designers, and quilters about what they would like to see," she explains. "For example, when I decided to offer trunk shows of my designs, the information I gathered from networking enabled me to offer inexpensive, innovative, and exciting programs to shop owners.

"I used the same process when I began teaching for guilds, retreats, and conferences. I gathered information on quilting seminars and took quilting classes myself. Today, in seeking new teaching work, I e-mail or telephone the program chair or board and kindly ask if I may forward my resume and lecture/workshop packet for consideration. I explain that I am a young, upbeat designer with several very exciting classes to offer. I have never been turned down. Even if I learn a seminar has already contracted its instructors, I ask to be considered for future events."

Many quilting Web sites are listed in Resources, but these are only a fraction of the many that exist (and about one-quarter of those that I use regularly). I have helped others and many have helped me. I decided what type of computerized sewing machine to buy and joined a mailing list to learn how to use it. You may also wish to join a list about your specific sewing machine, another about reproduction fabrics, yet another about teaching, and many that deal with advertising, marketing, and promoting yourself.

Quilt show calendars fill the Internet. You can select an event, fill out an enrollment form, and also pay for your classes, airfare, and hotel all from your home office computer! You can find, buy, bid on, and sell anything on the Internet. You can research, study, order books, ask questions, and answer them. From my own home office, the quilting world is at my fingertips. The Internet can do the same for you as a hobbyist or a part-time pro. It's up to you. There is no limit to the potential it offers you if you eventually decide to quilt for both fun and profit.

A Mini-Course in Crafts-Business Basics

by Barbara Brabec

▼▼▼

THIS SECTION OF THE BOOK will familiarize you with important areas of legal and financial concern and enable you to ask the right questions if and when it is necessary to consult with an attorney, accountant, or other business adviser. Although the tax and legal information included here has been carefully researched by the author and is accurate to the best of her knowledge, it is not the business of either the author or publisher to render professional services in the area of business law, taxes, or accounting. Readers should therefore use their own good judgment in determining when the services of a lawyer or other professional would be appropriate to their needs.

Information presented applies specifically to businesses in the United States. However, because many U.S. and Canadian laws are similar, Canadian readers can certainly use the following information as a start-up business plan and guide to questions they need to ask their own local, provincial, or federal authorities.

Contents

7. Insurance Tips

Homeowner's or Renter's Insurance

Liability Insurance

Insurance on Crafts Merchandise

Auto Insurance

8. Important Regulations Affecting Artists and Craftspeople

Consumer Safety Laws

Labels Required by Law

The Bedding and Upholstered Furniture Law

FTC Rule for Mail-Order Sellers

9. Protecting Your Intellectual Property

Perspective on Patents

What a Trademark Protects

What Copyrights Protect

Copyright Registration Tips

Respecting the Copyrights of Others

Using Commercial Patterns and Designs

10. To Keep Growing, Keep Learning

Motivational Tips

A "Things to Do" Checklist with Related Resources

- Business Start-Up Checklist
- Government Agencies
- Crafts and Home-Business Organizations
- Recommended Craft Business Periodicals
- Other Services and Suppliers
- Recommended Business Books
- Helpful Library Directories

1. Starting Right

In preceding chapters of this book, you learned the techniques of a particular art or craft and realized its potential for profit. You learned what kind of products are likely to sell, how to price them, and how and where you might sell them.

Now that you've seen how much fun a crafts business can be (and how profitable it might be if you were to get serious about selling what you make!) you need to learn about some of the "nitty-gritty stuff" that goes hand in hand with even the smallest business based at home. It's easy to start selling what you make and it's satisfying when you earn enough money to make your hobby self-supporting. Many crafters go this far and no further, which is fine. But even a hobby seller must be concerned about taxes and local, state, and federal laws. And if your goal is to build a part- or full-time business at home, you must pay even greater attention to the topics discussed in this section of the book.

Everyone loves to make money . . . but actually starting a business frightens some people because they don't understand what's involved. It's easy to come up with excuses for why we don't do certain things in life; close inspection of those excuses usually boils down to fear of the unknown. We get the shivers when we step out of our comfort zone and try something we've never done before. The simple solution to this problem lies in having the right information at the right time. As someone once said, "Knowledge is the antidote to fear."

The quickest and surest way to dispel fear is to inform yourself about the topics that frighten you. With knowledge comes a sense of power, and that power enables you to move. Whether your goal is merely to earn extra income from your crafts hobby or launch a genuine home-based business, reading the following information will help you get started on the right legal foot, avoid financial pitfalls, and move forward with confidence.

When you're ready to learn more about art or crafts marketing or the operation of a home-based crafts business, a visit to your library or bookstore will turn up many interesting titles. In addition to the special resources listed by this book's author, you will find my list of recommended business books, organizations, periodicals, and other helpful resources later in this chapter. This information is arranged in a checklist you can use as a plan to get your business up and running.

Before you read my "Mini-Course in Crafts-Business Basics," be assured that I understand where you're coming from because I was once there myself.

For a while I sold my craft work, and this experience led me to write my first book, *Creative Cash*. Now, 20 years later, this crafts-business classic ("my baby") has reached its sixth edition. Few of those who are totally involved in a crafts business today started out with a business in mind. Like me, most began as hobbyists looking for something interesting to do in their spare time, and one thing naturally led to another. I never imagined those many years ago

Social Security Taxes

When your craft business earnings are more than $400 (net), you must file a Self-Employment Tax form (Schedule SE) and pay into your personal Social Security account. This could be quite beneficial for individuals who have some previous work experience but have been out of the workplace for a while. Your re-entry into the business world as a self-employed worker, and the additional contributions to your Social Security account, could result in increased benefits upon retirement.

Because so many senior citizens are starting home-based businesses these days, it should be noted that there is a limit on the amount you can earn before losing Social Security benefits. The good news is that this dollar limit increases every year, and once you are past the age of 70, you can earn any amount of income and still receive full benefits. For more information, contact your nearest Social Security office.

when I got serious about my crafts hobby that I was putting myself on the road to a full-time career as a crafts writer, publisher, author, and speaker. Because I and thousands of others have progressed from hobbyists to professionals, I won't be at all surprised if someday you, too, have a similar adventure.

2. Taxes and Record Keeping

"Ambition in America is still rewarded . . . with high taxes," the comics quip. Don't you long for the good old days when Uncle Sam lived within his income and without most of yours?

Seriously, taxes are one of the first things you must be concerned about as a new business owner, no matter how small your endeavor. This section offers a brief overview of your tax responsibilities as a sole proprietor.

Is Your Activity a "Hobby" or a "Business"?

Whether you are selling what you make only to get the cost of your supplies back, or actually trying to build a profitable business, you need to understand the legal difference between a profitable hobby and a business, and how each is related to your annual tax return.

The IRS defines a hobby as "an activity engaged in primarily for pleasure, not for profit." Making a profit from a hobby does not automatically place you "in business" in the eyes of the Internal Revenue Service, but the activity will be *presumed* to have been engaged in for profit if it results in a profit in at least three years out of five. Or, to put it another way, a "hobby business" automatically becomes a "real business" in the eyes of the IRS at the point where you can state that you are (1) trying to make a profit, (2) making regular business transactions, and (3) have made a profit three years out of five.

As you know, all income must be reported on your annual tax return. How it's reported, however, has everything to do with the amount of taxes you must pay on this income. If hobby income is less than $400, it must be entered on the 1040 tax form, with taxes payable accordingly. If the amount is greater than this, you must file a Schedule C form with your 1040 tax form. This is to your advantage, however, because taxes are due only on your *net profit*. Because you can deduct expenses up to the amount of your hobby income, there may be little or no tax at all on your hobby income.

Self-Employment Taxes

Whereas a hobby cannot show a loss on a Schedule C form, a business can. Business owners must pay not only state and federal income taxes on their profits, but self-employment taxes as well. (See sidebar, "Social Security Taxes," page 205.) Because self-employed people pay Social Security taxes at twice the level of regular, salaried workers, you should strive to lower your annual gross profit figure on the Schedule C form through every legal means possible. One way to do this is through careful record keeping of all expenses related to the operation of your business. To quote IRS publications, expenses are deductible if they are "ordinary, necessary, and somehow connected with the operation and potential profit of your business." In addition to being able to deduct all expenses related to the making and selling of their products, business owners can also depreciate the cost of tools and equipment, deduct the overhead costs of operating a home-based office or studio (called the Home Office Deduction), and hire their spouse or children.

Given the complexity of our tax laws and the fact that they are changing all the time, a detailed discussion of all the tax deductions currently available to small business owners cannot be included in a book of this nature. Learning, however, is as easy as reading a book such as *Small Time Operator* by Bernard Kamoroff (my favorite tax and accounting guide), visiting the IRS Web site, or consulting your regular tax adviser.

You can also get answers to specific tax questions 24 hours a day by calling the National Association of Enrolled Agents (NAEA). Enrolled agents (EAs) are licensed by the Treasury Department to represent taxpayers before the IRS. Their rates for doing tax returns are often less than what you would pay for an accountant or CPA.

An important concept to remember is that even the smallest business is entitled to deduct expenses related to its business, and the same tax-saving strategies used by "the big guys" can be used by small business owners. Your business may be small now or still in the dreaming stage, but it could be larger next year and surprisingly profitable a few years from now. Therefore it is in your best interest to always prepare for growth, profit, and taxes by learning all you

Keeping Tax Records

Once you're in business, you must keep accurate records of all income and expenses, but the IRS does not require any special kind of bookkeeping system. Its primary concern is that you use a system that clearly and accurately shows true income and expenses. For the sole proprietor, a simple system consisting of a checkbook, a cash receipts journal, a cash disbursements ledger, and a petty cash fund is quite adequate. Post expenses and income regularly to avoid year-end pile-up and panic.

If you plan to keep manual records, check your local office supply store or catalogs for the *Dome* series of record-keeping books, or use the handy ledger sheets and worksheets included in *Small Time Operator*. (This classic tax and accounting guide by CPA Bernard Kamoroff includes details on how to keep good records and prepare financial reports.) If you have a computer, there are a number of accounting software programs available, such as Intuit Quicken, MYOB (Mind Your Own Business) Accounting, and Intuit Quick-

can about the tax laws and deductions applicable to your business. (See also sidebar, "Keeping Tax Records.")

Sales Tax Is Serious Business

If you live in a state that has a sales tax (all but five states do), and sell products directly to consumers, you are required by law to register with your state's Department of Revenue (Sales Tax division) for a resale tax number. The fee for this in most states ranges from $5 to $25, with some states requiring a bond or deposit of up to $150.

Depending on where you live, this tax number may also be called a Retailer's Occupation Tax Registration Number, resale license, or use tax permit. Also, depending on where you live, the place you must call to obtain this number will have different names. In California, for example, you would contact the State Board of Equalization; in Texas, it's called the State Comptroller's Office.

Books, the latter of which is one of the most popular and best bookkeeping systems for small businesses. The great advantage of computerized accounting is that financial statements can be created at the press of a key after accounting entries have been made.

Regardless of which system you use, always get a receipt for everything and file receipts in a monthly envelope. If you don't want to establish a petty cash fund, spindle all of your cash receipts, tally them at month's end, and reimburse your personal outlay of cash with a check written on your business account. On your checkbook stub, document the individual purchases covered by this check.

At year's end, bundle your monthly tax receipt envelopes and file them for future reference, if needed. Because the IRS can audit a return for up to three years after a tax return has been filed, all accounting and tax records should be kept at least this long, but six years is better. Personally, I believe you should keep all your tax returns, journals, and ledgers throughout the life of your business.

Within your state's revenue department, the tax division may have a name such as sales and use tax division or department of taxation and finance. Generally speaking, if you check your telephone book under "Government," and look for whatever listing comes closest to "Revenue," you can find the right office.

If your state has no sales tax, you will still need a reseller's permit or tax exemption certificate to buy supplies and materials at wholesale prices from manufacturers, wholesalers, or distributors. Note that this tax number is only for supplies and materials used to make your products, not for things purchased at the retail level or for general office supplies.

Once registered with the state, you will begin to collect and remit sales and use tax (monthly, quarterly, or annually, as determined by your state) on all *taxable sales*. This does not mean *all* of your gross income. Different states tax different things. Some states put a sales tax on certain services, but generally you will never have to pay sales tax on income from articles sold to magazines, on teaching or consulting fees, or subscription income (if you happen to publish a newsletter). In addition, sales taxes are not applicable to:

- **Items sold on consignment through a charitable organization, shop, or other retail outlet, including craft malls and rent-a-space shops (because the party who sells directly to the consumer is the one who must collect and pay sales tax).**

- **Products you wholesale to others who will be reselling them to consumers. (Be sure to get their tax-exemption ID number for your own files, however, in case you are ever questioned as to why you did not collect taxes on those sales.)**

As you sell throughout the year, your record-keeping system must be set up so you can tell which income is taxable and which is tax-exempt for reporting on your sales tax return.

Collecting Sales Tax at Craft Shows

States are getting very aggressive about collecting sales tax, and agents are showing up everywhere these day, especially at the larger craft fairs, festivals, and small business conferences. As I was writing this chapter, a posting on the Internet stated that in New Jersey the sales tax department is routinely contacting show promoters about a month before the show date to get the names and addresses of exhibitors. It is expected that other states will soon be following suit. For this reason, you should always take your resale or tax collection certificate with you to shows.

Although you must always collect sales tax at a show when you sell in a state that has a sales tax, how and when the tax is paid to the state can vary. When selling at shows in other states, you may find that the show promoter has obtained an umbrella sales tax certificate, in which case vendors would be asked to give management a check for sales tax at the end of the show for turning over to a tax agent. Or you may have to obtain a temporary sales tax certificate for a show, as advised by the show promoter. Some sellers who regularly do shows in two or three states say it's easier to get a tax ID number from each state and file an annual return instead of doing taxes on a show-by-show basis. (See sidebar, "Including Tax in the Retail Price," page 212.)

Collecting Sales Tax at a Holiday Boutique

If you're involved in a holiday boutique where several sellers are offering goods to the public, each individual seller will be responsible for collecting and remitting his or her own sales tax. (This means someone has to keep very good records during the sale so each seller receives a record of the sale and the amount of tax on that sale.) A reader who regularly has home boutiques told me that in her community she must also post a sign at her "cash station" stating that sales tax is being collected on all sales, just as craft fair sellers must do in some states. Again, it's important that you get complete details from your own state about its sales tax policies.

Collecting Tax on Internet Sales

Anything you sell that is taxable in your state is also taxable on the Internet. This is simply another method of selling, like craft fairs or mail-order sales. You don't have to break out Internet sales separately; simply include them in your total taxable sales.

3. The Legal Forms of Business

Every business must take one of four legal forms:

Sole Proprietorship
Partnership
LLC (Limited Liability Company)
Corporation

Including Tax in the Retail Price

Is it okay to incorporate the amount of sales tax into the retail price of items being sold directly to consumers? I don't know for sure because each state's sales tax law is different.

Crafters like to use round-figure prices at fairs because this encourages cash sales and eliminates the need for taking coins to make change. Some crafters tell their customers that sales tax has been included in their rounded-off prices, but you should not do this until you check with your state. In some states, this is illegal; in others, you may find that you are required to inform your customers, by means of a sign, that sales tax has been included in your price. Your may also have to print this information on customer receipts as well.

If you make such a statement and collect taxes on cash sales, be sure to report those cash sales as taxable income and remit the tax money to the state accordingly. Failure

As a hobby seller, you automatically become a sole proprietor when you start selling what you make. Although most professional crafters remain sole proprietors throughout the life of their business, some do form craft partnerships or corporations when their business begins to generate serious money, or if it happens to involve other members of their family. You don't need a lawyer to start a sole proprietorship, but it would be folly to enter into a partnership, corporation, or LLC without legal guidance. Here is a brief look at the main advantages and disadvantages of each type of legal business structure.

Sole Proprietorship

No legal formalities are involved in starting or ending a sole proprietorship. You're your own boss here, and the business starts when you say it does and ends automatically when you stop running it. As discussed earlier, income is reported annually on a Schedule C form

to do this would be a violation of the law, and it's easy to get caught these days when sales tax agents are showing up at craft fairs across the country.

Even if rounding off the price and including the tax within that figure turns out to be legal in your state, it will definitely complicate your bookkeeping. For example, if you normally sell an item for $5 or some other round figure, you must have a firm retail price on which to calculate sales tax to begin with. Adding tax to a round figure makes it uneven. Then you must either raise or lower the price, and if you lower it, what you're really doing is paying the sales tax for your customer out of your profits. This is no way to do business.

I suggest that you set your retail prices based on the pricing formulas given in this book, calculate the sales tax accordingly, and give your customers change if they pay in cash. You will be perceived as a professional when you operate this way, whereas crafters who insist always on "cash only" sales are sending signals to buyers that they don't intend to report this income to tax authorities.

and taxed at the personal level. The sole proprietor is fully liable for all business debts and actions. In the event of a lawsuit, personal assets are not protected.

Partnership

There are two kinds of partnerships: General and Limited.

A *general partnership* is easy to start, with no federal requirements involved. Income is taxed at the personal level and the partnership ends as soon as either partner withdraws from the business. Liability is unlimited. The most financially dangerous thing about a partnership is that the debts incurred by one partner must be assumed by all other partners. Before signing a partnership agreement, make sure the tax obligations of your partner are current.

In a *limited partnership,* the business is run by general partners and financed by silent (limited) partners who have no liability beyond an investment of money in the business. This kind of partnership is more complicated to establish, has special tax withholding regulations, and requires the filing of a legal contract with the state.

LLC (Limited Liability Company)

This legal form of business reportedly combines the best attributes of other small business forms while offering a better tax advantage than a limited partnership. It also affords personal liability protection similar to that of a corporation. To date, few craft businesses appear to be using this business form.

Corporation

A corporation is the most complicated and expensive legal form of business and not recommended for any business whose earnings are less than $25,000 a year. If and when your business reaches this point, you should study some books on this topic to fully understand the pros and cons of a corporation. Also consult an accountant or attorney for guidance on the type of corporation you should select—a "C" (general corporation) or an "S" (subchapter S corporation). One book that offers good perspective on this topic is *INC Yourself—How to Profit by Setting Up Your Own Corporation.*

The main disadvantage of incorporation for the small business owner is that profits are taxed twice: first as corporate income and again when they are distributed to the owner-shareholders as dividends. For this reason, many small businesses elect to incorporate as subchapter S corporations, which allows profits to be taxed at owners' regular individual rates. (See sidebar, "The Limited Legal Protection of a Corporation," below.)

The Limited Legal Protection of a Corporation

Business novices often think that by incorporating their business they can protect their personal assets in the event of a lawsuit. This is true if you have employees who do something wrong and cause your business to be sued. As the business owner, however, if you personally do something wrong and are sued as a result, you might in some cases be held legally responsible, and the "corporation door" will offer no legal protection for your personal assets.

Or, as CPA Bernard Kamoroff explains in *Small Time Operator,* "A corporation will not shield you from personal liability that you normally should be responsible for, such as not having car insurance or acting with gross negligence. If you plan to incorporate solely or primarily with the intention of limiting your legal liability, I suggest you find out first exactly how limited the liability really is for your particular venture. Hire a knowledgeable lawyer to give you a written opinion." (See section 7,"Insurance Tips.")

4. Local and State Laws and Regulations

This section will acquaint you with laws and regulations that affect the average art or crafts business based at home. If you've unknowingly broken one of these laws, don't panic. It may not be as bad as you think. It is often possible to get back on the straight and narrow merely by filling out a required form or by paying a small fee of some kind. What's important is that you take steps now to comply with the laws that pertain to your particular business. Often, the fear of being caught when you're breaking a law is often much worse than doing whatever needs to be done to set the matter straight. In the end, it's usually what you don't know that is most likely to cause legal or financial problems, so never hesitate to ask questions about things you don't understand.

Even when you think you know the answers, it can pay to "act dumb." It is said that Napoleon used to attend meetings and pretend to know nothing about a topic, asking many probing questions. By feigning ignorance, he was able to draw valuable information and insight out of everyone around him. This strategy is often used by today's small business owners, too.

Business Name Registration

If you're a sole proprietor doing business under any name other than your own full name, you are required by law to register it on both the local and state level. In this case, you are said to be using an "assumed," "fictitious," or "trade" name. What registration does is enable authorities to connect an assumed name to an individual who can be held responsible for the actions of a business. If you're doing business under your own name, such as Kay Jones, you don't have to register your business name on either the local or state level. If your name is part of a longer name, however (for example, Kay Jones Designs), you should check to see if your county or state requires registration.

Local Registration

To register your name, contact your city or county clerk, who will explain what you need to do to officially register your business on the local level. At the same time, ask if you need any special municipal or county licenses or permits to operate within the law. (See next section, "Licenses and Permits.") This office can also tell you how and where to write to register your name at the state level. If you've been operating under an assumed name for a while and are worried because you didn't register the name earlier, just register it now, as if the business were new.

Registration involves filling out a simple form and paying a small fee, usually around $10 to $25. At the time you register, you will get details about a classified ad you must run in a general-circulation newspaper in your county. This will notify the public at large that you are now operating a business under an assumed name. (If you don't want your neighbors to know what you're doing, simply run the ad in a newspaper somewhere else in the county.) After publication of this ad, you will receive a Fictitious Name Statement that you must send to the county clerk, who in turn will file it with your registration form to make your business completely legitimate. This name statement or certificate may also be referred to as your DBA ("doing business as") form. In some areas, you cannot open a business checking account if you don't have this form to show your bank.

State Registration

Once you've registered locally, contact your secretary of state to register your business name with the state. This will prevent its use by a corporate entity. At the same time, find out if you must

▼▼▼

Picking a Good Business Name

If you haven't done it already, think up a great name for your new business. You want something that will be memorable—catchy, but not too cute. Many crafters select a simple name that is attached to their first name, such as "Mary's Quilts" or "Tom's Woodcrafts." This is fine for a hobby business, but if your goal is to build a full-time business at home, you may wish to choose a more professional-sounding name that omits your personal name. If a name sounds like a hobby business, you may have difficulty getting wholesale suppliers to take you seriously. A more professional name may also enable you to get higher prices for your products. For example, the above names might be changed to "Quilted Treasures" or "Wooden Wonders."

Don't print business cards or stationery until you find out if someone else is already using the name you've chosen. To find out if the name has already been registered, you

▲▲▲

obtain any kind of state license. Generally, home-based craft businesses will not need a license from the state, but there are always exceptions. An artist who built an open-to-the-public art studio on his property reported that the fine in his state for operating this kind of business without a license was $50 a day. In short, it always pays to ask questions to make sure you're operating legally and safely.

Federal Registration

The only way to protect a name on the federal level is with a trademark, discussed in section 9.

Licenses and Permits

A "license" is a certificate granted by a municipal or county agency that gives you permission to engage in a business occupation. A "permit" is similar, except that it is granted by local authorities. Until recently, few craft businesses had to have a license or permit

▼▼▼

can perform a trademark search through a search company or hire an attorney who specializes in trademak law to conduct the search for you. And if you are planning to eventually set up a Web site, you might want to do a search to see if that domain name is still available on the Internet. Go to www.networksolutions.com to do this search. Business names have to be registered on the Internet, too, and they can be "parked" for a fee until you're ready to design your Web site.

It's great if your business name and Web site name can be the same, but this is not always possible. A crafter told me recently she had to come up with 25 names before she found a domain name that hadn't already been taken. (Web entrepreneurs are grabbing every good name they can find. Imagine my surprise when I did a search and found that two different individuals had set up Web sites using the titles of my two best-known books, *Creative Cash* and *Homemade Money*.)

▲▲

of any kind, but a growing number of communities now have new laws on their books that require home-based business owners to obtain a "home occupation permit." Annual fees for such permits may range from $15 to $200 a year. For details about the law in your particular community or county, call your city or country clerk (depending on whether you live within or outside city limits).

Use of Personal Phone for Business

Although every business writer stresses the importance of having a business telephone number, craftspeople generally ignore this advice and do business on their home telephone. Although it's okay to use a home phone to make outgoing business calls, you cannot advertise a home telephone number as your business phone number without being in violation of local telephone regulations. That means you cannot legally put your home telephone number on a business card or business stationery or advertise it on your Web site.

That said, let me also state that most craftspeople totally ignore this law and do it anyway. (I don't know what the penalty for breaking this law is in your state; you'll have to call your telephone company for that information and decide if this is something you want to do.) Some phone companies might give you a slap on the wrist and tell you to stop, while others might start charging you business line telephone rates if they discover you are advertising your personal phone number.

The primary reason to have a separate phone line for your business is that it enables you to freely advertise your telephone number to solicit new business and invite credit card sales, custom order inquiries, and the like. Further, you can deduct 100 percent of the costs of a business telephone line on your Schedule C tax form, while deductions for the business use of a home phone are severely limited. (Discuss this with your accountant.)

If you plan to connect to the Internet or install a fax machine, you will definitely need a second line to handle the load, but most crafters simply add an additional personal line instead of a business line. Once on the Internet, you may have even less need for a business phone than before because you can simply invite contact from buyers by advertising your e-mail address. (Always include your e-mail and Internet addresses on your business cards and stationery.)

If your primary selling methods are going to be consignment shops, craft fairs, or craft malls, a business phone number would be necessary only if you are inviting orders by phone. If you present a holiday boutique or open house once or twice a year, there should be no problem with putting your home phone number on promotional fliers because you are, in fact, inviting people to your home and not your business (similar to running a classified ad for a garage sale).

If and when you decide a separate line for your business is necessary, you may find it is not as costly as you think. Telephone companies today are very aware of the number of people who are working at home, and they have come up with a variety of affordable packages and second-line options, any one of which might be perfect for your craft business needs. Give your telephone company a call and see what's available.

Zoning Regulations

Before you start any kind of home-based business, check your home's zoning regulations. You can find a copy at your library or at city hall. Find out what zone you're in and then read the information under "Home Occupations." Be sure to read the fine print and note the penalty for violating a zoning ordinance. In most cases, someone who is caught violating zoning laws will be asked to cease and desist and a penalty is incurred only if this order is ignored. In other cases, however, willful violation could incur a hefty fine.

Zoning laws differ from one community to another, with some of them being terribly outdated (actually written back in horse-and-buggy days). In some communities, zoning officials simply "look the other way" where zoning violations are concerned because it's easier to do this than change the law. In other places, however, zoning regulations have recently been revised in light of the growing number of individuals working at home, and these changes have not always been to the benefit of home-based workers or self-employed individuals. Often there are restrictions as to (1) the amount of space in one's home a business may occupy (impossible to enforce, in my opinion), (2) the number of people (customers, students) who can come to your home each day, (3) the use of non-family employees, and so on. If you find you cannot advertise your home as a place of business, this problem can be easily solved by renting a P.O. box or using a commercial mailbox service as your business address.

Although I'm not suggesting that you violate your zoning law, I will tell you that many individuals who have found zoning to be a problem do ignore this law, particularly when they have a quiet business that is unlikely to create problems in their community.

Zoning officials don't go around checking for people who are violating the law; rather, they tend to act on complaints they have received about a certain activity that is creating problems for others. Thus, the best way to avoid zoning problems is to keep a low profile by not broadcasting your home-based business to neighbors. More important, never annoy them with activities that emit fumes or odors, create parking problems, or make noise of any kind.

Although neighbors may grudgingly put up with a noisy hobby activity (such as sawing in the garage), they are not likely to tolerate the same noise or disturbance if they know it's related to a home-based business. Likewise, they won't mind if you have a garage sale every year, but if people are constantly coming to your home to buy from your home shop, open house, home parties, or holiday boutiques every year, you could be asking for trouble if the zoning laws don't favor this kind of activity.

5. General Business and Financial Information

This section offers introductory guidelines on essential business basics for beginners. Once your business is up and running, however, you need to read other craft-business books to get detailed information on the following topics and many others related to the successful growth and development of a home-based art or crafts business.

Making a Simple Business Plan

As baseball star Yogi Berra once said, "If you don't know where you are going, you might not get there." That's why you need a plan.

Like a road map, a business plan helps you get from here to there. It doesn't have to be fancy, but it does have to be in written form. A good business plan will save you time and money while helping you stay focused and on track to meet your goals. The kind of business plan a craftsperson makes will naturally be less complicated than the business plan of a major manufacturing company, but the elements are basically the same and should include:

- *History*—how and why you started your business
- *Business description*—what you do, what products you make, why they are special
- *Management information*—your business background or experience and the legal form your business will take
- *Manufacturing and production*—how and where products will be produced and who will make them; how and where supplies and materials will be obtained, and their estimated costs; labor costs (yours or other helpers); and overhead costs involved in the making of products
- *Financial plan*—estimated sales and expense figures for one year
- *Market research findings*—a description of your market (fairs, shops, mail order, Internet, and so on), your customers, and your competition
- *Marketing plan*—how you are going to sell your products and the anticipated cost of your marketing (commissions, advertising, craft fair displays, and so on)

If this all seems a bit much for a small crafts business, start managing your time by using a daily calendar/planner and start a notebook you can fill with your creative and marketing ideas, plans, and business goals. In it, write a simple mission statement that answers the following questions:

- What is my primary mission or goal in starting a business?
- What is my financial goal for this year?
- What am I going to do to get the sales I need this year to meet my financial goal?

The most important thing is that you start putting your dreams, goals, and business plans on paper so you can review them regularly.

It's always easier to see where you're going if you know where you've been.

When You Need an Attorney

Many business beginners think they have to hire a lawyer the minute they start a business, but that would be a terrible waste of money if you're just starting a simple art or crafts business at home, operating as a sole proprietor. Sure, a lawyer will be delighted to hold your hand and give you the same advice I'm giving you here (while charging you $150 an hour or more for his or her time). With this book in hand, you can easily take care of all the "legal details" of a small business start-up. The day may come, however, when you do need legal counsel, such as when you:

Form a Partnership or Corporation

As stated earlier, an attorney's guidance is necessary in the formation of a partnership. Although many people have incorporated without a lawyer using a good how-to book on the topic, I wouldn't recommend doing this because there are so many details involved, not to mention different types of corporate entities.

Defend an Infringement of a Copyright or Trademark

You don't need an attorney to get a simple copyright, but if someone infringes on one of your copyrights, you will probably need legal help to stop the infringer from profiting from your creativity. You can file your own trademark application (if you are exceedingly careful about following instructions), but it would be difficult to protect your trademark without legal help if someone tries to steal it. In both cases, you would need an attorney who specializes in copyright, patent, and trademark law. (If you ever need a good attorney who understands the plight of artists and crafters, contact me by e-mail at barbara@crafter.com and I'll refer you to

Get a Safety Deposit Box

The longer you are in business, the more important it will be to safeguard your most valuable business records. When you work at home, there is always the possibility of fire or damage from some natural disaster, be it a tornado, earthquake, hurricane, or flood. You will worry less if you keep your most valuable business papers, records, computer disks, and so forth off-premises, along with other items that would be difficult or impossible to replace. Some particulars I have always kept in my business safety deposit box include master software disks and computer back-up tapes; original copies of my designs and patterns, business contracts, copyrights, insurance policies, and a photographic record of all items insured on our homeowner's policy. Remember: Insurance is worthless if you cannot prove what you owned in the first place.

the attorney who has been helpful to me in protecting my common-law trademark to *Homemade Money*, my home-business classic. The 6th edition of this book includes the details of my trademark infringement story.)

Negotiate a Contract

Many craft hobbyists of my acquaintance have gone on to write books and sell their original designs to manufacturers, suddenly finding themselves with a contract in hand that contains a lot of confusing legal jargon. When hiring an attorney to check any kind of contract, make sure he or she has experience in the particular field involved. For example, a lawyer specializing in real estate isn't going to know a thing about the inner workings of a book publishing company and how the omission or inclusion of a particular clause or phrase might impact the author's royalties or make it difficult to get publishing rights back when the book goes out of print. Although I have no experience in the licensing industry, I presume the same thing holds true here. What I do know for sure is that the problem with most contracts is not so much what's *in* them, as what *isn't.* Thus you need to be sure the attorney you hire for specialized contract work has done this kind of work for other clients.

Hire Independent Contractors

If you ever grow your business to the point where you need to hire workers and are wondering whether you have to hire employees or can use independent contractors instead, I suggest you to seek counsel from an attorney who specializes in labor law. This topic is very complex and beyond the scope of this beginner's guide, but I do want you to know that the IRS has been on a campaign for the past several years to abolish independent contractors altogether. Many small businesses have suffered great financial loss in back taxes and penalties because they followed the advice of an accountant or regular attorney who didn't fully understand the technicalities of this matter.

If and when you do need a lawyer for general business purposes, ask friends for a reference, and check with your bank, too, because it will probably know most of the attorneys with private practices in your area. Note that membership in some small business organizations will also give you access to affordable prepaid legal services. If you ever need serious legal help but have no funds to pay for it, contact the Volunteer Lawyers for the Arts.

Why You Need a Business Checking Account

Many business beginners use their personal checking account to conduct the transactions of their business, *but you must not do this* because the IRS does not allow co-mingling of business and personal income. If you are operating as a business, reporting income on a Schedule C form and taking deductions accordingly, the lack of a separate checking account for your business would surely result in an IRS ruling that your endeavor was a hobby and not a business. That, in turn, would cost you all the deductions previously taken on earlier tax returns and you'd end up with a very large tax bill. Don't you agree that the cost of a separate checking account is a small price to pay to protect all your tax deductions?

You do not necessarily need one of the more expensive business checking accounts; just a *separate account* through which you run all business income and expenditures. Your business name does not have to be on these checks so long as only your name (not your spouse's) is listed as account holder. You can save money on your checking account by first calling several banks and savings and loan institutions and comparing the charges they set for imprinted checks, deposits, checks written, bounced checks, and other services. Before you open your account, be sure to ask if the bank can set you up to take credit cards (merchant account) at some point in the future.

Accepting Credit Cards

Most of us today take credit cards for granted and expect to be able to use them for most everything we buy. It's nice to be able to offer credit card services to your craft fair customers, but it is costly and thus not recommended for beginning craft sellers. If you get into selling at craft fairs on a regular basis, however, at some point you may find you are losing sales because you don't have "merchant status" (the ability to accept credit cards as payment).

Some craftspeople have reported a considerable jump in sales once they started taking credit cards. That's because some people who buy with plastic may buy two or three items instead of one, or are willing to pay a higher price for something if they can charge it. Thus, the higher your prices, the more likely you are to lose sales if you can't accept credit cards. As one jewelry maker told me, "I always seem to get the customers who have run out of cash and left their checkbook at home. But even when they have a check, I feel uncomfortable taking a check for $100 or more."

A list follows of the various routes you can travel to get merchant status. You will have to do considerable research to find out which method is best for you. All will be costly, and you must have sufficient sales, or the expectation of increased sales, to consider taking credit cards in the first place. Understand, too, that taking credit cards in person (called face-to-face transactions where you have the card in front of you) is different from accepting credit cards by phone, by mail, or through a Web site (called non–face-to-face transactions). Each method of selling is treated differently by bankcard providers.

Merchant Status from Your Bank

When you're ready to accept credit cards, start with the bank where you have your business checking account. Where you bank, and where you live, has everything to do with whether you can get merchant status from your bank. Home-business owners in small towns often have less trouble than do those in large cities. One crafter told me Bank of America gave her merchant status with no problem, but some banks simply refuse to deal with anyone who doesn't operate out of a storefront. Most banks now insist that credit card sales be transmitted electronically, but a few still offer manual printers and allow merchants to send in their sales slips by mail. You will be given details about this at the time you apply for merchant status. All banks will require proof that you have a going business and will want to see your financial statements.

Merchant Status Through a Crafts Organization

If you are refused by your bank because your business is home based or just too new, getting bankcard services through a crafts or home-business organization is the next best way to go. Because such organizations have a large membership, they have some negotiating power with the credit card companies and often get special deals for their members. As a member of such an organization, the chances are about 95 percent that you will automatically be accepted into its bankcard program, even if you are a brand new business owner.

One organization I can recommend to beginning sellers is the National Craft Association. Managing Director Barbara Arena tells me that 60 percent of all new NCA members now take the MasterCard/VISA services offered by her organization. "Crafters who are unsure about whether they want to take credit cards over a long period of time have the option of renting equipment," says Barbara. "This enables them to get out of the program with a month's notice. NCA members can operate on a software basis through their personal computer (taking their laptop computer to shows and calling in sales on their cell phone) or use a swipe machine. Under NCA's program, crafters can also accept credit card sales on their Internet site."

For more information from NCA and other organizations offering merchant services, see "Knitting, Craft, and Business Organizations" on page 270.

Merchant Status from Credit Card Companies

If you've been in business for a while, you may find you can get merchant status directly from American Express or Novus Services, Inc., the umbrella company that handles the Discover, Bravo, and Private Issue credit cards. American Express says that in some cases it can grant merchant status immediately upon receipt of some key information given on the phone. As for Novus, many crafters have told me how easy it was to get merchant status from this company. Novus says it needs only your Social Security number and information to check your credit rating. If Novus accepts you, it can also get you set up to take VISA and MasterCard as well if you meet the special acceptance qualifications of these two credit card companies. (Usually, they require you to be in business for at least two years.)

Merchant Status from an Independent
Service Organization Provider (ISO)

ISOs act as agents for banks that authorize credit cards, promoting their services by direct mail, through magazine advertising, telemarketing, and on the Internet. Most of these bankcard providers are operating under a network marketing program (one agent representing one agent representing another, and so on). They are everywhere on the Internet, sending unsolicited e-mail messages to Web site owners. In addition to offering the merchant account service itself, many are also trying to get other Web site owners to promote the same service in exchange for some kind of referral fee. I do not recommend that you get merchant status through an ISO because I've heard too many horror stories about them. If you want to explore this option on the Internet, however, use your browser's search button and type "credit cards + merchant" to get a list of such sellers.

In general, ISOs may offer a low discount rate but will sock it to you with inflated equipment costs, a high application fee, and extra fees for installation, programming, and site inspection. You will also have to sign an unbreakable three- or four-year lease for the electronic equipment.

As you can see, you must really do your homework where bankcard services are concerned. In checking out the services offered by any of the providers noted here, ask plenty of questions. Make up a chart that lets you compare what each one charges for application and service fees, monthly charges, equipment costs, software, discount rates, and transaction fees.

Transaction fees can range from 20 to 80 cents per ticket, with discount rates running anywhere from 1.67 percent to 5 percent. Higher rates are usually attached to non–face-to-face credit card transactions, paper transaction systems, or a low volume of sales. Any rate higher than 5 percent should be a danger signal because you could be dealing with an unscrupulous seller or some kind of illegal third-party processing program.

I'm told that a good credit card processor today may cost around $800, yet some card service providers are charging two or three times that amount in their leasing arrangements. I once got a quote from a major ISO and found it would have cost me $40 a month to lease the terminal—$1,920 over a period of four years—or I could buy it for just $1,000. In checking with my bank, I learned I could get the same equipment and the software to run it for just $350!

In summary, if you're a nervous beginner, the safest way to break into taking credit cards is to work with a bank or organization that offers equipment on a month-by-month rental arrangement. Once you've had some experience in taking credit card payments, you can review your situation and decide whether you want to move into a leasing arrangement or buy equipment outright.

6. Minimizing the Financial Risks of Selling

This book contains a good chapter on how and where to sell your crafts, but I thought it would be helpful for you to have added perspective on the business management end of selling through various outlets, and some things you can do to protect yourself from financial loss and legal hassles.

First you must accept the fact that all businesses occasionally suffer financial losses of one kind or another. That's simply the nature of business. Selling automatically carries a certain degree of risk in that we can never be absolutely sure that we're going to be paid for anything until we actually have payment in hand. Checks may bounce, wholesale buyers may refuse to pay their invoices, and consignment shops can close unexpectedly without returning merchandise to crafters. In the past few years, a surprising number

State Consignment Laws

Technically, consigned goods remain the property of the seller until they are sold. When a shop goes out of business, however, consigned merchandise may be seized by creditors in spite of what your consignment agreement may state. You may have some legal protection here, however, if you live in a state that has a consignment law designed to protect artists and craftspeople in such instances. I believe such laws exist in the states of CA, CO, CT, IL, IA, KY, MA, NH, NM, NY, OR, TX, WA, and WI. Call your secretary of state to confirm this or, if your state isn't listed here, ask whether this law is now on the books. Be sure to get full details about the kind of protection afforded by this law because some states have different definitions for what constitutes "art" or "crafts."

of craft mall owners have stolen out of town in the middle of the night, taking with them all the money due their vendors, and sometimes the vendors' merchandise as well. (This topic is beyond the scope of this book, but if you'd like more information on it, see my *Creative Cash* book and back issues of my *Craftsbiz Chat* newsletter on the Internet at www.crafter.com/brabec).

Now, I don't want you to feel uneasy about selling or suspicious of every buyer who comes your way, because that would take all the fun out of selling. But I *do* want you to know that bad things sometimes happen to good craftspeople who have not done their homework (by reading this book, you are doing *your* homework). If you will follow the cautionary guidelines that follow, you can avoid some common selling pitfalls and minimize your financial risk to the point where it will be negligible.

Selling to Consignment Shops

Never consign more merchandise to one shop than you can afford to lose, and do not send new items to a shop until you see that payments are being made regularly according to your written consignment agreement. It should cover the topics of:

- Insurance (see "Insurance Tips," section 7)
- Pricing (make sure the shop cannot raise or lower your retail price without your permission)
- Sales commission (40 percent is standard; don't work with shop owners who ask for more than this. It makes more sense to wholesale products at 50 percent and get payment in 30 days)
- Payment dates
- Display of merchandise
- Return of unsold merchandise (some shops have a clause stating that if unsold merchandise is not claimed within 30 to 60 days after a notice has been sent, the shop can dispose of it any way it wishes)

Above all, make sure your agreement includes the name and phone number of the shop's owner (not just the manager). If a shop fails and you decide to take legal action, you want to be sure your lawyer can track down the owner. (See sidebar, "State Consignment Laws," page 204.)

Selling to Craft Malls

Shortly after the craft mall concept was introduced to the crafts community in 1988 by Rufus Coomer, entrepreneurs who understood the profit potential of such a business began to open malls all over the country. But there were no guidebooks and everyone was flying by the seat of his or her pants, making up operating rules along the way. Many mall owners, inexperienced in retailing, have since gone out of business, often leaving crafters holding the bag. The risks of selling through such well-known chain stores as Coomers or American Craft Malls are minimal, and many independently owned malls have also established excellent reputations in the industry. What you need to be especially concerned about here are new malls opened by individuals who have no track record in this industry.

I'm not telling you *not* to set up a booth in a new mall in your area—it might prove to be a terrific outlet for you—but I am cautioning you to keep a sharp eye on the mall and how it's being operated. Warning signs of a mall in trouble include:

- less than 75 percent occupancy
- little or no ongoing advertising
- not many shoppers
- crafters pulling out (usually a sign of too few sales)
- poor accounting of sales
- late payments

If a mall is in trouble, it stands to reason that the logical time for it to close is right after the biggest selling season of the year, namely Christmas. Interestingly, this is when most of the shady mall owners have stolen out of town with crafters' Christmas sales in their pockets. As stated in my *Creative Cash* book:

> If it's nearing Christmastime, and you're getting uncomfortable vibes about the financial condition of a mall you're in, it might be smart to remove the bulk of your merchandise— especially expensive items—just before it closes for the holidays. You can always restock after the first of the year if everything looks rosy.

Avoiding Bad Checks

At a crafts fair or other event where you're selling directly to the public, if the buyer doesn't have cash and you don't accept credit cards, your only option is to accept a check. Few crafters have bad check problems for sales held in the home (holiday boutique, open house, party plan, and such), but bad checks at craft fairs are always possible. Here are several things you can do to avoid accepting a bad check:

- Always ask to see a driver's license and look carefully at the picture on it. Write the license number on the check.

- If the sale is a for a large amount, you can ask to see a credit card for added identification, but writing down the number will do no good because you cannot legally cover a bad check with a customer's credit card. (The customer has a legal right to refuse to let you copy the number as well.)

- Look closely at the check itself. Is there a name and address printed on it? If not, ask the customer to write in this information by hand, along with his or her phone number.

- Look at the sides of the check. If at least one side is not perforated, it could be a phony check.

- Look at the check number in the upper right-hand corner. Most banks who issue personalized checks begin the numbering system with 101 when a customer reorders new checks. The Small Business Administration says to be more cautious with low sequence numbers because there seems to be a higher number of these checks that are returned.

- Check the routing number in the lower left-hand corner and note the ink. If it looks shiny, wet your finger and see if the ink rubs off. That's a sure sign of a phony check because good checks are printed with magnetic ink that does not reflect light.

Collecting on a Bad Check

No matter how careful you are, sooner or later, you will get stuck with a bad check. It may bounce for three reasons:

> nonsufficient funds (NSF)
> account closed
> no account (evidence of fraud)

I've accepted tens of thousands of checks from mail-order buyers through the years and have rarely had a bad check I couldn't collect with a simple phone call asking the party to honor his or her obligation to me. People often move and close out accounts before all checks have cleared, or they add or subtract wrong, causing their account to be overdrawn. Typically, they are embarrassed to have caused a problem like this.

When the problem is more difficult than this, your bank can help. Check to learn its policy regarding bounced checks. Some automatically put checks through a second time. If a check bounces at this point, you may ask the bank to collect the check for you. The check needs to be substantial, however, because the bank fee may be $15 or more if they are successful in collecting the money.

If you have accepted a check for a substantial amount of money and believe there is evidence of fraud, you may wish to do one of the following:

- **Notify your district attorney's office**
- **Contact your sheriff or police department (because it is a crime to write a bad check)**
- **Try to collect through small claims court**

For more detailed information on all of these topics, see *The Crafts Business Answer Book*.

7. Insurance Tips

As soon as you start even the smallest business at home, you need to give special attention to insurance. This section offers an introductory overview of insurance concerns of primary interest to crafts-business owners.

Homeowner's or Renter's Insurance

Anything in the home being used to generate income is considered to be business-related and thus exempt from coverage on a personal policy. Thus your homeowner's or renter's insurance policy will not cover business equipment, office furniture, supplies, or inventory of finished goods unless you obtain a special rider. Such riders, called a "Business Pursuits Endorsement" by some companies, are inexpensive and offer considerable protection. Your insurance agent will be happy to give you details.

As your business grows and you have an ever-larger inventory of supplies, materials, tools, and finished merchandise, you may find it necessary to buy a special in-home business policy that offers broader protection. Such policies may be purchased directly from insurance companies or through craft and home-business organizations that offer special insurance programs to their members.

Liability Insurance

There are two kinds of liability insurance. *Product* liability insurance protects you against lawsuits by consumers who have been injured while using one of your products. *Personal* liability insurance protects you against claims made by individuals who have suffered bodily injury while on your premises (either your home or the place where you are doing business, such as in your booth at a crafts fair).

Your homeowner's or renter's insurance policy will include some personal liability protection, but if someone were to suffer bodily injury while on your premises for *business* reasons, that coverage might not apply. Your need for personal liability insurance will be greater if you plan to regularly present home parties, holiday boutiques, or open house sales in your home where many people might be coming and going throughout the year. If you sell at craft fairs, you would also be liable for damages if someone were to fall and be injured in your booth or if something in your booth falls and injures another person. For this reason, some craft fair promoters now require all vendors to have personal liability insurance.

As for product liability insurance, whether you need it depends largely on the type of products you make for sale, how careful you are to make sure those products are safe, and how and where you sell them. Examples of some crafts that have caused injury to consumers and resulted in court claims in the past are stuffed toys with wire or pins that children have swallowed; items made of yarn or fiber that burned rapidly; handmade furniture that collapsed when someone put an ordinary amount of weight on them; jewelry with sharp points or other features that cut the wearer, and so on. Clearly, the best way to avoid injury to consumers is to make certain your products have no health hazards and are safe to use. (See discussion of consumer safety laws in section 8.)

Few artists and craftspeople who sell on a part-time basis feel they can afford product liability insurance, but many full-time craft professionals, particularly those who sell their work wholesale, find it a necessary expense. In fact, many wholesale buyers refuse to buy from suppliers that do not carry product liability insurance.

I believe the least expensive way to obtain both personal and product liability insurance is with one of the comprehensive in-home or craft-business policies offered by a craft- or home-business organization. Such policies generally offer a million dollars of both personal and product liability coverage. (See "Things to Do" Checklist on page 265 and Resources for some organizations you can contact for more information. Also check with your insurance agent about the benefits of an umbrella policy for extra liability insurance.)

Insurance on Crafts Merchandise

As a seller of art or crafts merchandise, you are responsible for insuring your own products against loss. If you plan to sell at craft fairs, in craft malls, rent-a-space shops, or consignment shops, you may want to buy an insurance policy that protects your merchandise both at home or away. Note that while craft shops and malls generally have fire insurance covering the building and its fixtures, this coverage cannot be extended to merchandise offered for sale because it is not the property of the shop owner. (Exception: Shops and malls in shopping centers are mandated by law to buy fire insurance on their contents whether they own the merchandise or not.)

This kind of insurance is usually part of the home- or crafts-business insurance policies mentioned earlier.

Auto Insurance

Be sure to talk to the agent who handles your car insurance and explain that you may occasionally use your car for business purposes. Normally, a policy issued for a car that's used only for pleasure or driving to and from work may not provide complete coverage for an accident that occurs during business use of the car, particularly if the insured is to blame for the accident. For example, if you were delivering a load of crafts to a shop or on your way to a crafts fair and had an accident, would your business destination and the "commercial merchandise" in your car negate your coverage in any

Insuring Your Art or Crafts Collection

The replacement cost insurance you may have on your personal household possessions does not extend to "fine art," which includes such things as paintings, antiques, pictures, tapestries, statuary, and other articles that cannot be replaced with new articles. If you have a large collection of art, crafts, memorabilia, or collector's items, and its value is more than $1,500, you may wish to have your collection appraised so it can be protected with a separate all-risk endorsement to your homeowner's policy called a "fine arts floater."

way? Where insurance is concerned, the more questions you ask, the better you'll feel about the policies you have.

8. Important Regulations Affecting Artists and Craftspeople

Government agencies have a number of regulations that artists and craftspeople must know about. Generally, they relate to consumer safety, the labeling of certain products, and trade practices. Following are regulations of primary interest to readers of books in Prima's For Fun & Profit series. If you find a law or regulation related to your particular art or craft interest, be sure to request additional information from the government agency named there.

Consumer Safety Laws

All product sellers must pay attention to the Consumer Product Safety Act, which protects the public against unreasonable risks of injury associated with consumer products. The Consumer Product Safety Commission (CPSC) is particularly active in the area of toys and consumer goods designed for children. All sellers of handmade products must be doubly careful about the materials they use for children's products because consumer lawsuits are common where products for children are concerned. To avoid this problem, simply comply with the consumer safety laws applicable to your specific art or craft.

Toy Safety Concerns

To meet CPSC's guidelines for safety, make sure any toys you make for sale are:

- Too large to be swallowed
- Not apt to break easily or leave jagged edges

- Free of sharp edges or points
- Not put together with easily exposed pins, wires, or nails
- Nontoxic, nonflammable, and nonpoisonous

The Use of Paints, Varnishes, and Other Finishes

Since all paint sold for household use must meet the Consumer Product Safety Act's requirement for minimum amounts of lead, these paints are deemed to be safe for use on products made for children, such as toys and furniture. Always check, however, to make sure the label bears a nontoxic notation. Specialty paints must carry a warning on the label about lead count, but "artist's paints" are curiously exempt from CPS's lead-in-paint ban and are not required to bear a warning label of any kind. Thus you should *never* use such paints on products intended for use by children unless the label specifically states they are *nontoxic* (lead-free). Acrylics and other water-based paints, of course, are nontoxic and completely safe for use on toys and other products made for children. If you plan to use a finishing coat, make sure it is nontoxic as well.

Fabric Flammability Concerns

The Flammable Fabrics Act is applicable only to those who sell products made of fabric, particularly products for children. It prohibits the movement in interstate commerce of articles of wearing apparel and fabrics that are so highly flammable as to be dangerous when worn by individuals, and for other purposes. Most fabrics comply with this act, but if you plan to sell children's clothes or toys, you may wish to take an extra step to be doubly sure the fabric you are using is safe. This is particularly important if you plan to wholesale your products. What you should do is ask your fabric supplier for a *guarantee of compliance with the Flammability Act.* This guarantee is generally passed along to the buyer by a statement on the invoice that reads "continuing guaranty under the Flammable Fabrics Act." If you do not find such a statement on your invoice, you should ask the fabric manufacturer, wholesaler, or distributor to furnish you with their "statement of compliance" with the flammability standards. The CPSC can also tell you if a particular manufacturer has filed a continuing guarantee under The Flammable Fabrics Act.

Labels Required by Law

The following information applies only to crafters who use textiles, fabrics, fibers, or yarn products to make wearing apparel, decorative accessories, household furnishings, soft toys, or any product made of wool.

Different governmental agencies require the attachment of certain tags or labels to products sold in the consumer marketplace, whether manufactured in quantity or handmade for limited sale. You don't have to be too concerned about these laws if you sell only at local fairs, church bazaars, and home boutiques. As soon as you get out into the general consumer marketplace, however—doing large craft fairs, selling through consignment shops, craft malls, or wholesaling to shops—it would be wise to comply with all the federal labeling laws. Actually, these laws are quite easy to comply with because the required labels are readily available at inexpensive prices, and you can even make your own if you wish. Here is what the federal government wants you to tell your buyers in a tag or label:

- **What's in a product, and who has made it. The Textile Fiber Products Identification Act (monitored both by the Bureau of Consumer Protection and the Federal Trade Commission) requires that a special label or hangtag be attached to all textile wearing apparel and household furnishings, with the exception of wall hangings. "Textiles" include products made of any fiber, yarn, or fabric, including garments and decorative accessories, quilts, pillows, placemats, stuffed toys, rugs, and so on. The tag or label must** include (1) the name of the manufacturer and (2) the generic names and percentages of all fibers in the product in amounts of 5 percent or more, listed in order of predominance by weight.

■ How to take care of products. Care Labeling Laws are part of the Textile Fiber Products Identification Act, details about which are available from the FTC. If you make wearing apparel or household furnishings of any kind using textiles, suede, or leather, you must attach a permanent label that explains how to take care of the item. This label must indicate whether the item is to be dry-cleaned or washed. If it is washable, you must indicate whether in hot or cold water, whether bleach may or may not be used, and the temperature at which it may be ironed.

■ Details about products made of wool. If a product contains wool, the FTC requires additional identification under a separate law known as the Wool Products Labeling Act of 1939. FTC rules require that the labels of all wool or textile products clearly indicate when imported ingredients are used. Thus, the label for a skirt knitted in the United States from wool yarn imported from England would read, "Made in the USA from imported products" or similar wordage. If the wool yarn was spun in the United States, a product made from that yarn would simply need a tag or label stating it was "Made in the USA" or "Crafted in USA" or some similarly clear terminology.

The Bedding and Upholstered Furniture Law

This is a peculiar state labeling law that affects sellers of items that have a concealed filling. It requires the purchase of a license, and products must have a tag that bears the manufacturer's registry number.

Bedding laws have long been a thorn in the side of crafters because they make no distinction between the large manufacturing company that makes mattresses and pillows, and the individual crafts producer who sells only handmade items. "Concealed filling" items include not just bedding and upholstery, but handmade pillows and quilts. In some states, dolls, teddy bears, and stuffed soft sculpture items are also required to have a tag.

Fortunately, only 29 states now have this law on the books, and even if your state is one of them, the law may be arbitrarily enforced. (One exception is the state of Pennsylvania, which is reportedly sending officials to craft shows to inspect merchandise to see if it is properly labeled.) The only penalty that appears to be connected with a violation of this law in any state is removal of merchandise from store shelves or craft fair exhibits. That being the case, many crafters choose to ignore this law until they are challenged. If you learn you must comply with this law, you will be required to obtain a state license that will cost between $25 and $100, and you will have to order special "bedding stamps" that can be attached to your products. For more information on this complex topic, see *The Crafts Business Answer Book*.

FTC Rule for Mail-Order Sellers

Even the smallest home-based business needs to be familiar with Federal Trade Commission (FTC) rules and regulations. A variety of free booklets are available to business owners on topics related to advertising, mail-order marketing, and product labeling (as discussed earlier). In particular, crafters who sell by mail need to pay attention to the FTC's Thirty-Day Mail-Order Rule, which states that one must ship customer orders within 30 days of receiving payment for the order. This rule is strictly enforced, with severe financial penalties for each violation.

Unless you specifically state in your advertising literature how long delivery will take, customers will expect to receive the product within 30 days after you get their order. If you cannot meet this shipping date, you must notify the customer accordingly, enclosing a postage-paid reply card or envelope, and giving them the option to cancel the order if they wish. Now you know why so many catalog sellers state, "Allow six weeks for delivery." This lets them off the hook in case there are unforeseen delays in getting the order delivered.

9. Protecting Your Intellectual Property

"Intellectual property," says Attorney Stephen Elias in his book, *Patent, Copyright & Trademark,* "is a product of the human intellect that has commercial value."

This section offers a brief overview of how to protect your intellectual property through patents and trademarks, with a longer discussion of copyright law, which is of the greatest concern to individuals who sell what they make. Because it is easy to get patents, trademarks, and copyrights mixed up, let me briefly define them for you:

- A *patent* is a grant issued by the government that gives an inventor the right to exclude all others from making, using, or selling an invention within the United States and its territories and possessions.

- A *trademark* is used by a manufacturer or merchant to identify his or her goods and distinguish them from those manufactured or sold by others.

- A *copyright* protects the rights of creators of intellectual property in five main categories (described in this section).

Perspective on Patents

A patent may be granted to anyone who invents or discovers a new and useful process, machine, manufacture or composition of matter, or any new and useful improvement thereof. Any new, original, and ornamental design for an article of manufacture can also be patented. The problem with patents is that they can cost as much as

$5,000 or more to obtain, and once you've got one, they still require periodic maintenance through the U.S. Patent and Trademark Office. To contact this office, you can use the following Web sites: www.uspto.com or www.lcweb.loc.gov.

Ironically, a patent doesn't even give one the right to sell a product. It merely excludes anyone else from making, using, or selling your invention. Many business novices who have gone to the trouble to patent a product end up wasting a lot of time and money because a patent is useless if it isn't backed with the right manufacturing, distribution, and advertising programs. As inventor Jeremy

A Proper Copyright Notice

Although a copyright notice is not required by law, you are encouraged to put a copyright notice on every original thing you create. Adding the copyright notice does not obligate you to formally register your copyright, but it does serve to warn others that your work is legally protected and makes it difficult for anyone to claim they have "accidentally stolen" your work. (Those who actually do violate a copyright because they don't understand the law are called "innocent infringers" by the Copyright Office.)

A proper copyright notice includes three things:

1. The word *copyright,* its abbreviation *copr.,* or the copyright symbol, ©

2. The year of first publication of the work (when it was first shown or sold to the public)

3. The name of the copyright owner. Example: © 2000 by Barbara Brabec. (When the words *All Rights Reserved* are added to the copyright notation, it means that copyright protection has been extended to include all of the Western Hemisphere.)

The copyright notice should be positioned in a place where it can easily be seen. It can be stamped, cast, engraved, painted, printed, wood-burned, or simply written by hand in permanent ink. In the case of fiber crafts, you can attach an inexpensive label with the copyright notice and your business name and logo (or any other information you wish to put on the label).

Gorman states in *Homemade Money,* "Ninety-seven percent of the U.S. patents issued never earn enough money to pay the patenting fee. They just go on a plaque on the wall or in a desk drawer to impress the grandchildren fifty years later."

What a Trademark Protects

Trademarks were established to prevent one company from trading on the good name and reputation of another. The primary function of a trademark is to indicate origin, but in some cases it also serves as a guarantee of quality.

You cannot adopt any trademark that is so similar to another that it is likely to confuse buyers, nor can you trademark generic or descriptive names in the public domain. If, however, you come up with a particular word, name, symbol, or device to identify and distinguish your products from others, you may protect that mark by trademark provided another company is not already using a similar mark. Brand names, trade names, slogans, and phrases may also qualify for trademark protection.

Many individual crafters have successfully registered their own trademarks using a how-to book on the topic, but some would say never to try this without the help of a trademark attorney. It depends on how much you love detail and how well you can follow directions. Any mistake on the application form could cause it to be rejected, and you would lose the application fee in the process. If this is something you're interested in, and you have designed a mark you want to protect, you should first do a trademark search to see if someone else is already using it. Trademark searches can be done using library directories, an online computer service (check with your library), through private trademark search firms, or directly on the Internet through the Patent and Trademark Office's online search service (see "Things to Do" Checklist and Resources). All of these searches together could still be inconclusive, however, because many companies have a stash of trademarks in reserve waiting for just the right product. As I understand it, these "nonpublished" trademarks are in a special file that only an attorney or trademark search service could find for you.

Like copyrights, trademarks have their own symbol, which looks like this: ®. This symbol can be used only once the trademark has been formally registered through the U.S. Patent and Trademark Office. Business owners often use the superscript initials "TM" with a mark to indicate they've claimed a logo or some other mark, but this offers no legal protection. While this does not guarantee trademark protection, it does give notice to the public that you are claiming this name as your trademark. However, after you've used a mark for some time, you do gain a certain amount of common-law protection for that mark. I have, in fact, gained common-law protection for the name of my *Homemade Money* book and successfully defended it against use by another individual in my field because this title has become so closely associated with my name in the home-business community.

Whether you ever formally register a trademark or not will have much to do with your long-range business plans, how you feel about protecting your creativity, and what it would do to your business if someone stole your mark and registered it in his or her own name. Once you've designed a trademark you feel is worth protecting, get additional information from the Patent and Trademark Office and read a book or two on the topic to decide whether this is something you wish to pursue. (See "Things to Do" Checklist and Resources.)

What Copyrights Protect

As a serious student of the copyright law, I've pored through the hard-to-interpret copyright manual, read dozens of related articles and books, and discussed this subject at length with designers, writers, teachers, editors, and publishers. I must emphasize, however, that I am no expert on this topic, and the following information does not constitute legal advice. It is merely offered as a general guide to a very complex legal topic you may wish to research further on your own at some point. In a book of this nature, addressed to hobbyists and beginning crafts-business owners, a discussion of copyrights must be limited to three basic topics:

- What copyrights do and do not protect
- How to register a copyright and protect your legal rights
- How to avoid infringing on the rights of other copyright holders

One of the first things you should do now is send for the free booklets offered by the Copyright Office (see "Things to Do" Checklist and Resources). Various free circulars explain copyright basics, the forms involved in registering a copyright, and how to submit a copyright application and register a copyright. They also discuss what you cannot copyright. Rather than duplicate all the free information you can get from the Copyright Office with a letter or phone call, I will only briefly touch on these topics and focus instead on addressing some of the particular copyright questions crafters have asked me in the past.

Things You Can Copyright

Some people mistakenly believe that copyright protection extends only to printed works, but that is not true. The purpose of the copyright law is to protect any creator from anyone who would use his creative work for his own profit. Under current copyright law, claims are now registered in seven classes, five of which pertain to crafts:

1. *Serials* (Form SE)—periodicals, newspapers, magazines, bulletins, newsletters, annuals, journals, and proceedings of societies.
2. *Text* (Form TX)—books, directories, and other written works, including the how-to instructions for a crafts project. (You

could copyright a letter to your mother if you wanted to—
or your best display ad copy, or any other written words that
represent income potential.)

3. *Visual Arts* (Form VA)—pictorial, graphic, or sculptural
   works, including fine, graphic, and applied art; photographs,
   charts; technical drawings; diagrams; and models. (Also included in this category are "works of artistic craftsmanship
   insofar as their form but not their mechanical or utilitarian
   aspects are concerned.")

4. *Performing Arts* (Form PA)—musical works and accompany-
   ing words, dramatic works, pantomimes, choreographic
   works, motion pictures, and other audiovisual works.

5. *Sound Recordings* (Form SR)—musical, spoken, or other
   sounds, including any audio- or videotapes you might
   create.

Selling How-To Projects to Magazines

If you want to sell an article, poem, or how-to project to a magazine, you need not
copyright the material first because copyright protection exists from the moment you
create that work. Your primary consideration here is whether you will sell "all rights"
or only "first rights" to the magazine.

The sale of first rights means you are giving a publication permission to print your article, poem, or how-to project once, for a specific sum of money. After publication, you
then have the right to resell that material or profit from it in other ways. Although it is
always desirable to sell only "first rights," some magazines do not offer this choice.

If you sell all rights, you will automatically lose ownership of the copyright to your
material and you can no longer profit from that work. Professional designers often
refuse to work this way because they know they can realize greater profits by publishing their own pattern packets or design leaflets and wholesaling them to shops.

Things You Cannot Copyright

You can't copyright ideas or procedures for doing, making, or building things, but the *expression* of an idea fixed in a tangible medium may be copyrightable—such as a book explaining a new system or technique. Brand names, trade names, slogans, and phrases cannot be copyrighted, either, although they might be entitled to protection under trademark laws.

The design on a craft object can be copyrighted, but only if it can be identified separately from the object itself. Objects themselves (a decorated coffee mug, a box, a tote bag) cannot be copyrighted.

Copyright Registration Tips

First, understand that you do not have to formally copyright anything because copyright protection exists from the moment a work is created, whether you add a copyright notice or not.

So why file at all? The answer is simple: If you don't file the form and pay the fee (currently $30), you'll never be able to take anyone to court for stealing your work. Therefore, in each instance where copyright protection is considered, you need to decide how important your work is to you in terms of dollars and cents, and ask yourself whether you value it enough to pay to protect it. Would you actually be willing to pay court costs to defend your copyright, should someone steal it from you? If you never intend to go to court, there's little use in officially registering a copyright; but because it costs you nothing to add a copyright notice to your work, you are foolish not to do this. (See sidebar, "Protecting Your Copyrights," page 252.)

If you do decide to file a copyright application, contact the Copyright Office and request the appropriate forms. When you file the copyright application form (which is easy to complete), you must include with it two copies of the work. Ordinarily, two actual copies of copyrighted items must be deposited, but certain items are exempt from deposit requirements, including all three-dimensional sculptural works and any works published only as reproduced in or on jewelry, dolls, toys, games, plaques, floor coverings, textile and other fabrics, packaging materials, or any useful article. In these cases, two photographs or drawings of the item are sufficient.

Note that the Copyright Office does not compare deposit copies to determine whether works submitted for registration are similar to any material already copyrighted. It is the sender's responsibility to determine the originality of what's being copyrighted. (See discussion of "original" in the next section, under "Respecting the Copyrights of Others.")

Protecting Your Copyrights

If someone ever copies one of your copyrighted works, and you have registered that work with the Copyright Office, you should defend it as far as you are financially able to do so. If you think you're dealing with an innocent infringer—another crafter, perhaps, who has probably not profited much (if at all) from your work—a strongly worded letter on your business stationery (with a copy to an attorney, if you have one) might do the trick. Simply inform the copyright infringer that you are the legal owner of the work and the only one who has the right to profit from it. Tell the infringer that he or she must immediately cease using your copyrighted work, and ask for a confirmation by return mail.

If you think you have lost some money or incurred other damages, consult with a copyright attorney before contacting the infringer to see how you can best protect your rights and recoup any financial losses you may have suffered. This is particularly important if the infringer appears to be a successful business or corporation. Although you may have no intention of ever going to court on this matter, the copyright infringer won't know that, and one letter from a competent attorney might immediately resolve the matter at very little cost to you.

Mandatory Deposit Requirements

Although you do not have to officially register a copyright claim, it *is* mandatory to deposit two copies of all "published works" for the collections of the Library of Congress within three months after publication. Failure to make the deposit may subject the copyright owner to fines and other monetary liabilities, but it does not affect copyright protection. No special form is required for this mandatory deposit.

Note that the term *published works* pertains not just to the publication of printed matter, but to the public display of any item. Thus you "publish" your originally designed craftwork when you first show it at a craft fair, in a shop, on your Web site, or any other public place.

Respecting the Copyrights of Others

Just as there are several things you must do to protect your "intellectual creations," there are several things you must not do if you wish to avoid legal problems with other copyright holders.

Copyright infringement occurs whenever anyone violates the exclusive rights covered by copyright. If and when a copyright case goes to court, the copyright holder who has been infringed upon must prove that his or her work is the original creation and that the two works are so similar that the alleged infringer must have copied it. This is not always an easy matter, for *original* is a difficult word to define. Even the Copyright Office has trouble here, which is why so many cases that go to court end up setting precedents.

In any copyright case, there will be discussions about "substantial similarity," instances where two people actually have created the same thing simultaneously, loss of profits, or damage to one's business or reputation. If you were found guilty of copyright infringement, at the very least you would probably be ordered to pay to the original creator all profits derived from the sale of the copyrighted work to date. You would also have to agree to refund any orders you might receive for the work in the future. In some copyright cases where the original creator has experienced considerable financial loss, penalties for copyright infringement have been as high as $100,000. As you can see, this is not a matter to take lightly.

This is a complex topic beyond the scope of this book, but any book on copyright law will provide additional information if you should ever need it. What's important here is that you fully understand the importance of being careful to respect the legal rights of others. As a crafts-business owner, you could possibly infringe on someone else's designs when you (1) quote someone in an article, periodical, or book you've written; (2) photocopy copyrighted materials; or (3) share information on the Internet. Following is a brief discussion of these topics.

1. **Be careful when quoting from a published source.** If you're writing an article or book and wish to quote someone's words from any published source (book, magazine, Internet, and so on), you should always obtain written permission first. Granted, minor quotations from published sources are okay when they fall under the Copyright Office's Fair Use Doctrine, but unless you completely understand this doctrine, you should protect yourself by obtaining permission before you quote anyone in one of your own written works. It is not necessarily the quantity of the quote, but the value of the quoted material to the copyright owner.

   In particular, never *ever* use a published poem in one of your written works. To the poet, this is a "whole work," much the same as a book is a whole work to an author. Although the use of one or two lines of a poem, or a paragraph from a book may be considered "fair use," many publishers now require written permission even for this short reproduction of a copyrighted work.

2. **Photocopying can be dangerous.** Teachers often photocopy large sections of a book (sometimes whole books) for distribution to their students, but this is a flagrant violation of the copyright law. Some publishers may grant photocopying of part of a work if it is to be used only once as a teaching aid, but written permission must always be obtained first.

   It is also a violation of the copyright law to photocopy patterns for sale or trade because such use denies the creator the profit from a copy that might have been sold.

3. **Don't share copyrighted information on the Internet.** People everywhere are lifting material from *Reader's Digest* and other copyrighted publications and "sharing" them on the Internet through e-mail messages, bulletin boards, and the like. *This is a very dangerous thing to do.* "But I didn't see a copyright notice," you might say, or "It indicated the author was anonymous." What you must remember is that *everything* gains copyright protection the moment it is created, whether a copyright notice is attached to it or not. Many "anonymous" items on the Internet are actually copyrighted poems and articles put there by someone who not only violated the copyright law but compounded the matter by failing to give credit to the original creator.

   If you were to pick up one of those "anonymous" pieces of information and put it into an article or book of your own, the original copyright owner, upon seeing his or her work in your publication, would have good grounds for a lawsuit. Remember, pleading ignorance of the law is never a good excuse.

   Clearly there is no financial gain to be realized by violating the rights of a copyright holder when it means that any day you might be contacted by a lawyer and threatened with a lawsuit. As stated in my *Crafts Business Answer Book & Resource Guide:*

▼▼▼

Changing Things

Many crafters have mistakenly been led to believe that they can copy the work of others if they simply change this or that so their creation doesn't look exactly like the one they have copied. But many copyright court cases have hinged on someone taking "a substantial part" of someone else's design and claiming it as their own. As explained earlier, if your "original creation" bears even the slightest resemblance to the product you've copied—and you are caught selling it in the commercial marketplace—there could be legal problems.

Crafters often combine the parts of two or three patterns in an attempt to come up with their own original patterns, but often this only compounds the possible copyright problems. Let's imagine you're making a doll. You might take the head from one pattern, the arms and legs from another, and the unique facial features from another. You may think you have developed an original creation (and perhaps an original pattern

▲▲▲

The best way to avoid copyright infringement problems is to follow the "Golden Rule" proposed by a United States Supreme Court justice: "Take not from others to such an extent and in such a manner that you would be resentful if they so took from you."

Using Commercial Patterns and Designs

Beginning crafters who lack design skills commonly make products for sale using commercial patterns, designs in books, or how-to instructions for projects found in magazines. The problem here is that all of these things are published for the general consumer market and offered for *personal use* only. Because they are all protected by copyright, that means only the copyright holder has the right to profit from their use.

That said, let me ease your mind by saying that the sale of products made from copyrighted patterns, designs, and magazine how-to projects is probably not going to cause any problems *as long*

you might sell), but you haven't. Because the original designer of any of the features you've copied might recognize her work in your "original creation" or published pattern, she could come after you for infringing on "a substantial part" of her design. In this case, all you've done is multiply your possibilities for a legal confrontation with three copyright holders.

"But I can't create my own original designs and patterns!" you moan. Many who have said this in the past were mistaken. With time and practice, most crafters are able to develop products that are original in design, and I believe you can do this, too. Meanwhile, check out Dover Publications' *Pictorial Archive* series of books (see the "Things to Do" Checklist and Resources). Here you will find thousands of copyright-free designs and motifs you can use on your craft work or in needlework projects. And don't forget the wealth of design material in museums and old books that have fallen into the public domain. (See sidebar, "What's in the Public Domain?" on page 260.)

as sales are limited, and they yield a profit only to you, the crafter. That means no sales through shops of any kind where a sales commission or profit is received by a third party, and absolutely no wholesaling of such products.

It's not that designers and publishers are concerned about your sale of a few craft or needlework items to friends and local buyers; what they are fighting to protect with the legality of copyrights is their right to sell their own designs or finished products in the commercial marketplace. You may find that some patterns, designs, or projects state "no mass-production." You are not mass-producing if you make a dozen handcrafted items for sale at a craft fair or holiday boutique, but you would definitely be considered a mass-producer if you made dozens, or hundreds, for sale in shops.

Consignment sales fall into a kind of gray area that requires some commonsense judgment on your part. This is neither wholesaling nor selling direct to consumers. One publisher might consider such sales a violation of a copyright while another might not.

Whenever specific guidelines for the use of a pattern, design, or how-to project is not given, the only way to know for sure if you are operating on safe legal grounds is to write to the publisher and get written permission on where you can sell reproductions of the item in question.

Now let's take a closer look at the individual types of patterns, designs, and how-to projects you might consider using once you enter the crafts marketplace.

Craft, Toy, and Garment Patterns

Today, the consumer has access to thousands of sewing patterns plus toy, craft, needlework, and woodworking patterns of every kind and description found in books, magazines, and design or project leaflets. Whether you can use such patterns for commercial use depends largely on who has published the pattern and owns the copyright, and what the copyright holder's policy happens to be for how buyers may use those patterns.

To avoid copyright problems when using patterns of any kind, the first thing you need to do is look for some kind of notice on the pattern packet or publication containing the pattern. In checking some patterns, I found that those sold by *Woman's Day* state specifically that reproductions of the designs may not be sold, bartered, or traded. *Good Housekeeping,* on the other hand, gives permission to use their patterns for "income-producing activities." When in doubt, ask!

Whereas the general rule for selling reproductions made from commercial patterns is "no wholesaling and no sales to shops," items made from the average garment pattern (such as an apron, vest, shirt, or simple dress) purchased in the local fabric store *may* be an exception. My research suggests that selling such items in your local consignment shop or craft mall isn't likely to be much of a problem because the sewing pattern companies aren't on the lookout for copyright violators the way individual craft designers and major corporations are. (And most people who sew end up changing those patterns and using different decorations to such a degree that pattern companies might not recognize those patterns even if they were looking for them.

On the other hand, commercial garment patterns that have been designed by name designers should never be used without permission. In most cases, you would have to obtain a licensing agreement for the commercial use of such patterns.

Be especially careful about selling reproductions of toys and dolls made from commercial patterns or design books. Many are likely to be for popular copyrighted characters being sold in the commercial marketplace. In such cases, the pattern company will have a special licensing arrangement with the toy or doll manufacturer to sell the pattern, and reproductions for sale by individual crafters will be strictly prohibited.

Take a Raggedy Ann doll, for example. The fact that you've purchased a pattern to make such a doll does not give you the right to sell a finished likeness of that doll any more than your purchase of a piece of artwork gives you the right to re-create it for sale in some other form, such as notepaper or calendars. Only the original creator has such rights. You have simply purchased the *physical property* for private use.

How-To Projects in Magazines and Books

Each magazine and book publisher has its own policy about the use of its art, craft, or needlework projects. How those projects may be used depends on who owns the copyright to the published projects. In some instances, craft and needlework designers sell their original designs outright to publishers of books, leaflets, or magazines. Other designers authorize only a one-time use of their projects, which gives them the right to republish or sell their designs to another market or license them to a manufacturer. If guidelines about selling finished products do not appear somewhere in the magazine or on the copyright page of a book, you should always write and get permission to make such items for sale. In your letter, explain how many items you would like to make, and where you plan to sell them, as that could make a big difference in the reply you receive.

In case you missed the special note on the copyright page of this book, you *can* make and sell all of the projects featured in this and any other book in Prima's FOR FUN & PROFIT series.

As a columnist for *Crafts Magazine,* I can also tell you that its readers have the right to use its patterns and projects for money-making purposes, but only to the extent that sales are limited to places where the crafter is the only one who profits from their use. That means selling directly to individuals, with no sales in shops of any kind where a third party would also realize some profit from a sale. Actually, this is a good rule-of-thumb guideline to use if you plan to sell only a few items of any project or pattern published in any magazine, book, or leaflet.

What's in the Public Domain?

For all works created after January 1, 1978, the copyright lasts for the life of the author or creator plus 50 years after his or her death. For works created before 1978, there are different terms, which you can obtain from any book in your library on copyright law.

Once material falls into the public domain, it can never be copyrighted again. As a general rule, anything with a copyright date more than 75 years ago is probably in the public domain, but you can never be sure without doing a thorough search. Some characters in old books—such as Beatrix Potter's *Peter Rabbit*—are now protected under the trademark law as business logos. For more information on this, ask the Copyright Office to send you its circular, "How to Investigate the Copyright Status of a Work."

Early American craft and needlework patterns of all kind are in the public domain because they were created before the copyright law was a reality. Such old patterns may

In summary, products that aren't original in design will sell, but their market is limited, and they will never be able to command the kind of prices that original-design items enjoy. Generally speaking, the more original the product line, the greater one's chances for building a profitable crafts business.

As your business grows, questions about copyrights will arise, and you will have to do a little research to get the answers you need. Your library should have several books on this topic and there is a wealth of information on the Internet. (Just use your search button and type "copyright information.") If you have a technical copyright question, remember that you can always call the Copyright Office and speak to someone who can answer it and send you additional information. Note, however, that regulations prohibit the Copyright Office from giving legal advice or opinions concerning the rights of persons in connection with cases of alleged copyright infringement.

show up in books and magazines that are copyrighted, but the copyright in this case extends only to the book or magazine itself and the way in which a pattern has been presented to readers, along with the way in which the how-to-make instructions have been written. The actual patterns themselves cannot be copyrighted by anyone at this point.

Quilts offer an interesting example. If a contemporary quilt designer takes a traditional quilt pattern and does something unusual with it in terms of material or colors, this new creation would qualify for a copyright, with the protection being given to the quilt as a work of art, not to the traditional pattern itself, which is still in the public domain. Thus you could take that same traditional quilt pattern and do something else with it for publication, but you could not publish the contemporary designer's copyrighted version of that same pattern.

10. To Keep Growing, Keep Learning

Everything we do, every action we take, affects our life in one way or another. Reading a book is a simple act, indeed, but trust me when I say that your reading of this particular book *could ultimately change your life.* I know this to be true because thousands of men and women have written to me over the years to tell me how their lives changed after they read one or another of my books and decided to start a crafts business. My life has changed, too, as a result of reading books by other authors.

Many years ago, the purchase of a book titled *You Can Whittle and Carve* unleashed a flood of creativity in me that has yet to cease. That simple book helped me to discover unknown craft talents, which in turn led me to start my first crafts business at home. That experience prepared me for the message I would find a decade later in the book, *On Writing Well* by William Zinsser. This author changed my life by giving me the courage to try my hand at writing professionally. Dozens of books later, I had learned a lot about the art and craft of writing well and making a living in the process.

Now you know why I believe reading should be given top priority in your life. Generally speaking, the more serious you become about anything you're interested in, the more reading you will need to do. This will take time, but the benefits will be enormous. If a crafts business is your current passion, this book contains all you need to know to get started. To keep growing, read some of the wonderful books recommended in the Resources. (If you don't find the books you need in your local library, ask your librarian to obtain them for you through the inter-library loan program.) Join one or more of the organizations recommended. Subscribe to a few periodicals or magazines, and "grow your business" through networking with others who share your interests.

Motivational Tips

As you start your new business or expand a money-making hobby already begun, consider the following suggestions:

- *Start an "Achievement Log."* Day by day, our small achievements may seem insignificant, but viewed in total after several weeks or months, they give us important perspective. Reread your achievement log periodically in the future, especially on days when you feel down in the dumps. Make entries at least once a week, noting such things as new customers or accounts acquired, publicity you've gotten, a new product you've designed, the brochure or catalog you've just completed, positive feedback received from others, new friendships, and financial gains.

- *Live your dream.* The mind is a curious thing—it can be trained to think success is possible or to think that success is only for other people. Most of our fears never come true, so allowing our minds to dwell on what may or may not happen cripples us, preventing us from moving ahead, from having confidence, and from living out our dreams. Instead of "facing fear," focus on the result you want. This may automatically eliminate the fear.

- *Think positively.* As Murphy has proven time and again, what can go wrong will, and usually at the worst possible moment. It matters little whether the thing that has gone wrong was caused by circumstances beyond our control or by a mistake in judgment. What does matter is how we deal with the problem at hand. A positive attitude and the ability to remain flexible at all times are two of the most important ingredients for success in any endeavor.

- *Don't be afraid to fail.* We often learn more from failure than from success. When you make a mistake, chalk it up to experience and consider it a good lesson well learned. The more you learn, the more self-confident you will become.

- *Temper your "dreams of riches" with thoughts of reality.* Remember that "success" can also mean being in control of your own life, making new friends, or discovering a new world of possibilities.

▼▼▼

Online Help

Today, one of the best ways to network and learn about business is to get on the Internet. The many online resources included in the "Things to Do" Checklist in the next section will give you a jump-start and lead to many exciting discoveries.

For continuing help and advice from Barbara Brabec, be sure to visit her Web site at www.crafter.com/brabec. There you will find her monthly *Craftsbiz Chat* newsletter, reprints of some of her crafts marketing and business columns, recommended books, and links to hundreds of other arts and craft sites on the Web. Reader questions may be e-mailed to barbara@crafter.com for discussion in her newsletter, but questions cannot be answered individually by e-mail.

You can also get Barbara's business advice in her monthly columns in *Crafts Magazine* and *The Crafts Report*.

▲▲▲

Until now you may have lacked the courage to get your craft ideas off the ground, but now that you've seen how other people have accomplished their goals, I hope you feel more confident and adventurous and are ready to capitalize on your creativity. By following the good advice in this book, you can stop dreaming about all the things you want to do and start making plans to do them!

I'm not trying to make home-business owners out of everyone who reads this book, but my goal is definitely to give you a shove in that direction if you're teetering on the edge, wanting something more than just a profitable hobby. It's wonderful to have a satisfying hobby, and even better to have one that pays for itself; but the nicest thing of all is a real home business that lets you fully utilize your creative talents and abilities while also adding to the family income.

"The things I want to know are in books," Abraham Lincoln once said. "My best friend is the person who'll get me a book I ain't read." You now hold in your hands a book that has taught you many things you wanted to know. To make it a *life-changing book,* all you have to do is act on the information you've been given.

I wish you a joyful journey and a potful of profits!

A "Things to Do" Checklist

INSTRUCTIONS: Read through this entire section, noting the different things you need to do to get your crafts business "up and running." Use the checklist as a plan, checking off each task as it is completed and obtaining any recommended resources. Where indicated, note the date action was taken so you have a reminder about any follow-up action that should be taken.

Business Start-Up Checklist

__Call city hall or county clerk

    __to register fictitious business name

    __to see if you need a business license or permit

    __to check on local zoning laws
    (info also available in your library)

    *Follow up:*_____

__Call state capitol

    __secretary of state: to register your business name;
    ask about a license

    __Department of Revenue: to apply for sales tax number

    *Follow up:*_____

__Call your local telephone company about

    __cost of a separate phone line for business

    __cost of an additional personal line for Internet access

    __any special options for home-based businesses

    *Follow up:*_____

__Call your insurance agent(s) to discuss

    __business rider on house insurance
    (or need for separate in-home insurance policy)
    __benefits of an umbrella policy for extra liability insurance
    __using your car for business
    (how this may affect your insurance)

    *Follow up:*_____

__Call several banks or S&Ls in your area to

    __compare cost of a business checking account
    __ get price of a safe-deposit box for valuable business records

    *Follow up:*_____

__Visit office and computer supply stores to check on

    __manual bookkeeping systems, such as the
    Dome Simplified Monthly
    __accounting software
    __standard invoices and other helpful business forms

    *Follow up:*_____

__Call National Association of Enrolled Agents at (800) 424-4339

    __to get a referral to a tax professional in your area
    __to get answers to any tax questions you may have (no charge)

    *Follow up:*_____

__Contact government agencies for information relative to your
business.

    (See "Government Agencies" checklist.)

__Request free brochures from organizations

    (See "Craft- and Home-Business Organizations.")

__Obtain sample issues or subscribe to selected publications

    (See "Recommended Craft Business Periodicals.")

__Obtain other information of possible help to your business

(See "Other Services and Suppliers.")

__Get acquainted with the business information available to you in your library.

(See list of "Recommended Business Books" and "Helpful Library Directories.")

Government Agencies

__Consumer Product Safety Commission (CPSC), Washington, DC 20207. (800) 638-2772. Information Services: (301) 504-0000. Web site: www.cpsc.gov. (Includes a "Talk to Us" e-mail address where you can get answers to specific questions.) If you make toys or other products for children, garments (especially children's wear), or use any kind of paint, varnish, lacquer, or shellac on your products, obtain the following free booklets:

__*The Consumer Product Safety Act of 1972*
__*The Flammable Fabrics Act*

Date Contacted:_____Information Received:_____

*Follow up:*_____

__Copyright Office, Register of Copyrights, Library of Congress, Washington, DC 20559. To hear recorded messages on the Copyright Office's automated message system (general information, registration procedures, copyright search info, and so on), call (202) 707-3000. You can also get the same information online at www.loc.gov/copyright.

To get free copyright forms, a complete list of all publications available, or to speak personally to someone who will answer your special questions, call (202) 797-9100. In particular, ask for:

__Circular R1, *The Nuts and Bolts of Copyright*
__Circular R2 (a list of publications available)

Date Contacted:_____Information Received:_____

*Follow up:*_____

__Department of Labor. If you should ever hire an employee
or independent contractor, contact your local Labor Department, Wage & Hour Division, for guidance on what you must
do to be completely legal. (Check your phone book under
"U.S. Government.")

Date Contacted:_____Information Received:_____

*Follow up:*_____

__Federal Trade Commission (FTC), 6th Street and Pennsylvania
Avenue, NW, Washington, DC 20580. Web site: www.ftc.gov. Request
any of the following booklets relative to your craft or business:

__*Textile Fiber Products Identification Act*

__*Wool Products Labeling Act of 1939*

__*Care Labeling of Textile Wearing Apparel*

__*The Hand Knitting Yarn Industry* (booklet)

__*Truth-in-Advertising Rules*

__*Thirty-Day Mail-Order Rule*

Date Contacted:_____Information Received:_____

Follow up _____

__Internal Revenue Service (IRS). Check the Internet at
www.irs.gov to read the following information online or
call your local IRS office to get the following booklets and
other free tax information:

__*Tax Guide for Small Business—#334*

__*Business Use of Your Home—#587*

__*Tax Information for Direct Sellers*

Date Contacted:_____Information Received:_____

*Follow up*_____

__Patent and Trademark Office (PTO), Washington, DC 20231.
Web site: www.uspto.gov.

For patent and trademark information 24 hours a day, call
(800) 786-9199 (in northern Virginia, call (703) 308-9000) to hear
various messages about patents and trademarks or to order the
following booklets:

__*Basic Facts About Patents*
__*Basic Facts About Trademarks*

To search the PTO's online database of all registered trademarks,
go to www.uspto.gov/tmdb/index.html.

Date Contacted:_____Information Received:_____

*Follow up:*_____

__Social Security Hotline. (800) 772-1213. By calling this number,
you can hear automated messages, order information booklets,
or speak directly to someone who can answer specific questions.

Date Contacted:_____Information Received:_____

*Follow up*_____

__U.S. Small Business Administration (SBA). (800) U-ASK-SBA.
Call this number to hear a variety of prerecorded messages on
starting and financing a business. Weekdays, you can speak personally to an SBA adviser to get answers to specific questions
and request such free business publications as:

__*Starting Your Business* —#CO-0028

__*Resource Directory for Small Business Management*—#CO-0042
  (a list of low-cost publications available from the SBA)

The SBA's mission is to help people get into business and stay
there. One-on-one counseling, training, and workshops are available through 950 small business development centers across the
country. Help is also available from local district offices of the

SBA in the form of free business counseling and training from SCORE volunteers. The SBA office in Washington has a special Women's Business Enterprise section that provides free information on loans, tax deductions, and other financial matters. District offices offer special training programs in management, marketing, and accounting.

A wealth of business information is also available online at www.sba.gov and www.business.gov (the U.S. Business Adviser site). To learn whether there is an SBA office near you, look under U.S. Government in your telephone directory, or call the SBA's toll-free number.

Date Contacted:_____Information Received:_____

*Follow up:*_____

__SCORE (Service Corps of Retired Executives). (800) 634-0245. There are more than 12,400 SCORE members who volunteer their time and expertise to small business owners. Many craft businesses have received valuable in-depth counseling and training simply by calling the organization and asking how to connect with a SCORE volunteer in their area.

In addition, the organization offers e-mail counseling via the Internet at www.score.org. You simply enter the specific expertise required and retrieve a list of e-mail counselors who represent the best match by industry and topic. Questions can then be sent by e-mail to the counselor of your choice for response.

Date Contacted:_____Information Received:_____

*Follow up:*_____

Crafts and Home-Business Organizations

In addition to the regular benefits of membership in an organization related to your art or craft (fellowship, networking, educational conferences or workshops, marketing opportunities, and so on), membership may also bring special business services, such as insurance programs, merchant card services, and discounts on supplies and materials. Each of the following organizations will send you membership information on request.

__The American Association of Home-Based Businesses, P.O. Box 10023, Rockville, MD 20849. (800) 447-9710. Web site: www.aahbb.org. This organization has chapters throughout the country. Members have access to merchant card services, discounted business products and services, prepaid legal services, and more.

Date Contacted:_____Information Received:_____

*Follow up:*_____

__American Crafts Council, 72 Spring Street, New York, NY 10012. (800)-724-0859. Web site: www.craftcouncil.org. Membership in this organization will give you access to a property and casualty insurance policy that will cost between $250 and $500 a year, depending on your city, state, and the value of items being insured in your art or crafts studio. The policy includes insurance for a craftsperson's work in the studio, in transit, or at a show; a million dollars' coverage for bodily injury and property damage in studio or away; and a million dollars' worth of product liability insurance. This policy is from American Phoenix Corporation; staff members will answer your specific questions when you call (800) 274-6364, ext. 337.

Date Contacted:_____Information Received:_____

*Follow up:*_____

__Arts & Crafts Business Solutions, 2804 Bishop Gate Drive, Raleigh, NC 27613. (800) 873-1192. This company, known in the industry as the Arts Group, offers a bankcard service specifically for and tailored to the needs of the arts and crafts marketplace. Several differently priced packages are available, and complete information is available on request.

Date Contacted:_____Information Received:_____

*Follow up:*_____

__Home Business Institute, Inc., P.O. Box 301, White Plains, NY 10605-0301. (888) DIAL-HBI; Fax: (914) 946-6694. Web site: www.hbiweb.com. Membership benefits include insurance programs (medical insurance and in-home business policy that includes some liability insurance); savings on telephone services, office supplies, and merchant account enrollment; and free advertising services.

Date Contacted:_____Information Received:_____

*Follow up:*_____

__National Craft Association (NCA), 1945 E. Ridge Road, Suite 5178, Rochester, NY 14622-2647. (800) 715-9594. Web site: www.craft assoc.com. Members of NCA have access to a comprehensive package of services, including merchant account services; discounts on business services and products; a prepaid legal program; a check-guarantee merchant program; checks by fax, phone, or e-mail; and insurance programs. Of special interest to this book's readers is the "Crafters Business Insurance" policy (through RLI Insurance Co.) that includes coverage for business property; art/craft merchandise or inventory at home, in transit, or at a show; theft away from premises; up to a million dollars in both personal and product liability insurance; loss of business income; and more. Members have the option to select the exact benefits they need. Premiums range from $150 to $300, depending on location, value of average inventory, and the risks associated with one's art or craft.

Date Contacted:_____Information Received:_____

*Follow up:*_____

Recommended Craft Business Periodicals

Membership in an organization generally includes a subscription to a newsletter or magazine that will be helpful to your business. Here are additional craft periodicals you should sample or subscribe to:

__*The Crafts Report—The Business Journal for the Crafts Industry,* Box 1992, Wilmington, DE 19899. (800) 777-7098. On the Internet at www.craftsreport.com. A monthly magazine covering all areas of craft-business management and marketing (includes my column, Barbara Brabec's "BusinessWise" column).

__*Craft Supply Magazine—The Industry Journal for the Professional Crafter,* Krause Publications, Inc., 700 East State Street, Iowa, WI 54990-0001. (800) 258-0929. Web site: www.krause.com. A monthly magazine that includes crafts business and marketing articles and wholesale supply sources.

__*Home Business Report,* 2949 Ash Street, Abbotsford, B.C., V2S 4G5 Canada. (604) 857-1788; Fax: (604) 854-3087. Canada's premier home-business magazine, relative to both general and craft-related businesses.

__*SAC Newsmonthly,* 414 Avenue B, P.O. Box 159, Bogalusa, LA 70429-0159. (800) TAKE-SAC; Fax: (504) 732-3744. A monthly national show guide that also includes business articles for professional crafters.

__*Sunshine Artist* magazine, 2600 Temple Drive, Winter Park, FL 32789. (800) 597-2573; Fax: (407) 539-1499. Web site: www.sun shineartist.com. America's premier show and festival guide.

Each monthly issue contains business and marketing articles of interest to both artists and craftspeople.

Other Services and Suppliers

Contact any of the following companies that offer information or services of interest to you.

__American Express. For merchant account information, call the Merchant Establishment Services Department at (800) 445-AMEX.

Date Contacted:_____Information Received:_____

*Follow up:*_____

__Dover Publications, 31 E 2nd Sreet, Mineola, NY 11501. Your source for thousands of copyright-free designs and motifs you can use in your craftwork or needlecraft projects. Request a free catalog of books in the *Pictorial Archive* series.

Date Contacted:_____Information Received:_____

*Follow up:*_____

__Novus Services, Inc. For merchant account information, call (800) 347-6673.

Date Contacted:_____Information Received:_____

*Follow up:*_____

__Volunteer Lawyers for the Arts (VLA), 1 E 53rd Street, New York, NY 10022. Legal hotline: (212) 319-2910. If you ever need an attorney, and cannot afford one, contact this nonprofit organization, which has chapters all over the country. In addition to providing legal aid for performing and visual artists and craftspeople (individually or in groups), the VLA also provides a range of educational services, including issuing publications concerning taxes, accounting, and insurance.

Date Contacted:_____Information Received:_____

*Follow up:*_____

__Widby Enterprises USA, 4321 Crestfield Road, Knoxville, TN 37921-3104. (888) 522-2458. Web site: www.widbylabel.com. Standard and custom-designed labels that meet federal labeling requirements.

Date Contacted:_____Information Received:_____

*Follow up:*_____

Recommended Business Books

When you have specific business questions not answered in this beginner's guide, check your library for the following books. Any not on library shelves can be obtained through the library's inter-library loan program.

__*Business and Legal Forms for Crafts* by Tad Crawford (Allworth Press)

__*Business Forms and Contracts (in Plain English) for Crafts People* by Leonard D. DuBoff (Interweave Press)

__*Crafting as a Business* by Wendy Rosen (Chilton)

__*The Crafts Business Answer Book & Resource Guide: Answers to Hundreds of Troublesome Questions About Starting, Marketing & Managing a Homebased Business Efficiently, Legally & Profitably* by Barbara Brabec (M. Evans & Co.)

__*Creative Cash: How to Profit from Your Special Artistry, Creativity, Hand Skills, and Related Know-How* by Barbara Brabec (Prima Publishing)

__*422 Tax Deductions for Businesses & Self-Employed Individuals* by Bernard Kamoroff (Bell Springs Publishing)

__*Homemade Money: How to Select, Start, Manage, Market, and Multiply the Profits of a Business at Home* by Barbara Brabec (Betterway Books)

__*How to Register Your Own Trademark with Forms* by Mark Warda, 2nd ed. (Sourcebooks)

__*INC Yourself: How to Profit by Setting Up Your Own Corporation,* by Judith H. McQuown (HarperBusiness)

__*Patent, Copyright & Trademark: A Desk Reference to Intellectual Property Law* by Attorney Stephen Elias (Nolo Press)

__*The Perils of Partners* by Irwin Gray (Smith-Johnson Publisher)

__*Small Time Operator: How to Start Your Own Business, Keep Your Books, Pay Your Taxes & Stay Out of Trouble* by Bernard Kamoroff (Bell Springs Publishing)

__*Trademark: How to Name a Business & Product* by McGrath and Elias (Nolo Press)

Helpful Library Directories

__*Books in Print* and *Guide to Forthcoming Books* (how to find out which books are still in print, and which books will soon be published)

__*Encyclopedia of Associations* (useful in locating an organization dedicated to your art or craft)

__*National Trade and Professional Associations of the U.S.* (more than 7,000 associations listed alphabetically and geographically)

__*The Standard Periodical Directory* (annual guide to U.S. and Canadian periodicals)

__*Thomas Register of American Manufacturers* (helpful when you're looking for raw material suppliers or the owners of brand names and trademarks)

__*Trademark Register of the U.S.* (contains every trademark currently registered with the U.S. Patent & Trademark Office)

Resources

▼▼

Recommended Books

Most of the recommended books in this section can be found in bookstores and libraries, or may be ordered by mail (see "Quilt Book Publishers"). Some books, however, have been published by the author and are available only by mail (see "Self-Published Books.")

Craft Business Books

Crafting for Dollars: Turn Your Hobby into Serious Cash, by Sylvia Landman (Rocklin, CA: Prima Publishing, 1996).

The Crafts Business Answer Book & Resource Guide, by Barbara Brabec (New York: M. Evans, 1998).

Creative Cash, 6th ed., by Barbara Brabec (Rocklin, CA: Prima Publishing, 1998).

Handmade for Profit, by Barbara Brabec (New York: M. Evans, 1996).

Homemade Money, 5th ed., rev., by Barbara Brabec (Cincinnati, OH: Betterway Books, 1997).

Make Your Quilting Pay for Itself, by Sylvia Landman (Cincinnati, OH: Betterway Books, 1997).

The Needlecrafter's Computer Companion, by Judy Heim (San Francisco: No Starch Press, 1995).

Books Featuring QAYG Methods

Heirloom Machine Quilting, by Harriet Hargrave (Concord, CA: C & T Publishing, 1995).

More Lap Quilting with Georgia Bonesteel, by Georgia Bonesteel (Birmingham, AL: Oxmoor House Publishers, 1985).

General Quilting Books

Appliqué 12 Easy Ways, by Ellie Sienkiewicz (Concord, CA: C & T Publishing, 1991).

The Block Book, by Judy Martin (Grinell, IA: Crosley-Griffith Publishing, 1998).

Colourwash Quilts, by Deirdre Amsden (Peoria, IL: That Patchwork Place, 1994).

The Complete Book of Machine Quilting, by Robbie and Tony Fanning (Radner, PA: Chilton Book Co., 1980).

Contemporary Quilting Techniques, by Pat Cairns (Radner, PA: Chilton Book Co., 1980).

Dream Sewing Spaces: Design & Organization, by Lynette Ranney Black (Portland, OR: Palmer/Pletsch Publishing, 1996).

Dye It, Paint It, Quilt It, by Joyce Mori and Cynthia Myerberg (Radner, PA: Chilton Book Co., 1996).

Floral Appliqué, by Nancy A. Pearson (Quilt House Publishing, 1994).

From Fiber to Fabric, by Harriet Hargrave (Concord, CA: C & T Publishing, 1997).

Impressionist Palette: Quilt Color & Design, by Gai Perry (Concord, CA: C & T Publishing, 1999).

Impressionist Quilts: A Color and Design Manual, by Gai Perry (Concord, CA: C & T Publishing, 1995).

Machine Quilting Made Easy, by Maurine Noble (Peoria, IL: That Patchwork Place, 1994).

Machine Quilting with Decorative Threads, by Maurine Noble and Elizabeth Hendricks (Peoria, IL: That Patchwork Place, 1998).

Make a Quilt in One Day, by Eleanor Burns (Little Rock, AR: Leisure Arts, 1989).

Mastering Machine Appliqué, by Harriet Hargrave (Concord, CA: C & T Publishing, 1991).

Memorabilia Quilting, by Jean Wells (Concord, CA: C & T Publishing, 1992).

Patchwork Patterns, by Jinny Beyers (EPM Publications Inc., 1979).

The Perfect Match: The Guide to Precise Machine Piecing, by Donna Lynn Thomas (Peoria, IL: That Patchwork Place, 1993).

The Quilter's Computer Companion, by Judy Heim and Gloria Hanson (Companion Paperback, 1998).

Quilting Patterns, by Joyce Scholtzhuer (McLean, VA: EPM Publications, 1984).

The Quiltmaker's Handbook, by Michael James (Englewood Cliffs, NJ: Prentice-Hall, 1978).

Quilts, Quilts and More Quilts, by Diana McClun and Laura Nownes (Concord, CA: C & T Publishing, 1997).

Scrap Quilts, by Judy Martin (Golden, CO: Leman Publications, 1985).

Scrap Quilts Using Fast Patch , by Anita Hallock (Radner, PA: Chilton Book Co., 1991).

Short-Cuts: A Concise Guide to Rotary Cutting, by Donna Lynn Thomas (Peoria, IL: That Patchwork Place, 1991).

Threadplay, by Libby Lehman (Peoria, IL: That Patchwork Place, 1997).

You Can Be a Super Quilter, by Carla J. Hassell (Radner, PA: Chilton Book Co. Wallace-Homestead Book Co., 1980).

Watercolor Impressions, by Pat Magret and Donna Slusser (Peoria, IL: That Patchwork Place, 1995).

Watercolor Quilts, by Pat Magret and Donna Slusser (Peoria, IL: That Patchwork Place, 1993).

Self-Published Books

(Available only by mail from author/
publisher. Request price and shipping
information.)

The Quilt as You Go Guide, by Nancy
Donahue. (Available from Patchwork
Patterns, P.O. Box 3461, Industry, CA
91744.)

Scraps Can Be Beautiful, by Jan
Halgrimson. (Available from Author
at P.O. Box 353, Edmonds, WA 90820.)

Quilt Book Publishers

Books Unlimited from ASN Publishing
1455 Linda Vista Drive
San Marcos, CA 92069
Orders only: (800) 345-1752
www.asnpub.com

C & T Publishing
1651 Challenge Drive
Concord, CA 94520
(800) 284-1114
www.ctpub.com

Publishers of quilting books, exclusively.

Dover Street Booksellers
8673 Commerce Drive, #13
P.O. Box 1563
Easton, MD 21601

Comprehensive quilting book catalog

That Patchwork Place
20205 144th Avenue NE
Bothell, WA 98041-0118
(800) 426-3126
www.patchwork.com
E-mail: info@patchwork.com

Publisher of quilt titles, exclusively;
see free catalog on the Web site.

Recommended Periodicals

Trade Journals

*Craft & Needlework Age Magazine
& Directory*
P.O. Box 420
Englishtown, NJ 07726

Comprehensive trade journal for all crafts,
including quilting.

Craft Supply Magazine
Krause Publications, Inc.
700 East State Street
Iola, WI 54990-0001
(800) 258-0929
www.krause.com

The industry journal for the professional
crafter.

Craftrends & Sew Business
Primedia Special Interest Publications
2 News Plaza, Box 1790
Peoria, IL 61656

Includes *Quilt Quarterly* publication
in a special section.

Professional Quilter
Morna McEver Golletz, Editor
221412 Rolling Hill Lane
Laytonsville, MD 20882
www.professionalquilter.com

Quarterly journal covering all aspects
of professional quilting, with profiles
of professional quilters.

Quilter's Newsletter
P.O. Box 59021
Boulder, CO 80323
Phone: (303) 278-1010

The Crafts Report
300 Water Street
Wilmington, DE 19899
(800) 777-7098
www.craftsreport.com

Business journal for fine crafts industry.
Includes national craft show listings.

General Crafts and Consumer Magazines

Crafts Magazine
P.O. Box 1790
Peoria, IL 61656

Crafts 'N Things
2400 Devon Ave., Suite 375
Des Plaines, IL 60018-4618

Crafting for Today
243 Newton-Sparta Road
Newton, NJ 07860

Let's Talk About Dollmaking
P.O. Box 662-LT
Point Pleasant, NJ 08742

Mimi Winer's journal for dollmakers.

Open Chain, The Creative Machine
P.O. Box 2634
Menlo Park, CA 94026-9926

Discusses using sewing machines for
quilting.

Quilting Periodicals

American Patchwork & Quilting
1912 Grand Avenue
Des Moines, IA 50309-3884

American Quilter Magazine
American Quilting Society
P.O. Box 3290
Paducah, KY 42002-3290
www.AQSquilt.com/

Art Quilt Magazine
P.O. Box 630927
Houston, TX 77263-0927

Australian Patchwork & Quilting
Stonehouse Publications (North
  American distributor)
11560 Timber Butte Road
Sweet Idaho, ID 83670

Creative Quilting Magazine
950 Third Avenue
New York, NY 10022

Miniature Quilts
Chitra Publications
2 Public Avenue
Montrose, PA 188801

New Zealand Quilter
Anne Scott, Editor/Publisher
P.O. Box 14-567
Kilbirnie, Wellington
New Zealand
E-mail: nzquilter@xtra.co.nz

Piecework Magazine
201 East Fourth Street
Loveland, CO 80537

Quilter's Newsletter
Box 59021
Boulder, CO 80323
www.quiltersnewsletter.com

Quilter's Quarterly Journal
National Quilting Association
Box 393
Ellicott City, MD 21041-0393
E-mail: nqa@erols.com

Quilting Today
Chitra Publications
2 Public Avenue
Montrose, PA 18801-1220

Quilt Magazine
1115 Broadway
New York, NY 10010

Quiltmaker Magazine
P.O. Box 58360
Boulder, CO 80323
(800) 477-6089
www.quiltmaker.com

Sew Many Quilts by Liz Porter
& Marianne Fons
Box 2262
Birmingham, AL 35201

Traditional Quilter
243 Sparta-Newton Road
Newton, NJ 07860

Traditional Quiltworks
2 Public Avenue
Montrose, PA 18801-1220
Published by Chitra Publications.

Library Directories

Following is a list of public library resources to help you research your market
and find suppliers.

*Ayers Directory of Newspapers
and Periodicals*

Lists magazines and newspapers printed
in the United States.

The Cumulative Book Index

Lists books published on a specific subject.

The Industrial Index

Lists article titles published in trade journals. Though such journals have limited
readership, they are highly specialized
and contain valuable information.

Standard Rate & Data Service

Lists television stations, radio, newspapers, magazines, and trade and business
publications, alphabetically and by category. It also lists the owner's name, address, dates of publication, advertising
rates, size and cost of advertising space
and display ads, and deadlines.

The Thomas Register

This directory, formerly available only in libraries, is now available as a CD-ROM.

(Get details on the Internet at www.thomasregister.com or call (888) 344-9066.)

Craft and Quilting Organizations

American Quilter's Society
P.O. Box 3290
Paducah, KY 42002-3290
http://www.AQSquilt.com/

Supports the Museum of the American Quilter's Society in addition to providing conventions, events, and awards for quilters. Dedicated to preserving the history of American quiltmaking. Offers membership and quarterly publication, *American Quilter.*

American Sewing Guild
P.O. Box 8568
Medford, OR 97504

Sponsors seminars, workshops, demonstrations, fashion shows, vendor malls.

Association of Crafts & Creative Industries (ACCI)
P.O. Box 2188
Zanesville, OH 43702-3388
E-mail: acci.info@creative-industries.com

Color Marketing Group
4001 N. Ninth Street, Suite 102
Arlington, VA 22203

A nonprofit international association of more than 1,200 design and color professionals, dedicated to forecasting and tracking color and design trends in the marketplace. Meets twice yearly.

Hobby Industry Association (HIA)
Box 348
Elmwood Park, NJ 07407
Phone: (201) 794-1133
Fax: (201) 797-0657
www.hobby.org

International Quilt Market & Festival
7660 Woodway, Suite 550
Houston, TX 77063
www.quilts.com
E-mail: shows@quilts.com
Phone: (713) 781-6864, ext. 301
Fax: (713) 781-8182

The Annual Fall International Quilt Festival and Quilt Market in Houston, Texas, the largest trade show in the country devoted exclusively to quilting. Rquest their informational brochure.

National Craft Association
1945 E. Ridge Road, Suite 5178
Rochester, NY 14622-2467
(800) 715-9594
www.craftassoc.com.

An organization dedicated to helping crafters succeed in business.

National Quilting Association, Inc.
P.O. Box 393
Ellicott City, MD 21041-0393
Fax: (410) 461-3693

NQA, the oldest national quilting organization, publishes *Quilting Quarterly,* provides workshops and programs (including certification), special newsletters for quilting teachers and judges, grants, and scholarships.

Quilt Festivals by Mancuso
Mancuso, Inc., Dept. WP
P.O. Box 667
New Hope, PA 18938
www.quiltfest.com

Sponsors several annual quilt shows throughout the United States.

Society of Craft Designers (SCD)
Box 3388
Zanesville, OH 43702-3388
Phone: (740) 452-4541
Fax: (740) 452-2552
E-mail: scd@offinger.com

Helps designers sell to magazines.

Recommended Web Sites

Web site addresses do change from time to time, so if you cannot connect with any of the following addresses, use an Internet search engine to look for the name of the business or individual.

Quilt-Related Web Sites

The following Web sites include online newsletters, bulletin boards, sources for patterns, books and supplies, craft shop and mall listings, and more.

About.com
Bookstore recommendations
bookstore.miningco.com

Alpha Mall Shopping
A bulletin board for free ads; directory of quilt shops.
www.alphamall.qc.ca

American Quilt Thimbles
www.americanquilts.com

America's Favorite Quilting Magazines
www.quiltmag.com

Aurora's *BeadAholic Quarterly* Newsletter
members.tripod.com/ ~ auroram

Barbara Brabec's CraftBiz Chat
Online business newsletter for crafters.
www.crafter.com/brabec

Checker
Online store for quilt patterns, books, and quilts.
www.Checkerlist.com/

Cloud Nine
Batting for quilters.
cloudnine.freeservers.com/

Colonial Quilt Connection
patriot.net/ ~ smithma7CQC

Duncan by Design
Fiber paints for quilters.
www.duncancrafts.com

Fabric Link
www.fabriclink.com

High Tech Quilting
Jan Cabral's collection of digital fabrics
and related computer quilt drawing
techniques.
www.keyweb.com/hightech

KD Fabrics Online
members.gnn.com/kdwilson/startidx.htm

Little Foot Limited Quilting Notions
www.littlefoot.net

Madeira Threads USA
members.gnn.com/madeira
    special.htm

Make It Southwest!
www.cyspacemalls.com/quilt/

Nancy's Notions
Complete line of sewing equipment
and notions.
www.nancysnotions.com/

The Patchwork Studio
www.islandnet.com/~agreig/

Pfaff Home Page
www.pfaff.com
To sign up for mailing list:
lyris.quiltropolis.com/scrips/lyris.pl?sub.
com

Pine Tree QuiltWorks
General online catalog of quilt supplies,
fabric, and books.
www.quiltworks.com/store/default.asp

Planet Patchwork
Excellent online quilters' newsletter.
planetpatchwork.com/index.html

Quiltart
Group of quiltmakers. Offers subscription
and membership for contemporary
quilters.
www.quiltart.com

QuiltBiz
Web site and daily newsletter for quilt
professionals, designers, teachers, and
shop owners.
www.nmia.com/~ozzg/quiltbiz.htm

The QuiltBroker
www.QuiltBroker.com/

The Quilt Connection
www.quiltconnection.com/index.html

Quilted Angel
Online quilting supplies and classes.
www.quiltedangel.com/html/guest_book.
html

Quilt Gallery
A gallery of unique contemporary quilts
and previews of new quilts.
www.penny-nii.com/

Quilt Hangers by Creative Wood Design
www.empnet.com/quilt/

QuiltNet
www.quilt.net

Quiltropolis Mail Lists
www.quiltropolis.com/NewMailinglists.
htm

Quilts on Line
www.quiltersnewsletter.com/

Stencil Company
Quilting stencils and quilting designs.
www.quiltingstencils.com/

A Stitch in Time
A newsletter about dolls, quilts, sewing.
www.cloudnet.com/ ~ astitch

Strip-Pieced Watercolor Magic
www.patchwork.com/library/books/
Magic.html

Sulky of America
Sulky threads and quilting/embroidery
    supplies.
www.sulky.com/

World Wide Quilting Page
ttsw.com/MainQuiltingPage.html

Individual Quilters and Other Artisans

If a mailing address is not listed following,
it means the individual prefers contact
only by e-mail or through their Web site.

Majorie Bevis, Marbling Artist
325 4th Street
Petaluma, CA 94952
(707) 762-7514
www.marbledfabrics.com

Caryl Bryer Fallert, Art Quilts
Box 945
Oswego, IL 60543
www.bryerpatch.com/

Patricia Anne Hammond
1136 Clover Valley Way
Edgewood, MD 21040
(410) 676-6419
E-mail: hearthst@erols.com

Kaye's Favorite Quilting, Sewing,
and Craft Links
P.O. Box 456
West Branch, MI 48661
(800) 248-KAYE
www.kayewood.com/links.html

Merry May
Schoolhouse Enterprises
P.O. Box 305
Tuckahoe, NJ 08250-0305
(609) 628-2231
E-mail: cluesew@jerseycape.com

Quilt Gallery of Debby Kratovil
www.his.com/ ~ queenb/gallery.html

Rob's Virtual Quilt Page
www.tvq.com/

Deanna Spingola's Watercolor Magic
    Quilting
www.spingola.com/ds/

Sylvia's Studio for Professional Crafters
    & Quilters
users.rcn.com/sylvias-studio
E-mail: sylvias-studio@rcn.com
Books, articles, audio tapes, free tips.

David Walker's Quilting Web site
w3.one.net/ ~ davidxix

Small and Home-Based Business Links

At Home Professionals
www.homeprofessionals.com

Business at Home
www.gohome.com

Small and Home-Based Business Links
www.bizoffice.com

Your Home Business
yourhomebiz.com

Online Quilt Groups

Contact the following online quilting chat-groups using any e-mail program. Type in the following addresses to contact each group directly and get instructions on how to join the group. All are inter-active, international quilt groups open to all quilters. People post and reply to messages. They are great places to ask quilt-ing questions.

Interquilt
mbishop@needles.com

Kaffeel-Klatsch
kaffeel-klatsch@quilt.com

National Arts and Crafts Resource Network
A free online crafts newsletter.
Acraftbiz@aol.com

Quilt Art
quiltart@quilt.net

QuiltBee
quiltbee@quilter.com

Quilt Biz
For professional quilters and shop owners.
ozzg@nmia.com

Quilting Supplies, Patterns, and Books

American Professional Quilting Systems for the Quilting Professional (Longarm Machines)
(800) 426-7233
www.apqs.com
E-mail: apqs@netins.net

Rosanne Andreas
The Beaded Phoenix
Box 292
Monsey, NY 10952
(888) 684-7248
www.bestweb.net/ ~ andreas

A beading supplier.

Ardco
252 Cedar Road
Poquoson, VA 23662

Manufacturers of metal, non-skid templates.

A to Z Designs
13882 Montecito Drive
Victorville, CA 92392

Specializes in dark and pastel fabrics for Amish quilting, plus frames and Dazor lamps.

Clotilde
2 Sew Smart Way, B8031
Stevens Point, WI 54481-8031
(800) 772-2891

Sewing/quilting notions (always a
20 percent discount).

Connecting Threads for the Busy Quilter
P.O. Box 8940
Vancouver, WA 98668-8940
(800) 574-6454

General quilting products.

Contemporary Quilting
173 Post Road
Fairfield, CT 06430

Specializing in fabric only.

Cotton Club
Box 2263
Boise, ID 83701-2263
www.cottonclub.com
E-mail: cotton@micron.net

More than a mail order catalog for quality
quilting fabrics, the Cotton Club offers
regular fabric memberships that include
special collections such as watercolor
sample packets. Full-sized 4-inch squares
are large enough to be included in quilts.
Quilting books at 20 percent off list price.

Country Quilter
344 Route 100
Somers, NY, 10589

Quilting pattern company featuring
whimsical quilt designs.

Crazy Quilter's Club and Catalog
69 Coolidge Avenue
Haverhill, MA 01832

Specializing in patterns and supplies for
crazy quilts.

Design Plus
907 Columbia Road
Fort Collins, CO 80525

Owner Heidi Wurst will mail color sheets
and actual samples of custom-made quilt
labels upon request. Makes and prints
labels to include quiltmaker's name,
address, phone, and other quilting details.

Dritz Corporation
Box 5028
Spartanburg, SC 29304

Sewing and quilting notions.

EZ International Quilt Shop
95 Mayhill Street
Saddle Brook, NJ 07662
www.ezquilt.com

Books, patterns, tools, and notions.
Specializes in plastic templates and rulers.

Fairfield Processing Company
88 Rose Hill Avenue
Box 1157
Danbury, CT 06810
(800) 243-0989
www.poly-fil.com
E-mail: fairfld@mail.snet.net

Batting, stuffing, and pillow forms.

John Flynn's Multi-Frame Quilting System
1000 Shiloh Overpass Road
Billings, MT 59106
(800) 745-3596
www.flynnquilt.com
E-mail: johnflynn@mcn.net

Gray Wind Publishing
308 W. U.S. Hwy 34
Phillips, NE 68865

Specializes in quilting books and patterns, including foundation paper-piecing patterns.

Fabric World
3841 Hinkleville Road
Paducah, KY 42001
(800) 845-8723
www.Hancocks-Paducah.com

Complete catalog of fabric, notions, batting, tools, and books.

Hobbs Bonded Fibers & Batting
Box 2521
Waco, TX 76702-2521
Fax: (254)772-7238

Home Craft Services
340 W. Fifth Street
Kansas, MO 64105

Offers pre-cut quilt pieces and kits.

Denise Schultz
Kate's Appliqué Paper Co.
97 Corte Lenosa
Greenbrae, CA 94904

Keepsake Quilting
Route 25B
Box 1618
Centre Harbor, NH 03226-1618

Comprehensive catalog of patterns, books, notions, and fabrics.

Kirk Collection
1513 Military Avenue
Omaha, NE 68111
E-mail: KirkColl@aol.com

Specializing in antique fabrics and quilts from 1850 to 1950, plus quality reproduction fabrics, wool and silk battings, books, and notions.

Linda Moran
Marble-T Design
3391 South Nastar Drive
Tucson, AZ 85730
Fax: (520) 571-7578
www.marbledfab.com
E-mail: marble@marbledfab.com

Specializes in marbled fabric for quilters.

Mace Motif
106 Manito Road
Manasquan, NY 08736

Catalog features rotary-cutting templates and stained-glass quilting books and patterns.

Newport Quilt and Gift Co.
644 SW Coast Hwy, Suite B
Newport, OR 97365

Offers watercolor flower blocks and fabric by mail.

Patchwork
6676 Amsterdam Road
Amsterdam, MT 59741
E-mail: ptchwrks@alpinet.net

Specializing in reproduction fabrics from 1775 through 1950.

Patchwork 'N Things
P.O. Box 3725
Granada Hills, CA 91394

Quilt supplies and notions.

PBH Foundation Patterns
1617 Ashby Avenue
Berkeley, CA 94703

Wholesale and retail paper foundation patterns.

Pieces of Dreams
Box 298
Running Springs, CA 92382

Hand-painted and space-dyed fabrics.

PineTree Quilting
585 Broadway
South Portland, ME 04106
www.quiltworks.com/store/default.asp
E-mail: aardvark@ime.net

Comprehensive catalog of natural fiber and poly battings; appliqué aids, fabric, pencils, and markers; templates and template plastic; needlecraft gloves; rotary cutters, clippers, and scissors; machine sewing needles; seven brands of hand-sewing needles and threads. They also sell all quilting books at 20% off retail (e-mail the book title and author's name for price quote).

Practical Patchwork
123 West Third Street
Mountain View, MO 65548

Offers fabric kits and fabric.

Quakertown Quilts
607 Friendswood Drive
Friendswood, TX 77546

Offers fabric, books, patterns, notions, classes, and services. Wholesale inquires welcome.

Qualin International
Box 31145
San Francisco, CA 94131
(415) 333-8500; Fax: (415) 282-8789

Importers of silk yardage, dyes, paints, and garments for painting.

QuiltBroker Internet Service
907 Columbia Road
Fort Collins, CO 80525
www.quiltbroker.com/

Specializes in selling new and previously owned quilts catering to interior designers and collectors.

Quilt Farm
Box 7877
St. Paul, MN 55107

Offers comprehensive array of tools, notions, fabrics, patterns, and books.

Quilt House
95 Mayhill Street
Saddle Brook, NJ 07663
(800) 660-0145
www.ezquilt.com

Specializing in tools and templates.

Quilter's Bookshelf
3244 N. Hackett Avenue
Milwaukee, WI 53211

Comprehensive selection of quilt books.

Quilter's Haven
Box 4873
Covina, CA 91723

General quilting supplies.

Quilter's Rule International
817 Mohr Avenue
Waterford, WI 53185
Fax: (414) 514-2100

Comprehensive selection of sewing and quilting supplies.

Shar Jorgensen
Quilting from the Heartland
9015 Hwy NW
Montevideo, MN 56265

Catalog of quilting templates and tools.

Quilts & Other Comforts
P. O. Box 4101
Golden, CO 80401-0100
www.qoc-catalog.com

One of the largest quilting supply catalogs of fabric, tools, templates, patterns, and books.

QuiltSmith, Ltd.
252 Cedar Road
Poquoson, VA 23662

Precision metal, non-skid quilting templates made by Ardco.

Quiltwork Patches
209 SW Second Street
Box 724
Corvallis, OR 97339

General quilting supplies.

Quiltworks
1055 E 79th Street
Minneapolis, MN 55420

Comprehensive catalog of books, patterns, and fabrics.

Skydyes
83 Richmond Lane
West Hartford, CT 06711

Hand-painted cotton and silk fabrics.

Stencils and Stuff
5198 TR 123
Millersburg, OH 44654

Stencils, thread, and notions.

Quilting Software

Cochenille Design Studio
Box 4276
Encinitas, CA 92023
E-mail: info@cochenille.com

Electric Quilt
The Electric Quilt Co.
1039 Melrose Street
Bowling Green, OH 43402
E-mail: acquiltco@wcnet.org

(See review of Electric Quilt V2 Software at www.204.249.244.10/EQ2 Review.html)

PC Quilt
Nina Antze
7061 Lynch Road
Sebastopol, CA 95472
E-mail: NinaA@aol.com

Designer Nina Antze designed this program first for IBM/DOS and later developed a version for Macintosh users called Baby Mac.

Quilter's Design Studio
Box 19946
San Diego, CA 92159-0946

For Windows and Macintosh.

Quilt-Pro
1825 Summit Avenue
Plano, TX 75023
(800) 884-1511
www.quiltpro.com

A Windows drawing program to create quilts. Call for a free demonstration disk and ordering information.

QuiltSoft
Box 19946
San Diego, CA 92159-0946

Windows drawing program.

Arts and Crafts Shows, Shops, and Malls

American Craft Guide to Craft Galleries
& Shops USA
ACC Publications
40 West 53rd Street
New York, NY 10019

Directory of 614 galleries/shops seeking fine arts and crafts.

American Craft Malls
103 Ash Creek
Azle, TX 76020
(817) 300-0152
www.procrafter.com/procraft
E-Mail: ProCrafter@aol.com

Coomers Malls
Coomers, Inc.
6012 Reef Point Lane
Ft. Worth, TX 76135
Phone: (888) 362-7238
www.coomers.com

Crafts Fair Guide
Lee Spiegel
Box 5062
Mill Valley, CA 94952
(800) 871-2341

A review of West Coast arts and crafts fairs with evaluations by participating craftspeople.

Craft Shop Directory
Archangel Crafts Co.
Twin Forks Office Park
6040-A Six Forks Road, Suite 263
Raleigh, NC 27609

Send $5.00 for listing of shops for craft products and 102 craft shops interested in consignment or wholesale buying. They specify whether they are looking for woodwork, fiber, toys, quilts, pottery, or jewelry.

Sunshine Artist
2600 Temple Drive
Winter Park, FL 32789
(407) 539-1399

This monthly magazine offers detailed descriptions of more than 2,000 art events throughout the nation, with critiques of shows from working artists and craftspeople.

Glossary

Album Quilt: A sampler quilt made of a variety of blocks often made by several people.

Appliqué: A piece of fabric stitched onto a larger piece of material.

Appliqué Background: The piece of fabric to which an appliqué design is stitched.

Art Pencil (white): A medium-soft pencil used for tracing designs onto dark fabrics.

Backing: The fabric on the back of the quilt.

Backstitch: A stitch taken at the beginning and end of a line of stitching to secure thread ends.

Basting: Large, running stitches that hold layers of fabric together for sewing or quilting.

Batting: The filler placed between the quilt top and backing, usually made of cotton, wool, silk, or polyester.

Binding: A narrow strip of fabric used to finish the raw edges of a quilt.

Blindstitch: Tiny, invisible stitches used for sewing one piece of fabric on top of another.

Block: A unit made of smaller patchwork pieces, then repeated to make the quilt top.

Border: Pieced, appliquéd, or plain band of fabric framing the outer edges of the quilt.

Bottom Border: The border on the lower or bottom edge of the quilt.

Calico: Cotton fabric printed with figured patterns, originally from India.

Cotton Polyester Sewing Thread: Thread used for general sewing.

Coverlet: A bed cover not large enough to cover the pillows or reach the floor.

Crosshatch: Two series of parallel lines that intersect. Usually marked on a quilt top with a ruler and marking pencil and used as a guide for hand or machine quilting.

Cutting Diagram: Drawing showing the layout of the pattern on the fabric.

Dangling Thread: A loose, unknotted thread left in an uncompleted quilting area to be re-threaded and used to complete the quilting once quilt is assembled.

Decorative Quilting: Stitched designs in feathers, flowers, leaves, or other shapes to quilt larger areas on a quilt when outline quilting alone is not sufficient to hold the sandwich together.

Dressmaker Pencil (white): A soft pencil used for tracing on dark fabrics.

Finger Rolling: A technique used to prepare appliqués for blindstitching.

Friendship Quilt: A quilt made up of blocks, each made by a different person.

Horizontal Row: A row of blocks across the width of the quilt.

Joining Squares: Squares of fabric connecting joining strips.

Joining Strips: Narrow strips of fabric connecting the quilt blocks.

Lap Quilt: To quilt without a frame, also known as **Quilt-As-You-Go (QAYG)** quilting.

Lattice Strips: Strips of fabric added between quilt blocks, also called sashing.

Miter: To join two strips of fabric at right angles and piece them together.

Monochromatic Color Scheme: A single color in several tints and shades and fabric prints.

Patchwork: The process of stitching small fabric pieces and shapes into a whole.

Piece: A small section of fabric (noun); to sew, by hand or machine, small pieces of fabric together (verb).

Piecework: A unit made by sewing small pieces together to form a larger unit.

Pillow Backing: The fabric on the back of a finished pillow.

Pillow Tuck Blocks: Narrow row of plain blocks specifically for tucking under the pillow.

Pin Baste: Basting with pins rather than thread.

Quilt: Two layers of fabric filled with batting and stitched together by hand or machine (noun); the act of stitching the two layers of a quilt together with batting in between (verb).

Quilt Diagram: A picture of a quilt drawn during the planning stages to place blocks.

Quilt Top: The top layer of a quilt or quilted project, pieced or appliquéd.

Quilt-As-You-Go Frame: Portable, collapsible quilting frame used to quilt one block at a time.

Quilt-As-You-Go Quilt: See **Lap Quilt.**

Quilting Design: A design traced on or applied to the fabric to follow when quilting.

Quilting Frame: A large frame used to hold an entire quilt's layers while it is being quilted.

Quilting Thread: Heavier, waxed thread manufactured especially for hand quilting.

Reverse Appliqué: The reverse of traditional appliqué, where fabric is cut away from the background fabric to expose one or more different fabric layers beneath.

Sashing: See **Lattice.**

Scrapbag Quilting: Using bits of leftover fabric scraps to create a quilt top.

Seam Allowance: The amount of fabric between the seam and the raw edge.

Seam Allowance Included: Seam allowance has been added to a given measurement.

Seam Allowance Not Included: Seam allowance has not been added to the measurement.

Seam Line: The stitching guideline to follow by hand or machine.

Selvage: The finished edges running on the straight grain of purchased fabric by the manufacturer. May contain the company name and other information. Should not be included in cutting pieces for quilting as it is doubled fabric and has no stretch.

Side Border: The border on the sides of the quilt.

Square: To have exact right angles at each of four corners.

Stay-Stitch: Machine stitching along a seam line to reinforce appliqué before clipping.

Stencil: A design aid that enables one to transfer a design to a quilt to be hand or machine quilted. Most stencils are made of cardboard or plastic and contain grooves that allow pencils to mark the lines.

Stitch-in-the-Ditch Quilting: Sewing over the seam line of joined pieces of fabric so the quilting falls between fabric sections and is not noticeable.

Template: Plastic or cardboard pattern from which several fabric pieces are cut.

Thread Baste: Basting with running stitches.

Tied Quilt: A quilt filled with batting but secured with tied knots rather than stitching.

Trapunto: A type of sculptured quilting worked on only two layers of fabric (without batting) and stuffed from the back layer through tiny slits and holes with batting or yarn.

Top Border: Borders at the upper or top edge of the quilt top.

Vertical Row: A row of blocks down the length of the quilt.

Whip Stitch: A quick stitch to sew—sort of the opposite of the hidden stitch. It generally joins two finished edges together, but is also used in quilting to stitch a binding to the quilt backing (when the visible stitching will not matter).

White Work: A quilt top made of one piece of white fabric intricately quilted with white thread.

Index

About the Author

SYLVIA ANN LANDMAN began her career in fiber arts as a dressmaker and a designer of custom knitting, crochet, and embroidery working from her home studio. Not long after, it became a teaching studio as well. Working full-time in the crafts field, Sylvia continues to teach in her home studio, at community colleges, and at workshops throughout the United States. She is the author of *Crafting for Dollars,* Prima Publishing, 1996, and *Make Your Quilting Pay for Itself,* F&W/Betterway, 1997. She also writes a regular column for *Quilting Quarterly Journal,* and frequently publishes her original craft and quilting designs.

About the Series Editor

BARBARA BRABEC is one of the world's leading experts on how to turn an art or crafts hobby into a profitable home-based business. She regularly communicates with thousands of creative people through her Web site and monthly columns in *Crafts Magazine* and *The Crafts Report*.

To Order Books

Please send me the following items:

Quantity	Title	U.S. Price	Total
_____	Decorative Painting For Fun & Profit	$ 19.99	$ _____
_____	Holiday Decorations For Fun & Profit	$ 19.99	$ _____
_____	Woodworking For Fun & Profit	$ 19.99	$ _____
_____	Knitting For Fun & Profit	$ 19.99	$ _____
_____	Quilting For Fun & Profit	$ 19.99	$ _____
_____	Soapmaking For Fun & Profit	$ 19.99	$ _____
_____	_____	$ _____	$ _____
_____	_____	$ _____	$ _____

Subtotal	$ _____
Deduct 10% when ordering 3–5 books	$ _____
7.25% Sales Tax (CA only)	$ _____
8.25% Sales Tax (TN only)	$ _____
5% Sales Tax (MD and IN only)	$ _____
7% G.S.T. Tax (Canada only)	$ _____
Shipping and Handling*	$ _____
Total Order	$ _____

*Shipping and Handling depend on Subtotal.

Subtotal	Shipping/Handling
$0.00–$29.99	$4.00
$30.00–$49.99	$6.00
$50.00–$99.99	$10.00
$100.00–$199.99	$13.50
$200.00+	Call for Quote

**Foreign and all Priority Request orders:
Call Customer Service
for price quote at 916-632-4400**

This chart represents the total retail price of books only (before applicable discounts are taken).

By Telephone: With American Express, MC, or Visa,
call 800-632-8676 or 916-632-4400. Mon–Fri, 8:30–4:30.
www.primapublishing.com
By E-mail: sales@primapub.com
By Mail: Just fill out the information below and send with your remittance to:
Prima Publishing • P.O. Box 1260BK • Rocklin, CA 95677

Name _____

Address _____

City_____ State _____ ZIP _____

MC/Visa/American Express# _____ Exp._____

Check/money order enclosed for $ _____ Payable to Prima Publishing

Daytime telephone _____

Signature _____